Mechanic Accents

Dime Novels and Working-Class Culture in America

MICHAEL DENNING

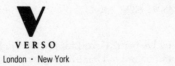

VERSO

London · New York

First published by Verso 1987
© Michael Denning

Verso
UK: 6 Meard Street, London W1V 3HR
USA: 29 West 35th Street, New York, NY 10001 2291

Verso is the imprint of New Left Books

British Library Cataloguing in Publication Data

Denning, Michael, *1954-*
     Mechanic accents : dime novels and working
     class culture in America. — (Haymarket).
     1. American fiction — 19th century —
     History and criticism
     I. Title
     813'.009   PS377

Library of Congress Cataloging-in-Publication Data

Denning, Michael.
     Mechanic accents.

     Includes Index.
     1. American fiction—19th century—History and criticism.
2. Dime Novels—United States—History and criticism.
3. Popular literature—United States—History and criticism.
4. Labor   and   laboring   classes—United   States—Books   and
reading—History—19th   century.   5. Literature   and   society—
United States—History—19th century. I. Title,
PS374.D5D44   1987   813'.3'09   87-14989

ISBN 0-86091-178-0
ISBN 0-86091-889-0 (pbk.)

Typeset by Leaper & Gard Ltd, Bristol, England.
Printed and bound in Great Britain by Biddles Ltd, Guildford.

For my mother

The Haymarket Series

Editors: Mike Davis
Michael Sprinker

The Haymarket Series is a new publishing initiative by Verso offering original studies of politics, history and culture focused on North America. The series presents innovative but representative views from across the American left on a wide range of topics of current and continuing interest to socialists in North America and throughout the world. A century after the first May Day, the American left remains in the shadow of those martyrs whom this series honours and commemorates. The studies in the Haymarket Series testify to the living legacy of activism and political commitment for which they gave up their lives.

Already Published

BLACK AMERICAN POLITICS: From the Washington Marches to Jesse Jackson by *Manning Marable*

PRISONERS OF THE AMERICAN DREAM: Politics and Economy in the History of the US Working Class by *Mike Davis*

MARXISM IN THE US: Remapping the History of the American Left by *Paul Buhle*

THE YEAR LEFT: *Volume One*: 1984 U.S. Elections; Politics and Culture in Central America.

THE YEAR LEFT: *Volume Two*: Toward a Rainbow Socialism.

FIRE IN THE AMERICAS: *by Roger Burbach and Orlando Nunez*

YOUTH, IDENTITY, POWER: The Chicano Generation by
Carlos Muñoz, Jr.

Forthcoming
THE YEAR LEFT: *Volume Three*: Reshaping the American Left;
Media Politics.

ORIGINS OF THE AMERICAN FAMILY
by *Stephanie Coontz*

THE 'FIFTH' CALIFORNIA: Political Economy of a State-
Nation by *Mike Davis*

LABORING ON: The US Working Class Since 1960 by *Kim
Moody*

THE PARADOX OF AMERICAN SOCIAL DEMOCRACY
by *Robert Brenner*

Contents

Acknowledgements

I am indebted to many friends and colleagues whose comments and suggestions have strengthened this book; rather than trying to name them all, and in order to emphasize its origins in the collective intellectual work of the left academy, I will simply thank my fellow members of the following groups who read, heard and discussed parts of it: the New Haven Marxist Literary Group, the Connecticut Valley MARHO: The Radical Historians Organization, the editorial board of *Social Text*, the Union Square Marxist study group at Columbia, the Commercial Culture seminar at the New York Institute for the Humanities, and the St. Cloud Summer Institutes on Culture and Society. I also want to thank Columbia University's Columbus Circle, the *Zentrum für Nordamerika-Forschung* in Frankfurt, the Center for the Humanities at Wesleyan University, the Pembroke Center at Brown University, the Strong Museum, and David Montgomery's labor history seminar for listening to and discussing parts of this work.

I am also very grateful to Edward T. LeBlanc, editor of *Dime Novel Round-Up*, for his help in finding and xeroxing dime novels, for an afternoon of answering many questions, and for the generous sharing of his unpublished bibliographic listings. And I am indebted to the staffs of the Yale American Studies Program, of Yale's Sterling and Beinecke Libraries, of the Columbia English Department, and of Wesleyan's Center for the Humanities, for their professional help and support. An essay drawing on this book was published in *History Workshop Journal* #22 (Autumn 1986), and in Kurt Shell and Gunter Lenz, eds., *The Crisis of Modernity: Recent Critical Theories of Culture and Society in the United States and Germany*, (Frankfurt: Campus Verlag and Boulder: Westview Press, 1986).

Several people read the entire manuscript and offered vital criticisms and suggestions: I thank Jean-Christophe Agnew, Peter

Buckley, Amy Kaplan, David Montgomery (a suggestive paragraph in one of his essays inspired the project), Janice Radway, Richard Slotkin, Sean Wilentz, and the Haymarket editors, Michael Sprinker and Mike Davis. I particularly want to thank Alan Trachtenberg, who encouraged and directed the dissertation on which this is based, and whose interpretations of American cultural history deeply influenced it; Fred Jameson, both for his personal and intellectual support and for his part in the reinvention of Marxist cultural studies in the United States, a development to which this work owes much; Dean Bergeron, whose example as radical, teacher, and historian provided the foundation for this work; and Hazel Carby, who has shared it from the beginning.

Introduction

It is only the cheap stories, which you call dime novels, for which
the demand is, and always will be inexhaustible, and which must
be depended on for the regeneration of American literature.

Capt. Fred. Whittaker, 1884
Author of *Larry Locke, The Man of Iron;
or, A Fight for Fortune.
A Story of Labor and Capital.*

[The question of] so-called 'popular literature,' that is, ... the
success of serial literature (adventure stories, detective stories,
thrillers) among the masses, ... represents the major part of the
problem of a new literature as the expression of moral and
intellectual renewal, for only from the readers of serial literature
can one select a sufficient and necessary public for creating the
cultural base of the new literature. It appears to me that the
problem is this: how to create a body of writers who are,
artistically, to serial literature what Dostoyevsky was to Sue and
Soulie, or, with respect to the detective story what Chesterton
was to Conan Doyle and Wallace? With this aim in mind, one
must abandon many prejudices, but above all it should be
remembered not only that one cannot have a monopoly but also
that one is faced with a formidable organization of publishing
interests.

The most common prejudice is this: that the new literature has
to identify itself with an artistic school of intellectual origins, as
was the case with Futurism. The premiss of the new literature
cannot but be historical, political, popular. It must aim at
elaborating that which already is, whether polemically or in some
other way does not matter. What does matter, though, is that it
sink its roots into the humus of popular culture as it is, with its
tastes and tendencies and with its moral and intellectual world,
even if it is backward and conventional.

Antonio Gramsci, 1933-1934
'Problems of Criticism'

These fragile, rare, and highly fugitive books will be useful likewise to anyone interested in proletarian literature. ... The dime novel ... is the nearest thing we have had in this country to what is now so much discussed, a true 'proletarian' literature, that is, a literature written for the great masses of people and actually read by them.

Merle Curti, 1937
'Dime Novels and the American Tradition'

A sign that has been withdrawn from the pressures of the social struggle — which, so to speak, crosses beyond the pale of class struggle — inevitably loses force, degenerating into allegory and becoming the object not of live social intelligibility but of philological comprehension. The historical memory of mankind is full of such worn out ideological signs incapable of serving as arenas for the clash of live social accents. However, inasmuch as they are remembered by the philologist and the historian, they may be said to retain the last glimmers of life.

V.N. Voloshinov, 1930
Marxism and the Philosophy of Language

The dime novel and story-paper literature, wrote a reviewer in *The Atlantic Monthly* in 1879, 'is an enormous field of mental activity, the greatest literary movement, in bulk, of the age, and worthy of very serious consideration for itself. Disdained as it may be by the highly cultivated for its character, the phenomenon of its existence cannot be overlooked' (Bishop 1879, 383). A century later, the controversies over this 'literary movement' are as faded as the decaying dime novels themselves. But the questions surrounding the dime novel, one of the first mass media, one of the first culture industries, remain central to contemporary cultural politics. In this book I want to reconsider the popular narratives of the nineteenth century that are lumped under the term 'dime novel', the American equivalent of the French *feuilleton* or the British 'penny dreadful', and their place in the cultures of American working people between the 1840s and the 1890s. I approach these stories from two main perspectives; we might loosely define these, following Raymond Williams, as a concern for 'literature *in* society', seeing literature as a form of production, and a view of 'literature *and* society', seeing literature as embodying social consciousness. Thus, the book will weave together an economics and a poetics of the dime novel, an account of the novels as commodities, of the relations between author, publisher, and reader within the dime novel industry, and of the relations between these commodities and the culture industry as a whole, with an account of the novels as narratives, of the kinds of stories that were published, the conventions and formulae that recurred, the character systems that organized their worlds, the rhetorics and codes that structure their language.

In what follows, I ask two principal questions: what can be learned *about* these popular narratives, their production and consumption, and their place and function within working class cultures; and, what can be learned *from* them, as symbolic actions, about working class culture and ideology. To answer these questions I address theoretical arguments about the ways classes are represented and the ways classes represent their world to themselves, historical arguments about the development of a culture industry in the nineteenth century United States, and critical arguments about how to read these 'simple', 'popular' texts, and how they were read. For the same *Atlantic* reviewer who advised 'very serious consideration' of these tales warned: 'Though written almost exclusively for the use of the lower classes of society, the story papers are not accurate pictures of their life. They are not a mass of evidence from which, though rude, a valuable insight into their thoughts, feelings, and doings can be obtained by others who do not know them' (Bishop 1879, 389). This warning about the ruses of representation and the limits of literary criticism must be kept in mind; thus I will look not so much for 'accurate pictures of their life', as for the accents in which the stories are told, the disguises they use, and the figures that condense and displace workers' 'thoughts, feelings, and doings'. Yet these accents, disguises, and figures are ambiguous; in order to understand them it is necessary to situate them in the conflicts over and within working class cultures and the culture industry.

I will argue that these popular stories, which are products of the culture industry — 'popular', 'mass', or 'commercial' culture — can be understood neither as forms of deception, manipulation, and social control nor as expressions of a genuine people's culture, opposing and resisting the dominant culture. Rather they are best seen as a contested terrain, a field of cultural conflict where signs with wide appeal and resonance take on contradictory disguises and are spoken in contrary accents. Just as the signs of a dominant culture can be articulated in the accents of the people, so the signs of the culture of the working classes can be dispossessed in varieties of ventriloquism. Among

the principal sites of this struggle are the signs of class themselves, the rhetoric by which people understand the divisions of
the social world and situate themselves within it, the stories in
which conflicting groups of people become giant characters. In
what follows I will look at the dime novels and story papers as a
terrrain of these conflicting rhetorics, accents and disguises of
class, arguing that while they do not present 'accurate pictures'
of workers' lives, they can, if read historically, give valuable
insight into workers' 'thoughts, feelings, and doings'.

The history of popular culture is not simply an antiquarian
collecting and cataloguing of nostalgia artifacts; it is the history
of the social relations between the industries producing cheap
commodities for mass entertainment and recreation, the symbolic forms and practices, both traditional and newly-invented,
of working class communities, and the attempts by the dominant
culture to police and reform the culture of the 'lower classes'.
Part One will examine the dime novel's place in this history.
After reconsidering the way dime novels have been understood
and remembered in American culture (chapter one), it will
discuss the emergence of the dime novel industry, one of the
United States' first culture industries (chapter two), then
consider the relation between dime novels and their working
class readers (chapter three), and finally trace the attempts to
police and reform dime novels and working class reading
(chapter four). I will argue that the world of dime fiction was a
separate world — in terms of production, reading public, and
conventions, — not only from the literary fiction of the nineteenth century, but from the popular fiction of genteel culture,
the fiction serialized and reviewed in the *Atlantic*, *Century*,
Harpers and *Scribners*. Furthermore, though I neither claim that
dime novels were the self-representations of American workers
nor that dime novels were confined to a working class public, I
argue that since workers made up the bulk of the dime novel
public, their concerns and accents are inscribed in the cheap
stories.

Part Two opens with a theoretical discussion of the ways dime
novels were read and the ways they may be interpreted (chapter
five). It then examines five moments in the history of the cheap
stories from their birth in the first long wave of American
capitalist expansion in the 1840s to their gilded age during the
extended economic, political, and cultural crisis between 1873
and 1893. It begins with the 'mysteries of the city' of the 1840s,
and the contradictory attempt by one of the earliest 'stars' of the

fiction factory, George Lippard, to become a tribune of the mechanics who made up his audience (chapter six). It then turns to two sets of narratives of the 'great upheaval': the group of stories that were written about the celebrated Molly Maguire case in the 1870s out of which the detective story emerged (chapter seven); and the stories of tramps and outlaws that appeared in the context of the 1877 railroad strike (chapter eight). Finally, it looks at two groups of narratives of working class manhood and womanhood: the heroic masculine success tales of honest mechanics and Knights of Labor that appeared in the early 1880s (chapter nine); and the working-girl stories of virtue defended that effectively replaced domestic fiction and dominated the story papers and cheap libraries of the 1880s and 1890s (chapter ten).

Though I will look at only a small fraction of the tens of thousands of dime novels and story paper serials published in these years, I hope to demonstrate that the formulas and figures that recur in these mysteries of the city and stories of labor and capital hold a central place in the cheap stories generally, and that the great upheavals of the gilded age transformed the 'mystery of the city' into a 'story of labor and capital'. Furthermore, I hope to show that the formulas and figures that recur in these dime novels are marked by the imprint of their working class audience, and that an attention to the allegorical ways in which they were read can allow us to uncover their disguises and hear their mechanic accents. Though these stories may have passed from 'live social intelligibility' into 'philological comprehension', the contested terrain at the intersection of the culture industry and the cultures of the working classes remains the terrain of our conflicts, and the precondition for a 'new literature as the expression of moral and intellectual renewal', a new culture.

PART ONE

Books For the Million!

1

The Figure of the Dime Novel in American Culture

The dreadful damage wrought to-day in every city, town, and village of these United States by the horrible and hideous stuff set weekly before the boys and girls of America by the villainous sheets which pander greedily and viciously to the natural taste of young readers for excitement, the irreparable wrong done by these vile publications, is hidden from no one.

Brander Matthews, 1883

The saffron-backed Dime Novels of the late Mr. Beadle, ill-famed among the ignorant who are unaware of their ultra-Puritan purity, ... began to appear in the early years of the Civil War; and when I was a boy in a dismal boarding school at Sing Sing, in the winters of 1861-1863, I reveled in their thrilling and innocuous record of innocent and imminent danger. ... I make no doubt that if the Dime Novels of my school-days had been in circulation in Shakespeare's boyhood the Bard would have joyed in them.

Brander Matthews, 1923

Dime novels: this figure conjures powerful images in American culture. Standing for the whole of nineteenth-century cheap sensational fiction, it evokes nostalgic images of boys' books, read on the sly, but fundamentally harmless and whole-some: tales of the west in the adventures of Buffalo Bill and Deadwood Dick, of rags-to-riches in the Horatio Alger saga and of the schoolboy fun of Frank Merriwell at Yale. Within a few years of their demise in the 1890s they were recalled as signs of a lost innocence, unspoiled fragments of an age before mass culture; the nineteenth-century debates about their immoral and disreputable nature seemed a comic extravagance of Victorian gentility. As the two quotations from Brander Matthews — an influential American literary critic of the time — demon-strate, the immediate menace of cheap sensational fiction to genteel culture was repressed, generating a screen memory of

9

thrilling and innocuous boyhood pleasures. And through the twentieth century, dime novels have been kept alive more by collectors and enthusiasts than by literary critics or cultural historians. In the face of this memory, it is necessary to unravel the synecdoche: to see what is the part, and what the whole, and to see the history of its construction. For though I will refer to the entire body of commercial, mass-produced, sensational fiction of the nineteenth century as 'dime novels', to use the term uncritically can lead us to mistake drastically the nature of nineteenth-century popular fiction.

Popular fictional narratives appeared in three main formats between the 1840s and the 1890s: the story paper, the dime novel, and the cheap library. Though the formats overlapped in history and content — at some times all three sorts were on the market and many novels appeared in all three formats — they do mark three different moments in the cheap fiction publishing of the nineteenth century.

The story paper was an eight-page weekly newspaper, which cost five or six cents, and contained anywhere from five to eight serialized stories, as well as correspondence, brief sermons, humor, fashion advice, and bits of arcane knowledge. They were published mainly in New York and Philadelphia for a national audience, having emerged out of a gradual but incomplete separation of the news and story functions of the newspaper. They first appeared at the tail end of the newspaper revolution of the 1830s, when the penny press was established. The penny press — the *New York Sun* (founded 1833), *New York Herald* (founded 1835), and *Philadelphia Public Ledger* (founded 1836), among others — was, as Michael Schudson (1978, 30) summarizes, 'distinctive economically — in selling cheaply, in its distribution by newsboys, and in its reliance on advertising; politically — in its claims to independence from party; and substantively — in its focus on news, a genre it invented.' The conditions for the success of the penny press also contributed to the beginning of the story papers: technological developments in production and distribution with the emergence of the steam-driven cylinder press and an extensive rail and canal network, and social changes in the emergence of a new reading public, the artisans and mechanics of the eastern cities. The first story papers were *Brother Jonathan*, founded in New York by Park Benjamin and Rufus Griswold in 1839, and *New World*, founded by Benjamin and Griswold a few months later after leaving *Brother Jonathan* in a dispute. 'Both journals,' the historian James Barnes (1974, 11)

notes, 'far exceeded the circulation of other American periodicals, with the exception of *Graham's Magazine* and a few of the
leading daily newspapers.' In Boston, the *Nation* and the *Universal Yankee Nation* soon entered the field. These early story papers
were competitive and short-lived, relying largely on pirated
European novels despite their nationalist rhetoric. The foun-
dations for longer-lasting story papers came in the 1850s with the
establishment of Robert Bonner's *New York Ledger* (1855) and
Street & Smith's *New York Weekly* (1859). Their success established a format that was imitated by competitors for the next
forty years: Beadle & Adams' *Saturday Journal* (1870) (which
became *Beadle's Weekly* in 1882 and *Banner Weekly* in 1885); James
Elverson's *Saturday Night* (1865); George Munro's *Fireside
Companion* (1867); and Norman Munro's *Family Story Paper*
(1873). These papers, which had circulations in the hundreds of
thousands, were aimed at the entire family, containing a
carefully-balanced mixture of serialized adventure stories,
domestic romances, western tales, and historical romances.[1]

The second main format for cheap, sensational fiction was the
pamphlet novel, also pioneered by Park Benjamin when he
issued a twelve-and-a-half-cent 'shilling novelette' as an 'extra'
for readers of the *New World* in 1842. These fifty-page, 5-inch-by-
8½-inch pamphlets were widely imitated until increased postal
rates put many of them out of business in 1845 (Schick 1958, 49).
Nevertheless, the practice had been established well enough for
a small New York publisher of ten-cent song- and etiquette
books to issue a weekly series of pamphlet novels in 1860 under
the title 'Beadle's Dime Novels'. Within four years the *North
American Review* saw fit to review the Beadle books, and the
reviewer found their sales to be 'almost unprecedented in the
annals of booksellers. A dime novel is issued every month and
the series has undoubtedly obtained greater popularity than any
other series of works of fiction published in America' (W. Everett
1864, 304). These dime novels, 4-inch-by-6-inch pamphlets of
about 100 pages each known as 'yellow-backs', found a large
part of that unprecedented audience among soldiers in the
Civil War. Beadle and Adams had published four million dime
novels by 1865; sales of individual titles ranged from 35,000 to
80,000 (Schick 1958, 51). Competitors sprang up quickly; among
the more successful series were Sinclair Tousey's American Tales
(1863), Elliott, Thomas & Talbot's Ten Cent Novelettes (1863),
George Munro's Ten Cent Novels (1864) and Robert DeWitt's
Ten Cent Romances (1867).

The third main format for popular fiction was the cheap library. These were series of nickel and dime pamphlets of about 8 inches by 11 inches, consisting of either 16 or 32 pages of two- or three-columned print. They were introduced in 1875 when Donnelly, Lloyd & Co., a Chicago publisher, issued their Lakeside Library. When *Publisher's Weekly* surveyed the field in late 1877, they found 'fourteen "libraries" or series of these broadsheets, of which one outreaches a hundred numbers, while another is increasing just now at a regular rate of eight a week.' They continue: 'It is difficult to generalize as to what classes of readers buy these broadsheets, but we are inclined to believe, from what we can learn, that they are very largely the *clientele* of the weekly story papers. These have not been pushed of late years as they used to be, and their readers perhaps are ready for something new. The new libraries are also said to have pretty nearly disposed of what little remained of the dime-novel business' (The Cheap Libraries 1877). Not only were the readers the same, but so were the publishers. Beadle and Adams issued a Fireside Library, George Munro a Seaside Library, and Norman Munro a Riverside Library; but the field was dominated by Street & Smith, whose many series included the Log Cabin Library (1889), and the Nick Carter Library (1891); and Frank Tousey, who published the Five Cent Weekly Library (1878-1893) and the New York Detective Library (1883-1898), among others.

So, despite the changing formats, the continuities of readership, publishers, and the fiction itself — many stories were first serialized in the story papers, then printed as dime novels, and eventually reprinted in the libraries — justify the use of 'dime novels' to describe this body of narratives, a body quite separate from the genteel fiction of the Victorian middle classes, the novels reviewed and serialized in the major periodicals: *Century*, *Scribners*, *Harpers* and *The Atlantic*.

If this period can be said to have begun with the newspaper revolution that brought forth the penny press and its new reading public, its end is probably marked by several circumstances of the 1890s: John Lovell's attempt to create a cheap book trust by buying out many of the libraries for his U.S. Book Company in 1891, and his failure in the Panic of 1893; the International Copyright Agreement of 1891, which ended the pirating of British and European fiction that had generated much of the profit of the cheap books and series; the development of the Sunday newspaper; and the 'magazine revolution', the emergence of inexpensive slick and pulp magazines in the 1890s. By

1900, the *The Bookman* was noting 'the extinction of the dime novel' (Dred 1900).

If that is the whole for which the 'dime novel' stands as a synecdoche, the emphasis on the early westerns, tales of the frontier and of Indian fighting, as the dominant, most characteristic, and most interesting genre has established a prevalent view of that whole. The shift toward outlaw tales, tales of urban life, and detective stories is usually considered a degeneration of the dime novel (Bellows 1899; Smith 1950, 119-120). In addition, dime novels are characteristically thought of as books for boys and men; cheap romances for women are rarely read or studied.

This view, which dominated the first wave of studies and appreciations of nineteenth-century popular fiction, was triggered by Frank P. O'Brien's large collection of Beadle's dime novels. Part of this collection was auctioned to the public in 1920, while most of it was donated to the New York Public Library and purchased by the Huntington Library in the early 1920s. As Philip Durham (1966, ix) points out, 'realizing the tendency to look down on cheaply-printed popular literature, Dr. O'Brien was careful not to refer to his books as dime novels; the descriptive title of the catalogue was *American Pioneer Life*.' In the New York Public Library catalogue of the O'Brien collection, one finds a classic formulation of the 'dime novel'. They are 'literally saturated with the pioneer spirit of America. It [the collection] portrays the struggles, exploits, trials, dangers, feats, hardships, and daily lives of the American pioneers. ... It is a literature intensely nationalistic and patriotic in character; obviously designed to stimulate adventure, self-reliance and achievement; to exalt the feats of the pioneer men and women who settled the country; and to recite the conditions under which those early figures lived and did their work' (Beadle Collection 1922, 3-4). They are considered realistic novels: 'It has finally come to be realized that the pictures of pioneer life in the Far West, as presented by the Beadle books, are substantially accurate portrayals of the strange era and characters therein depicted. ... The Beadle books present a more accurate and vivid picture of the appearance, manner, speech, habits and methods of the pioneer western characters than do the more formal historians' (7). We find in this introduction the folk wisdom that 'uncounted armies of boys who lived between the Mississippi and the Atlantic were taken to the woodsheds by their fathers, and there subjected to severe physical and mental anguish as a result of the parental discovery that they were reading such "impossible trash"' (7). And we find the sense that the cheap libraries of the 1880s and 1890s are 'degenerate and feeble imitations of the earlier Beadle publications' (17). There is no attention to the romances published for girls and women.

Most subsequent considerations of the dime novel were based on the O'Brien collection and this view of the lineaments of nineteenth-century popular fiction. Newspaper humorist Irwin Cobb (1929, 194-195), in his 'A Plea for Old Cap Collier', defends the dime novels by comparing them to the style and substance of nineteenth-century school readers, and concludes: 'Read them for the thrills that are in them. Read them, remembering that if this country had not had a pioneer breed of Buckskin Sams and Deadwood Dicks we should have had no native school of dime novelists. Read them for their brisk and stirring movement; for the spirit of outdoor adventure and life which crowds them; for their swift but logical processions of sequences; for the phases of pioneer Americanism they rawly but graphically portray, and for their moral values.' In 1929, Edmund Pearson, a librarian, published the first book-length account of dime novels: *Dime Novels: or, Following an Old Trail in Popular Literature.* This slight, entertaining history, interspersed with liberal quotations and plot summaries, exemplifies the combination of nostalgia and nationalism that characterized many of these treatments. Such discussions are also marked by a disdain for their contemporary popular culture, measuring present degeneration against past glory;[2] they share this contempt with the more substantial contemporary treatments of popular fiction in Britain: Q.D. Leavis' *Fiction and the Reading Public* (1932), and George Orwell's 'Boys' Weeklies' (1939).

This view of dime novels also informed the first major scholarly and critical studies: Albert Johannsen's two-volume *The House of Beadle and Adams and its Dime and Nickel Novels* (1950), which contains lists of novels, indexes, and biographies of writers, and remains the finest bibliographic guide to dime novels; and Henry Nash Smith's essays on dime novel westerns in *Virgin Land* (1950). They too focused on a single publisher, Beadle and Adams; a single genre, the western; and a primarily male reading public.[3]

Furthermore, it is important to realize the centrality of the collecting and sale of dime novels to our understanding of them. A small group of collectors has been responsible for the physical preservation of this ephemeral literature and for all of the indexes and catalogs of stories that exist. Most of the major research library collections owe their existence to these collectors, not to library initiative. The main periodical dealing with nineteenth-century popular fiction, *Dime Novel Round-Up*, has been published since 1931 as a collector's journal. The bibliographic work of its present editor, Edward T. LeBlanc, is the foundation for any scholarly or critical examination.

However, when Albert Johannsen (1950, 2: 325) writes at length on the 'value' of dime novels, he is referring to their exchange value. He writes that 'another factor in determining the value of a novel ... is the story itself. Opinions differ as to the relative importance of the different groups of novels.' Johannsen goes on to list types, in order of descending 'value': early colonial and pioneer tales, western tales of scouts and Indian fighters, tales of Buffalo Bill and Calamity Jane, sea tales, tales of city life, detective stories. He concludes: 'And love stories, I presume, should go at the bottom of the list.' My reason for citing this is less to disagree with Johannsen (I assume that his was a relatively accurate sense of the rare book market of the late 1940s) than to point out its effects on historical writing. When dealing with an immense body of narratives — Beadle and Adams alone published 3,158 separate titles[4] — certain kinds of selection are necessary. And the kind of selection that has structured our understanding — the kind of synecdoche 'dime novel' is — has an historical and ideological foundation.

This is why I rehearse this history. For Beadle and Adams, though important, did not entirely dominate sensational fiction. Their success with tales of pioneers and the frontier must be balanced against the wider range of fiction — aristocratic costume romances, detective tales, working-girl stories, tales of the American Revolution, mysteries of the city, outlaw stories — which was published in the story papers, cheap libraries, and pamphlet novels, both before and after the heyday of Beadle's Dime Books. Several central judgements about dime novels are the result more of collectors' tastes than of historical analysis, tastes that owe much to the myths and ideologies of the 'western' in twentieth-century popular culture. Indeed the relative fading of westerns from contemporary popular culture may allow us to recognize the other genres and types that existed in the nineteenth century; there are signs that the dime novel detective tale is replacing the dime novel western in critical favor.[5]

Moreover, the sense that there was a shift in the dime novel from western themes to urban themes is belied by the tremendous popularity of the 'mysteries of the city' in the 1840s; and the judgment of degeneration seems an unwillingness to deal with the relation of the dime novel to the immigrant working classes. One can see this in a lament of the late 1920s:

> The period between 1870 and 1900 witnessed the rise of the train-robber and detective as the protagonists in paper-covered literature. It marks also the decline of the House of Beadle and the triumph of the cheaper elements in dime novel publishing. . . . As more competitors entered the field, which was still lucrative, the quality of the 'dimes' and 'half-dimes' was lowered until they became flaring atrocities. No longer was it possible for a Henry Ward Beecher to commend the editor of a dime novel. Presidents of the United States no longer pored over the yellow-backs. The pulpit and the polite press trained its heaviest 'grape' on the sub-literary weeklies, and in the last fifteen years [1913-1928] they have been harried and hunted off the news-stands into the dismal murk of second-hand speakeasies (Robinson 1928, 64-65).

However, the picture of the dime novel changes if we think of its readers not as small-town Tom Sawyers sneaking a 'read' behind the woodshed but as young factory workers; the nationalism and chauvinism of the cheap stories takes on a different cast when considered in relation to young immigrants. And any attention to the story papers shows the importance of girls' and women's reading in a picture of cheap sensational fiction of the nineteenth century. Finally, far from being an uncorrupted moment before the onset of mass culture, the dime novel industry is a central component of the emerging culture industry: Robert Bonner, Park Benjamin, and Erastus Beadle stand with P.T. Barnum and Albert Spaulding as early entrepreneurs of leisure. Therefore my concern will be with the 'mechanic accents' of these stories, with the intersection of the new mass culture and the culture of the new masses, with the place of dime novels within working class life. To view these books that collectors prize through the culture of craftworkers, factory operatives, and laborers rescues them from a kind of patronizing and patriotic nostalgia, and situates them not in a pastoral golden age but in the class conflicts of the gilded age.

2

Fiction Factories: The Production of Dime Novels

Why has our yellow-covered literature
Poured o'er the land its influence impure?
Why, but because 'twas cheap — its profits sure!

A.J.H. Duganne, 1851

Of course we all know that all kinds of factories exist in New
York, but until last week I never knew that the great metropolis
boasted of such a thing as a real and fully equipped literary
factory.... This literary factory is hidden away in one of the
by-streets of New York.... It employs over thirty people, mostly
girls and women. For the most part these girls are intelligent. It is
their duty to read all the daily and weekly periodicals in the land.
... Any unusual story of city life — mostly the misdoings of city
people — is marked by these girls and turned over to one of three
managers. These managers, who are men, select the best of the
marked articles, and turn over such as are available to one of a
corps of five women, who digest the happening given to them
and transform it to a skeleton or outline for a story. This shell, if it
may be so called, is then returned to the chief manager, who turns
to a large address-book and adapts the skeleton to some one of
the hundred or more writers entered on his book.... [The stories
are then sold] to the cheaper sensational weeklies, to boiler-plate
factories and to publishers of hair-curling libraries of adventure.
... This business is of the most profitable character to its owners.
The 'factory' does not care where its authors get their material
from, so long as the story, when finished, is calculated to please
the miscellaneous audience for which it is intended. 'Situations',
and of the most dramatic and startling character, must be
frequent, and two or three murders and a rescue or two in one
chapter are not a bit too many.

Edward Bok, 1892

This depiction of cheap story production by Edward Bok, the

editor of *Ladies Home Journal*, is an emblem of the tendencies within this early culture industry. Bok's observations come late in the century and are somewhat exceptional; nevertheless, from Edward Everett's (1860, 480-489) awed account of the mass production and distribution of the story paper, the *New York Ledger*, in 1860, to Bok's account of the division of labor in a story-writing factory, the writing of dime novels was viewed by literary figures as an extraordinary kind of industrial production. As the genteel literary critic George Woodberry wrote in 1891: 'the whole complexion of the thing is of a different world' (Ickstadt 1979, 93). In this chapter, I will look at this 'different world' of literary production, first by looking at the nature of the industry and the place of writers within it, and then by separating the dime novel from fiction writing generally and considering its relation to two other industries of culture and leisure — journalism and the melodramatic theater.

The dime novel industry was founded for the most part by a generation of artisan entrepreneurs. Robert Bonner (born 1824 in Ireland), Erastus Beadle (born 1821), Frederick Gleason (born 1816), George Munro (born 1815), Theophilus Beasley Peterson (born 1823), and Francis Shubael Smith (of Street & Smith) (born 1819) had all apprenticed in the printing trades and were journeymen compositors or stereotypers.[1] The craft of printing experienced a technological revolution in the 1830s and 1840s; the spread of stereotyping eroded the skills of compositors and the new steam-powered presses not only displaced many pressmen but increased the capital necessary for the larger printing plants. So at a time when the *New York Tribune* estimated that 'not more than one in twenty New York journeymen eventually opened his own shop, and those who did could at best hope to club together with friends to open a small, marginal business',[2] these small printers who turned failing newspapers into highly-advertised story papers and sold pamphlet novels for a dime became the first successful entrepreneurs of the cheap fiction industry.

Though some, like Robert Bonner, became notorious for flaunting their wealth, and others, like Street and Smith, established firms that remained successful into the twentieth century, most dime novel publishers found themselves in an uncertain and fluctuating business. In less than a decade, Jonas Winchester, the artisan printer who backed the storypaper, *New World*, and its 'extras', went from 'rather humble beginnings' to become 'one of the leading printers in New York City', only to fall to poverty and 'oblivion' (Barnes 1974, 11, 25). Cheap fiction publishers were always subject to postal regulations; the first cheap books of the 1840s had reduced their price by appearing as newspapers and newspaper supplements, with lower postal rates than books. Their demise came when the post office began to charge book rates for supplements in 1843, and then reduced postal rates for all books in 1845. This set off what Frank Schick (1958, 50) called 'the biggest boom American book publishing had ever known' between 1845 and 1857; as a result, 'by the late 1840s and early 1850s there was scarcely a trace of the cheap weeklies and their supplements' (Barnes 1974, 28). Throughout the nineteenth century, dime novel publishing remained subject to the efforts of the Post Office to regulate publishing competition by continually revising the postage rates and classifications governing books, magazines, and newspapers (Shove 1937).

Paradoxically, the dime novel business seemed to thrive in periods of depression. Cheap books were most successful when regular book publishing was in disarray, when prices were generally depressed, and when the cost of printing and writing labor was low. The first wave of cheap books emerged out of the depression that followed the Panic of 1837; the second wave, triggered by the New York story papers and Beadle's dime books, crested in the years after the Panic of 1857; and the third wave appeared with the swell of cheap nickel libraries in the depression that followed the Panic of 1873.[3]

The key to dime novel success, however, lay in distribution. Thus, one of the most successful firms in the industry was the American News Company, founded in 1864, which until 1904 held a virtual monopoly over the distribution of story papers, magazines and pamphlet novels to newsstands and dry goods stores, handling the publications of Beadle and Adams, Street and Smith, Robert Bonner, Norman Munro, and Frank Tousey, among others (Stern 1980, 303-305; Schick 1958, 103). Indeed whereas the first wave of cheap books and story papers in the 1840s was often limited to the market of a single city and survived only a few years, the distribution monopoly of the American News Company made the post-Civil War nickel and dime libraries a national industry.

Perhaps the most difficult aspect of the fiction industry to rationalize was the writing of the stories themselves. Throughout the period, cheap story publishers competed for the services of celebrated writers. Robert Bonner was famous for paying high prices to 'star' writers for exclusive contracts. In the early years, successful dime novelists like George Lippard, T.S. Arthur and Ned Buntline were able to begin their own story papers. But the tendency of the industry was to shift from selling an 'author', who was a free laborer, to selling a 'character', a trademark whose stories could be written by a host of anonymous hack writers and whose celebrity could be protected in court. Indeed, this subordination of the writer is inscribed in the stories themselves. In a study of dime westerns by Ned Buntline, Edward Ellis, Prentiss Ingraham and Edward Wheeler, Christine Bold (1983, 30) has argued that 'the development and decline of the story-telling voice mirror changes in the publishing world where authors gradually lost more and more of their authority over their fiction. ... Early dime novelists spent much time in their repetitive tales of captivity, chase and rescue on the frontier talking to the reader about the process of composition.' However, she argues, this individual narrative voice is effaced first by the characters themselves, and then by the discourse between publisher and consumer which frames the tales.

An overall view of the writers for the story papers, cheap libraries and dime novels has to be sketchy and speculative at this time. There are some autobiographical accounts, a few interviews, a handful of biographies (though usually of popular writers of the earliest period — George Lippard, E.D.E.N. Southworth, Ned Buntline — before the complete subordination of writers to company pseudonyms), and Albert Johannsen's biographical dictionary of the Beadle's authors.[4] For the most part, however, even rudimentary study has not been done. Collectors have devoted much time and research to sorting out pseudonyms, finding out which names are of real people, and under which names known writers published. My own survey of the existing accounts suggests several tentative conclusions. First, dime novels writers were able to support themselves by their writing for a time, but only the most prolific kept it up for an entire career and few seem to have made large sums of money. In his autobiography, *The Fiction Factory*, William Wallace Cook offers one of the few accounts of a rank-and-file sensational story writer. Beginning as a clerk, ticket agent and paymaster, Cook turned to fiction writing as a full time occupation in 1893, and supported himself for twenty years; his story alternates between flush times, when he hires stenographers to keep up with the demand, and hard times, when he is laid off as publishers cut back by reprinting old serials. Writing cheap stories was often combined with journalism, schoolteaching, and working for the popular theater. A number of dime novelists, including Frederick Whittaker, Edward Ellis and Charles Morris, wrote histories as well, usually local histories, or military accounts of the Civil War or the war against the Indians. A few, particularly children's writers, were social and moral reformers: their writing was tied to temperance, moral uplift and improvement of workers' conditions. Others saw themselves as tribunes of the popular classes; we will look in chapter six at the contrasting politics of George Lippard and Ned Buntline. John E. Barrett was a labor reformer and probably a member of the Knights of Labor, Elizabeth Oakes Smith was a women's rights activist (Johannsen 1950, 2: 259), and John Harvey Whitson once ran for office for the Greenback party (Adimari 1935, 100).

In his study of the writer in the nineteenth-century German book industry, Russell Berman (1983, 41) argues against 'the eternally returning cultural conservative complaint that the purportedly low quality of popular literature merely reflects the desires of the masses.' Rather, 'it was the experience of the book industry and its economic forms which led to the specific character of the maligned literature.' The memoirs of the dime novel writers support Berman's contention. Their accounts of the writing process share certain themes: quantity, speed, and fixed demands by the publishers. One finds Albert Aiken 'in a little den on an upper floor' of the 'worm-eaten old building' of Beadle & Adams where he 'used to grind out dime novels day after day with the steadiness of a machine' (Jenks 1904, 113), and Mrs Alex McVeigh Miller sending in her weekly installments of 'thirty pages of longhand writing on foolscap paper' (Lewis 1941, 3). William Wallace Cook began by receiving a title and synopsis for a serial, and would then write, adapt and revise installments to meet the ever-changing specifications of the publisher. Almost all the accounts tell the story of novels written at exceptional speed in marathon sessions, and all emphasize the sheer quantity of writing. Upton Sinclair claims to have written as much as the collected works of Sir Walter Scott in his dime novels days between 1897 and 1902 (Adimari 1956, 52), and William Wallace Cook (1912, 54) notes that he 'has written two 30,000-word stories a week for months at a time ... [and] has begun a Five Cent Library story at 7 o'clock in the morning and worked the clock around, completing the manuscript at 7 the next morning.'

The requirements of the publishers were stricly formulated; in

1893, Street & Smith wrote to the aspiring Cook:

> Our careful reading of the installment leads us to believe that you
> write easily, and can probably do suitable work for us. What we
> require for our libraries is something written up-to-date, with
> incidents new and original with which the daily press is teeming — if
> you will submit us such a story we shall be pleased to examine same,
> and if found suitable we will find a place for it at once. We pay for
> stories in this library $100. They should contain 40,000 words, and
> when issued appear under our own nom de plume (Pachon 1957, 69).

As a result, some writers discount their dime novel productions
as merely writing for money, though all defend the morality and
usefulness of dime novels. Eugene Sawyer tells an interviewer in
1902: Though my work was all trashy, it never pandered to any
depraved tastes. For a dime novel you require only three things
— a riotous imagination, a dramatic instinct and a right hand
that never tires. I never revised a line or crossed out a word'
(Burgess 1902, 533). William Wallace Cook (1912, 39) not only
defends the morality of the nickel thrillers against the dollar 'best
seller' — 'a difference in the price of two commodities does not
necessarily mark a moral difference in the commodities themselves' — but maintains that 'this is not "trash". It is literature
sold at a price which carries it everywhere, and the result is
untold good' (41). 'A writer is neither better nor worse than any
other man who happens to be in trade. He is a manufacturer' (26).

At times, one even finds traces of literary ideologies: Whitman
and Poe are continually invoked as the ideal of popular literary
figures the dime writers sought to emulate. The most eloquent
statement is Frederick Whittaker's (1884, 8) defense of the dime
novel in the *New York Tribune*. The *Tribune* had published an
editorial attacking the immorality and bad influence of dime
novels, that 'pestilent stuff'. While Whittaker's statement
includes the obligatory denial of the dime novel's immorality, it
is not based for the most part on moral grounds. Instead, he
intends 'to defend the class to which I belong. ... The only
writers who can make a living by literary labors alone are dime
novelists. ... Had Poe lived in these days, he would have been a
writer of dime novels; for his prose stories have all the qualities
which are required in a good dime.' He then argues: 'It is only
the cheap stories, which you call dime novels, for which the
demand is, and always will be inexhaustible, and which must be
depended on for the regeneration of American literature.' Here

even the term for these books is contested, as Whittaker refuses the term of abuse, 'what you call dime novels', for the proper terms, 'cheap stories' and 'American literature'.

Though there are certain *auteurs* who by force of personality established themselves as stars in this industry — Lippard, Buntline, Southworth, Libbey — the trend was toward industrial production based on division of labor and corporate trademarks, the pseudonyms of the market. In this light the paradigmatic 'authors' are 'Old Sleuth' and 'Bertha M. Clay'. Old Sleuth was the first successful and continuous detective character; the first story about Old Sleuth was written by Harlan Page Halsey for George Munro's *Fireside Companion* in 1872, and the success of the character led to the publication of a five-cent Old Sleuth Library, in 1885, which featured Old Sleuth in about a quarter of its biweekly issues. The stories were said to be written by 'Old Sleuth' himself, and this became the focus of a series of court cases when a number of firms, beginning with that of George Munro's brother, Norman Munro, attempted to use the term 'sleuth' in their own series. The first court decision 'perpetually enjoined Norman Munro from publishing any stories represented to have been written by Old Sleuth, Young Sleuth, the Young Badger, the Author of Old Sleuth, The Author of Young Badger, or either of them ... unless such stories were actually written by [Harlan P. Halsey].' But the cases got more complicated when Halsey left George Munro to write for Street & Smith's *New York Weekly*; now the case was not to defend the author against imitations but to maintain property rights in the name 'Old Sleuth' against the author himself. In cases against Street & Smith and Beadle & Adams, the courts finally decided that 'George Munro has "a certain property right" in the use of the phrase Old Sleuth and was entitled to protection under the "law governing common-law trade marks."'[5] Halsey had to write his detective stories for the *New York Weekly* under a different pseudonym, Judson Taylor.

'Bertha M. Clay,' one of the most popular writers of romances in the late nineteenth century, has a similar story. The name began in the late 1870s when the *New York Weekly* pirated the stories of 'C.M.B.', Charlotte M. Brame, from the London *Family Herald*, and ascribed them to 'Bertha M. Clay'. Their success led to the use of the name by Street & Smith not only for pirated Brame stories but for other romances written by the same house novelists who wrote the Nick Carter and Frank Merriwell stories: John R. Coryell, Frederick V. Dey, Gilbert Patten, William J.

Benners, and William Wallace Cook. Indeed, Cook (1912, 45-46) tells of his jump from 'a rapid-fire Ten-Cent Library story for young men to a bit of sentimental fiction for young women. ... The popular young lady authoress, "Stella Edwards" [this is the name Cook uses to refer to the company pseudonyms "Bertha Clay" and "Julia Edwards" in his autobiography], whose portrait in a decollete gown had been so often flaunted in the eyes of "her" public, was a myth. The "stuff" supposedly written by the charming "Stella Edwards" was ground out by men who were versatile enough to befool women readers, with a feminine style.' Though Charlotte Brame died in 1884, 'Bertha M. Clay' continued to 'write' into the twentieth century (Noel 1954, 186-190; Adimari 1958, 123).

Therefore in general these dime novels are best considered as an essentially anonymous, 'unauthored' discourse, not unlike journalism. Indeed, dime novels and newspapers are linked by more than the coincidence of new technologies and new reading publics. Many dime novelists were newspaper reporters and editors.[6] Moreover, as Bok's testimony about the fiction factory demonstrates, dime novel plots were often constructed out of the events reported in the daily and weekly newspapers of cities around the country. Indeed, William Wallace Cook (1912, 35) cites a letter from his publisher Street and Smith which suggests that he 'in future stories make no special effort to produce an unusual plot, but stick closer to the action and incident, taken as much as possible from newspapers, which are teeming with material of this character.' As a result Cook kept careful files of newspaper clippings as 'raw material' to draw on for plots and local color. If the production of dime novels is considered as a branch of journalism, the repeated formulas, the quantity and rapidity of the writing, the lack of a clear 'author', the appearance of current events in the stories, and the industrial conditions of dime novel writing become more comprehensible.[7]

Dime novels were also clearly connected to popular melo-dramas. A contemporary reviewer writes of 'the utilization, by paraphrasing them, of pieces which are having a successful run at the theaters. *The Two Orphans, Divorce, Under the Gas-Light,* and other such have appeared in this way. Reversing a common process, they are not "dramatized for the stage," but narrativized for the story paper.'[8] This crossing between dime novels and melodrama may indicate a common audience as well as a common body of stories; if so, the split between genteel and sensational fiction is reproduced in the growing split between

legitimate theater and melodrama. A major historian of melodrama takes the Astor Place Riots of 1849 (led in part by dime
novelist Ned Buntline) as the sign of the end of a theater which
united different classes in boxes, pits and galleries: 'one theater
was no longer large enough to appeal to all classes' (Grimsted
1968, 73). After 1850, the melodrama and the dime novel increasingly found a predominantly working class audience. Moreover,
the narrativization of stage productions indicates a new mode or
character in the reading of dime novels and story papers; reading
became a way of preserving and recapturing a public moment or
a favorite performance. Like the scripts of the melodramas
themselves, the thinness of dime novels, the absence of detailed
description, may reveal the memory of the nineteenth-century
theatrical spectacles with their elaborate special effects and
mechanisms — trains, fires and live animals on stage — while
prefiguring the close relation between popular fiction and the
modern cinema.

Bok's 'literary factory' is thus an apt phrase for what was an
emerging culture industry in the nineteenth century.[9] The term
'culture industry' comes from the work of the Frankfurt School
theorists, Max Horkheimer and Theodor Adorno (1944), and
recently it has been used persuasively in the examination of
nineteenth-century German culture (Hohendahl 1983). The
strength of the concept is twofold: it avoids a static and ahistorical dichotomy between elite culture and popular culture, since it
marks the decisive break from earlier elite and folk cultures and
emphasizes the effects of that break on both cultures; and it
draws attention to the commodification of culture — the restruc-
turing of cultural production by wage labor, a capitalist market,
and a capitalist labor process which divides, rationalizes, and
deskills work.

Although a view of dime novels as commodities in a growing
and interconnected culture industry can tell us much about the
conditions in which they were produced and, as I will demonstrate in the analyses to follow, about the forms that they took,
there are limits to the commodification argument, as its pro-
ponents themselves point out. Peter Hohendahl (1983: 6) writes
that:

> ... the thesis that the cultural sphere became more and more commodi-
> fied — which lies at the heart of the theory of Adorno and Hork-
> heimer — cannot explain the full extent of the changes that occurred
> after 1870 [in Germany]. It specifically overlooks the role of the state
> and of local administrations. In their attempt to rescue culture from

the onslaught of big business, they reorganized the cultural sphere, creating organizations that would administer the cultural participation of the masses. The public library movement in the early 1900s would be a good example for this build-up of administrative structures designed to save 'culture'.

Indeed the public library movement in the United States in the late nineteenth century, and particularly the controversies over the place of fiction in the library, are significant parts of the history of dime novels and the 'reformation' of working class culture. And though the American state was a diffuse and under-developed entity in the nineteenth century, it played a significant role in regulating popular fiction, particularly through Post Office regulations. Another non-commercial force that shaped the culture industry was the emergence of evangelical reformers, whether they acted as censors, like the celebrated Anthony Comstock; or as authors of alternative, 'moral' fiction in the same format, as in temperance novels and the morality tales of Oliver Optic and Horatio Alger.

Finally there was resistance within the culture industry itself, attempts to use the new means of fiction production against commodification. This is evident in some of the radical writers like Lippard, though attempts to articulate radical and populist politics in fiction are rare. It is more striking in the politics of publishers like the abolitionist James Redpath, whose ten-cent Books for the Camp Fires were aimed at Union soldiers and included a cheap edition of *Clotelle* by the black novelist William Wells Brown; and John Lovell, who used the cheap book form to publish not only sensational fiction but socialist and populist works. His Political and Scientific Series included the first cheap edition of Henry George's *Progress and Poverty* (Stern 1980, 204-205).

So if we accurately characterize the production of dime novels as a fiction factory, as part of an emerging culture industry, we should be careful not to assimilate it too quickly with an inexorable logic of capital or with notions of 'mass deception,' in the phrase of Adorno and Horkheimer. As in other capitalist industries, there are struggles both at the point of production, the writing of these dime novels; and at the point of consumption, the reading of cheap stories. So a history of dime novels is not simply a history of a culture industry; it also encompasses a history of their place in working class culture, and of their role in the struggles to reform that culture.

3

'The Unknown Public': Dime Novels and Working Class Readers

Who read these stories and what did they think of them? Though this question is now central to the study of popular culture, it remains a difficult and elusive one. In part, this is because of sketchy and uncertain evidence. Even when one can determine who the readers were, it is very difficult to determine how they interpreted their reading. But the difficulty also lies in the reluctance of cultural historians of the United States to use class categories to describe and analyze the reading public. As a result, they often end up with a simple dichotomy between the few and the many, the discriminating and the mass, the elite and the popular. However, the place of dime novels in American culture depends not only on the industrial character of their production but on the class character of their reading public. Thus, this chapter will attempt to characterize the readers of dime novels by exploring the relations between popular fiction and its working class audience.[1]

The question of who read dime novels becomes two questions in the context of the relation between popular fiction and working class culture. One begins from the artifacts: who were the audience of dime novels, story papers, and cheap libraries? The other begins from the reading public: what did working class people read in the late nineteenth century? My argument is that these two questions converge: that the bulk of the audience of dime novels were workers — craftworkers, factory operatives, domestic servants, and domestic workers — and that the bulk of workers' reading was sensational fiction.

Recent accounts of the readers of dime novels by literary critics and cultural historians tend to be rather vague. In his book on dime novel westerns, Daryl Jones (1978, 14) writes only that 'though dime novelists aimed their stories at a predominantly working-class audience, the appeal of the genre in fact pervaded the entire culture. Dime novels provided a source of entertainment and diversion for any individual of any social class who sought relief from the anxieties of the age.' Mary Noel (1954, 290-291), on the other hand, sees the story paper audience as 'middle class and American'. 'Whether or not the lowest economic group read the story papers must remain in doubt' — and she doubts it. Nina Baym (1984, 47), in an examination of antebellum reviews of fiction, concludes that 'in novel criticism, the audience seems to be divided into two groups, correlated loosely with presumed class member-ship. First, and more numerous, were ordinary or "mere" novel readers looking for pleasure and reading for story; second, there was a small group of cultivated, discreet, intelligent, educated, tasteful, thoughtful readers who wanted something more than, but not incompatible with (reviewers hoped), the tastes of the ordinary reader.' But Baym misses a third group only occasionally mentioned in the reviews she cites: the readers of cheap literature. Far more adequate than either the nostalgic image of a single 'American' reading public or the split between the few and the many is the picture sketched by Henry Nash Smith (1978, 8-9). He invokes the terminology of 'brows', noting an important distinction between:

> . . . the work of the new women novelists and yet another kind of fiction that proliferated during the 1840s — crude adventure stories repre-sented by Tom Sawyer's favorite, *The Black Avenger of the Spanish Main; or, The Fiend of Blood. A Thrilling Story of Buccaneer Times*, by 'Ned Buntline' (E.Z.C. Judson), published in 1847. For want of a more elegant terminology I shall call the sentimental fiction of Warner and Cummins, together with the system of values embodied in it, 'middlebrow', and Ned Buntline's work 'lowbrow'. In such a scheme, Hawthorne and Melville evidently must be categorized as 'highbrow'. Although not enough evidence has been accumulated to support confident statements about the sizes of these segments of the mid-nineteenth century reading public, it appears that the total sales of lowbrow fiction were the largest — especially after the Beadle & Adams dime novels began to appear in 1860; but a few best-selling middlebrow titles far outstripped any individual lowbrow items in circulation.

But Smith argues that the relation between 'brow levels' and social and economic classes is obscure: 'The notorious vagueness of class lines in the United States precludes any close linkage between brow levels and the actual social structure.'[2] A closer look at the nineteenth-century sources can make the relation between brows — a twentieth-century concept — and classes clearer.

Smith's picture of antebellum fiction readers is very similar to George Woodberry's survey of the fiction-reading public in 1891. Woodberry, a leading genteel literary critic, identified a three-tier public: the readers of 'pure literature', interested in the art of fiction proper; the readers of the popular success novels; and the readers of 'the literature of the "Unknown Public"', addressing itself to thousands of readers, whose authors were quite unknown, their subjects and methods strange, and that was all "written for money" — "the whole complexion of the thing is of a different world"' (Ickstadt 1979, 93). Woodberry echoes Edward Everett's (1860, 488) early comment that the story paper was the first attempt to reach the 'Unknown Public'. Indeed the 'Unknown Public' was one of a variety of epithets contemporaries used for the dime novel audience: the 'great people', the 'million', the 'submerged tenth'. The slogan of Beadle and Adams was 'Books for the Million!'. In his defense of the dime novel, Frederick Whittaker (1884, 8) speaks of 'the "great people" to whom the papers are constantly appealing. The readers of the dimes are farmers, mechanics, workwomen, drummers, boys in shops and factories, and a great many people who are so much appalled by the abuse of the daily press that they do not confess what they have been reading.' Dime novelist Eugene Sawyer, on the other hand, maintained: 'It is not, however, only the "submerged tenth" who reads cheap stories. I have been in bookshops and seen bankers and capitalists gravely paying their nickels for the same tales as their elevator boys read' (Burgess 1902, 532). Despite Sawyer's somewhat self-justifying assertion, W.H. Bishop (1879, 389) expressed the nineteenth-century consensus when he wrote in the *Atlantic* that the story papers and cheap libraries were 'written almost exclusively for the use of the lower classes of society.'

Nevertheless, more exact delineations of the audience are hard to find. The publishers themselves left little evidence more specific than Beadle's 'books for the million'. A bookseller noted that 'the people who buy the "libraries" are the people who take in the *New York Ledger,* . . . utterly unknown to bookstores.'[3] In 1871, the *New York Weekly* explicitly linked publishing stories about women sewing machine operators with seeking them as an audience:

Every sewing machine girl in the United States should not only read *Bertha Bascomb, the Sewing Machine Girl,* but should make it her especial business to see that everybody else reads it. The story is designed to benefit the working girl, and therefore every working girl in our broad land should constitute herself an agent for its distribution. Everybody will be better for reading this great story; and we confidently look for an addition of at least one hundred thousand extra readers to swell our already unprecedented circulation (Noel 1954, 278).

Moreover, one can assume that some part of the audience was made up of immigrants and ethnics, particularly Irish and Germans, since publishers issued series like Ten Cent Irish Novels and George Munro's Die Deutsche Library. There were, however, no dime novels aimed at Blacks; and I have not found evidence of any Black readership.[4] The audience clearly was predominantly young. W.H. Bishop (1879, 384) describes 'the traffic on publication days':

> A middle-aged woman, with a shawl over her head and half a peck of potatoes in a basket, stops in for one; a shop-girl on her way home from work; a servant from one of the good houses in the side streets. ... But with them, before them, and after them come boys. ... The most ardent class of patron ... are boys.

Nevertheless, except for the story papers and libraries explicitly aimed at boys and girls, this could not be called 'children's literature'. When William Wallace Cook (1912, 35) began writing dime fiction, he was criticized by the editor for writing for too young an audience: 'I hope you have not made the hero too juvenile, as this would be a serious fault. The stories in the Ten-Cent Library are not read by boys alone but usually by young men, and in no case should the hero be a kid.' Thus the 'people', the 'unknown public', the 'million', the audience of dime novels and story papers seems to be predominantly young, 'lowbrow', and internally divided by gender. It includes, depending on on's rhetoric, the 'producing classes' or the 'lower classes', encompassing German and Irish immigrants and ethnics but excluding Blacks and Chinese immigrants and ethnics.

If we turn to the other question — what did nineteenth-century working-class people read? — a complementary picture emerges from recent studies of literacy and from the two basic types of contemporary accounts of workers' reading; those of observers and reformers of working-class life, and those of workers in autobiographies and memoirs.[5] First, the success of the dime novel industry was in large part a result of the high levels of literacy among American workers. This was spurred not only by the availability of cheap reading matter but by the development of the 'common school' of universal primary education for whites in the years between 1830 and 1850. In their detailed examination of literacy in the nineteenth-century United States, Lee Soltow and Edward Stevens (1981, 51) find that there are three major reductions in illiteracy: 'the first following a decade of intense social reform, including common school reform (1850-1859), the second (more modest) appearing in the decade following the Civil War, when a number of states enacted compulsory education laws (1870-1879), and the third appearing in the decade following the passage of compulsory school attendance laws in most states and their enforcement in some (1880-1889).' Though the 1840 Census found that 97% of white adults over 21 in the Northeast, and 91% in the Northwest, were literate, this was based on a minimum standard of literacy. Soltow and Stevens, using a stricter standard and working from army enlistment files, find that 89% of northern artisans and 76% of northern farmers and laborers were literate in the period between 1830 and 1895 (52). 'Farmers and laborers, who were the two groups exhibiting the highest rates of illiteracy between 1799 and 1829, underwent rapid declines [in rates of illiteracy] . . . by the end of the century' (54). Indeed by 1870, just before the emergence of the cheap libraries, there were similar literacy rates among native-born and foreign-born men (though foreign-born women were substantially more illiterate than native-born women until 1890) (199). Together, common-school literacy and the fiction factory provided the conditions for written narratives to become a significant part of working-class amusement.

Indeed, one of the earliest observers of working-class reading, the Presbyterian minister James Alexander (1839, 66), who published two books about and for workers in 1838 and 1839, called attention to the new story papers:

The demand for this merely entertaining literature is evinced by the character of the large weekly newspapers, and low-priced magazines, which circulate most among operatives. I need not name these; our cities abound in them. The newspapers to which I allude are commonly issued on Saturday, and their immense sheet gives occupation to many a poor reader for the whole of Sunday. Now you will observe, that a large part of the outer form of these publications is frequently taken up with just that kind of reading which is fitted to make a sound mind sick, and a feeble mind crazy. Tales upon tales of love, of horror, of madness, and these often the effusions of the most unpractised and contemptible scribblers, who rejoice in this channel for venting their inanities, succeed one another week after week, and are the chief reading of persons whom I could name, for year after year.

Forty years later, the Unitarian minister Jonathan Baxter Harrison (1880, 167-171) noted in his 'Study of a New England Factory Town' that:

> The young people of the mills generally read the story papers, published (most of them) in New York City, and devoted to interminably 'continued' narratives, of which there are always three or four in process of publication in each paper.

I will look later at Harrison's characterization of the stories and his assessment of their effects in what is perhaps the most extensive observer's account of working class reading. For now, we should note his account of the mill workers' reading of story papers, his sense that they were young people's reading, and his assumption that his middle class audience would be unaware of their content. He goes on to observe that 'many hundreds of the older operatives, especially foreigners, of two or three nationalities, were reading a paper which is devoted to the liberation of the working-people of America. ... This paper has a large circulation among operatives, miners and city mechanics, in nearly all parts of the country. ... It always contains two or three serial stories by popular writers, which are designed to "float" the heavier articles devoted to the propagation of the doctrines of the agitators.' Finally he discusses a local labor-reform newspaper. The term 'newspaper' implied a wide variety of reading matter in the nineteenth century, so when 'newspapers' are said to be the principal reading matter of workers (e.g. Harvey 1974, 107), this may describe papers that consisted mainly of sensational fiction.

A decade later, the *Atlantic Monthly* published another series of articles on working class life. Lillie B. Chace Wyman (1888-1889, 607-608), in her 'Studies of Factory Life', finds a reading room started by mill operatives and patronized by immigrant men. The reading material was mainly newspapers. The few books, she writes, 'on examination, proved to be largely such as people are willing to give away, because they are of no interest to anybody.'

Another observer who notes newspaper reading is Emile Levasseur (1900, 393-435) of the French *Académie des Sciences Morales et Politiques*, who writes of the 1890s, 'the workman reads the newspaper as everyone else does in America. ... Daily papers cost 1 and 2 cents, weekly papers, 5 cents, as a rule. There is no doubt that the enormous development of the American newspaper in the last forty years has been due in part to the laboring classes.' He bases his conclusions not only on observation but on the federal and state government investigations of workers' budgets which show a high proportion of families making some expenditure for newspapers and books: a recent study of these budgets shows that in 1889, in ten northeastern states, 89.5 percent of native American working-class families and 87 percent of Irish-born working-class families had significant expenditures for newspapers and books (Modell 1978, 214).

An illuminating account of women's reading is given by Jennie Croly, a middle class patron and supporter of young working women. In testimony before the Senate Committee on Education and Labor in 1883, she said, in response to a question about working girls' recreation:

> In the first place, such girls do not care much about sitting down to read. If they have half a day of spare time they want to get out of doors, they want air ... as for reading, they want something very different from what they have in their daily lives, and so they run to the story papers that contain flashy stories; that tell about the fine ladies and how many dresses they have, and that tell about the worst murders and the most exciting incidents that they can get. And I do not blame them for it. They are crazy for something that is outside of themselves, and which will make them forget the hard facts of their daily lives (U.S. Senate, Committee on Education and Labor, 2: 613-614).

Other observers also note story paper reading, usually in passing. An example from early in the period is the Englishman James D. Burn (1865, 34), who notes the wide circulation of the *New York Ledger*, a paper 'solely occupied by light literature', and, in criticizing the boarding-house life that marks American working-class life, says that it encourages women to 'pass away the time by lounging over sensational literature' (6-7). At the end of the nineteenth century, Walter Wyckoff (1898a, 179-180), in his experiment with life as a transient casual laborer, finds an Irish logger, on a rainy day, 'reading a worn paper copy of one of the Duchess's novels, which is the only book that I have so far seen in camp.' He notes that 'most of the men here can read, but to not one of them is reading a resource.'

These accounts by observers of working-class reading need to be read skeptically, however, because all stand within a class conflict over the 'reform' of working-class reading, a conflict I will turn to in the next chapter. Thus one will find advocates of reform stressing the sensational and immoral character of working-class reading, while defenders of the working class will often cite examples of independent 'literary' and 'self-improving' reading.

As we turn to workers' memoirs and autobiographies, similar qualifications apply. Most people, when recalling books that influenced them, will recall literary and political readings more often than sensational fiction, particularly given the general disdain in which it is held: as dime novelist Frederick Whittaker (1884, 8) wrote, dime novels were read by 'a great many people who are so much appalled by the abuse of the daily press that they do not confess what they have been reading.' Furthermore, cheap stories are part of the texture of everyday life; they are not *events* that the autobiographer will tend to narrate. Nevertheless, one does find some accounts of reading sensational fiction in workers' autobiographies.

Some of the earliest accounts of workers' reading are in some ways the most exceptional: those of the Lowell mill girls. Drawn from the New England countryside, they were formed within a genteel Congregationalist culture, and the paternalism of the boarding-house system reinforced this culture. They also preceded the development of mass cheap literature, so their reading was almost entirely within the genteel literary system. So the reading cited by Lucy Larcom and Harriet Robinson includes the English poets and essayists, the literary reviews like *North American Review* and *Blackwood's*, the new women's magazines like *Godey's Ladies Book* and *Graham's Magazine,* and the Christian newspapers: the source for this reading is the circulating library. Harriet Robinson (1898, 57) writes:

> Novels were not very popular with us, as we inclined more to historical writings and to poetry. But such books as *Charlotte Temple, Eliza Wharton, Maria Monk, The Arabian Nights, The Mysteries of Udolpho, Abellino, the Bravo of Venice,* or *The Castle of Otranto* [this list includes popular Gothic and domestic novels], were sometimes taken from the circulating library, read with delight, and secretly lent from one young girl to another.

When she reflects on the mill girls of the present (1898), she writes that 'public libraries are provided, and they have more leisure to read than the mill-girls of forty years ago. But they do not seem to know how to improve it. Their leisure only gives them the more time to be idle in; more time to waste in the streets, or in reading cheap novels and stories' (122). Lucy

Larcom has a somewhat less censorious attitude; after detailing at length her reading in the English poets, she writes: 'And we were as fond of good story-books as any girls that live in these days of overflowing libraries.' Nevertheless after saying that she 'devoured a great many romances', she adds, 'there are so many books of fiction written nowadays, I do not see how the young people who try to read one tenth of them have any brains left for every-day use.' She herself had at least one encounter with the new story papers when she tells of reading Dickens's *Old Curiosity Shop* in a Philadelphia weekly paper.[6]

The most detailed accounts for later in the century are found in the series of short life stories published in *The Independent* between 1902 and 1906, and in the autobiographies of Rose Cohen, Abraham Bisno, and Dorothy Richardson. *The Independent*, a reform magazine, published a series of life stories of 'undistinguished Americans' in order to 'typify the life of the average worker in some particular vocation, and to make each story the genuine experience of a real person' (Katzman and Tuttle 1982, xi). In these testimonies, some written and some the result of interviews, one finds several references to reading. Sadie Frowne, a Polish immigrant and New York garment worker in a sweatshop, says, 'I can read quite well in English now and I look at the newspapers every day. I can read English books, too, sometimes. The last one that I read was *A Mad Marriage* by Charlotte Brame [an English novelist whose works were a staple of the story papers and romance libraries; the original 'Bertha M. Clay']. She's a grand writer and makes things just like real to you. You feel as if you were the poor girl yourself going to get married to a rich duke' (Katzman and Tuttle 1982, 56). A similar sentiment is expressed by a tailoress who does given-out work: 'What chance I get I read something light, like *The Fatal Wedding*. It is one of the best things I've had yet. *The Earl's Secret* is another good one. ... Sometimes I wonder how it would seem if I should have the luck that you read about in the novels — get rich all of a sudden and have your fine house and carriage as some of the girls have that I used to go with. I don't know as I would feel much better' (Stein and Taft 1971, 110).

Rose Cohen (1918), a Russian Jewish immigrant of the 1880s, tells of her early reading in her autobiography. It begins with her reading novels in Yiddish to her mother, novels that were rented from soda water stand keepers for five cents, never more than one a week: 'Mother always listened reluctantly, as if she felt it were a weakness to be so interested. Sometimes she would rise suddenly during the most interesting part and go away into the dark kitchen. But soon I would catch her listening from the doorway. And I lived now in a wonderful world. One time I was a beautiful countess living unhappily in a palace, another time I was a beggar's daughter singing in the street' (187-191). This account ends with her reading a Yiddish translation of *David Copperfield*. A later key moment is her first book read in English, a love story whose name she does not remember: 'I felt so proud that I could read an English book that I carried it about with me in the street. I took it along to the shop. I became quite vain' (249). This leads her to join the free library at the Educational Alliance, and to attempt, unsuccessfully at first, to read Shakespeare (252-254). But throughout her life story, changes in reading mark changes in life and sources of conflict: her father did not 'take kindly' to her reading, fearing that the reading of Gentile books would take her away from Judaism.

Abraham Bisno (1967, 49-50), a Russian Jewish immigrant and garment worker, gives an account of the place of cheap stories in his autobiography that is not dissimilar to that of Rose Cohen:

At fifteen [1881] I began to learn to read. Both in Jewish and in English. I learned English from signs and from advertisements I looked at during the slack period of the trade. Jewish I learned when there was no work and a man who peddled Jewish stories loaned them out weekly to me for five cents a week. He persuaded me to learn to read these stories because they were great romances. An agent of a Jewish newspaper got me to subscribe to a weekly paper. In those years I was very ignorant. I practically knew nothing of what was happening in the United States, and outside of my work and family experiences knew very little. The Jewish stories I read opened my eyes to new worlds. A man named Shomer wrote a great many Jewish romances copied from the French with a change only of names and habits from the French to the Jewish. He wrote a great many of them and I would read three or four a week, absorb their contents enthusiastically and eagerly.

The stories went like this: a poor girl, but very beautiful, fell in love with a rich young man, whose parents would not permit a marriage. Tragedy would follow. The boy would talk of suicide, the girl was miserable, until something happened where the girl was found to really be a heiress, the family smiled on her, they married and lived happily ever after. In a great many of them, there was an intriguing character who would cause either the boy or girl to distrust the other by false tale-bearing. He would be found out in his lies, and the differences were patched up again. Some tales of adventure and enterprise, but most of them about romantic love, the difficulties besetting the path of love, the difficulties ensuing, marriage, and everlasting happiness. But for me these were great finds. When there was no work I read them day and night and would tell about them to any who would listen.

Bisno's autobiography, which was never published during his life, is unusually frank and detailed in its depiction of everyday life; and his voracious reading of sensational fiction for its introduction to 'new worlds' is, I suggest, a typical experience. It is worth noting not only the physical resemblance between the dime novels and these Yiddish *shundromanen* of the 1880s, but the deep similarity of plots: the story Bisno recounts is very close to those written by Laura Jean Libbey. This similarity of plots, together with the absence of an international copyright agreement until 1891, made for a kind of 'world literature' as sensational novels were translated back and forth from English, French, German and Yiddish, translated not to be faithful to the 'original', but, as in the case of Shomer, to be adapted to local names, geography and customs. Moreover, that Bisno seems to have read more romances than tales of adventure or enterprise should make us realize that although cheap stories were clearly marked and marketed by the gender of the implied reader, this did not exclude significant cross-reading.

A somewhat different perspective emerges from Dorothy Richardson's *The Long Day: The Story of a New York Working Girl*. Because Richardson, of whom little is known, had a middle-class background, the story that emerges is less one of the development of her own reading than of the confrontation in the paper box factory between her genteel reading culture and the sensational reading of her workmates. She is asked, 'Don't you never read no story-books?'; but her 'confession of an omnivorous appetite for all sorts of story-books' leads not to a point of contact but to the great gap in the sorts of stories they read. She is told the story of *Little Rosebud's Lovers*, a novel by Laura Jean Libbey that I will examine in chapter ten, and hears of the merits of the stories of Charlotte Brame, Charles Garvice, and Effie Adelaide Rowlands, all mainstays of the story papers and the cheap libraries. When she recounts her reading, 'the names of a dozen or more of the simple, every-day classics that the schoolboy and -girl are supposed to have read' [Dickens, *Little Women*, *Gulliver's Travels*], her workmates have never heard of them. 'They were equally ignorant of the existence of the conventional Sunday-school romance ... and similar goody-goody writers for goody-goody girls; their only remarks being that their titles didn't sound interesting' (Richardson 1905, 75-86). Richardson concludes that:

> The literary tastes of my workmates at the box-factory [are] typical of other factories and other workshops, and also of the department store. A certain downtown section of New York City is monopolized by the publishers and binders of 'yellow-backs', which are turned out in bales and cartloads daily. Girls fed on such mental trash are bound to have distorted and false views of everything (299-300).

Richardson's dramatic account of the gap between herself and her workmates is a striking example of the class character of a divided reading public.

There are also passing references to the reading of sensational fiction in the autobiographies of labor leaders. Terence Powderly (1940, 15) recalls 'having read love stories in the old *New York Ledger*, and James J. Davis (1922, 75) writes of his siblings that 'we were fluent readers, much better readers than our parents, but we had no books. We took the *Youth's Companion*, and it was the biggest thing in our lives. Every week we were at the post-office when the *Companion* was due. We could hardly wait, we were so eager to see what happened next in the "continued" story.' But the reading that figures in most autobiographies is, not surprisingly, either tokens of self-improvement and self-culture or signs of the development of political and labor consciousness.

These testimonies to the reading of sensational fiction illuminate not only the audience of dime novels but the circumstances under which the reading of popular fiction took place, the situation of reading. This can tell something of the place of cheap stories in working-class culture, and indeed give the critic and historian some idea of how they ought be read and interpreted now. There were three main sites of reading: at home, at work, and while traveling. If these seem to exhaust all the possibilities, let me note first some sites where sensational fiction does *not* seem to have been read (though proving the absence of something is clearly less certain than establishing its presence): at school where little fiction was read; at religious institutions (here we must recall the wide range and circulation of Sunday School fiction); at saloons where evidence of reading seems limited to commercial or political newspapers; and at other sites of cultural and leisure activities such as sporting events, theatrical productions, and holiday picnics and parades.

The rise of railroad and streetcar travel both for commuting to work and for leisure gave a new place and opportunity for light, entertaining reading. As the distance between residential neighborhoods and factory districts grew in the late nineteenth century, more time was spent commuting, and cheap reading matter accompanied the journey: at the end of the century, Emile Levasseur observed workers reading newspapers on the New York streetcars. J.S. Ogilvie, a New York publisher who often reprinted serials that had appeared in Street & Smith's *New York Weekly*, became, according to one historian of cheap book publishing, 'the largest "purveyor" of "Railroad Literature" in the country' in the 1880s with ten and fifteen cent novels (Shove 1937, 95). Frank Leslie also aimed his cheap books, particularly *Frank Leslie's Home Library of Standard Works by the Most Celebrated Authors*, at railway consumption: 'Nearly every book bearing the Leslie imprint was in the class of cheap railroad literature and was handled by the American News Company. Through that company's system, and with the development of railroads throughout the country, cheap popular books could be retailed at newstands, station kiosks, and on the trains themselves, where train boys included books among the wares they offered. ... Leslie was keenly alive to the need for appropriate reading matter for the masses of people enjoying train travel in the 1870s' (Stern 1980, 184-6).

Nevertheless, if one considers the European experience of railway reading, the evidence is not so clear-cut. If in Britain, as Tony Davies (1983, 49) has remarked, 'the production of cheap fiction from the 1840s onward has two social destinations: the family home and the railway, corresponding perhaps to "respectable" and "disreputable" conceptions of the popular classes', in the United States the home was the key social destination. 'Railroad literature' does not appear to be as developed a category in American publishing as in England and France; there are few dime novel series or cheap libraries that have the word in the title.[7] Moreover Wolfgang Schivelbusch (1979, 69) has argued that 'a glance at the offerings of the English and French railway bookstalls shows that the reading public is almost exclusively bourgeois. An English survey of 1851 shows that, in contrast to the supply of trashy mass literature in the regular bookstores, the railway bookstalls and lending libraries in London carry highly respectable nonfiction, fiction, travel guides, etc.' It is still somewhat unclear whether, in the US, railway literature means cheap reprints of genteel and polite fiction for middle-class travellers or dime novels. However, the culture of the railroad is deeply inscribed in the dime novel, whether as the technical force that makes mass distribution possible, as the mode of transportation that encourages reading, or as the subject of innumerable novels themselves.

Most reading of sensational fiction, however, was probably done in the household. The story papers figure this in their titles, invoking the family as in *Family Story Paper* or the home and hearth as in the *Fireside Companion*. Their weekly publication schedules were aimed at Sunday reading, the only day off for workers, and one of the main reasons for the decline of the story papers toward the end of the century was the emergence of the Sunday newspaper. There seems to have been, in this period before broadcasting, much reading aloud in the family: the decline in reading aloud is one of the major changes in leisure habits that the Lynds found in comparing the 1920s to the 1890s. The story papers themselves encouraged reading aloud (Noel 1954, 292). And in a context where children often had a greater grasp of English than their parents, the account Rose Cohen gives of reading aloud to her mother while her mother worked in the home is probably not atypical.

The serialized narratives were probably read intermittently, with installments missed and less exciting narratives forgotten. In Germany, popular narratives — *colporteur* novels — were sold in installments door to door; thus Ronald Fullerton (1977) is able to show, by looking at sales figures, that relatively few novels were read in their entirety. Ironically, the historian who is often working from incomplete collections of the story papers may experience the stories in a way closer to that of the original readers than if the complete run were available. Fullerton also suggests that the popularity of serialized and installment novels was based not only on the price (indeed sometimes it was more expensive to buy all the installments of a novel than to buy the novel as a whole) but on the fact that story papers and pamphlet-sized novels were less intimidating in sheer size to someone with rudimentary reading skills than a full volume, let alone a three-volume novel.

Fiction reading was also part of the culture of the workplace. It was a way to relieve boredom; so one finds accounts of reading filling dead times, as when the original Beadle's dime novels found an audience among Civil War soldiers (Kaser 1984) or when William Wyckoff finds the logger reading a dime novel during a rainy day in a logging camp. Reading was a part of factory lunch breaks (see, for example, Lang 1948, 22). And it filled times of unemployment: Bisno says that he read 'during the slack periods of the trade' and 'when there was no work'. But there was also reading on the job itself. Lucy Larcom (1889, 175-6) tells of how, despite regulations against books in the mill, she and others pasted clippings from the weekly papers at their work places. Herbert Gutman (1976, 36) points out that 'Samuel Gompers recollected that New York City cigarmakers paid a fellow craftsman to read a newspaper to them while they worked.' And James Alexander (1838, 225-226), an evangelical minister addressing the 'American mechanic' in the late 1830s, writes:

> Reading aloud ... besides being a useful accomplishment, is highly advantageous to the health, and is recommended by the best physicians, as a preservative of the lungs. All this may be gained without any self-denial, by the custom of reading the papers, or other entertaining publications, during the intervals of labour. This is an advantage possessed by mechanics whose operations are sedentary and indoors; and this, I suppose, will go far to account for the fact, that learned men have so frequently proceeded from the shops of tailors and shoemakers.

One can conclude from this that in certain trades the practice was fairly widespread.[8]

The place of dime novels in working-class culture can also be inferred from the place of dime novels in labor newspapers. The labor papers often carried serialized fiction that resembled dime novels in title and subject matter. In contrast to the burgeoning star system of the story papers where the names of Sylvanus Cobb, Ned Buntline, or E.D.E.N. Southworth sold thousands of copies, the stories in labor papers often appeared without an author's name; however, this may be because the stories were pirated. Indeed the *New York Weekly* once accused Patrick Ford's *Irish World* of stealing a poem and illustration from them, an offense compounded by Ford's characterization of them as 'sensational' and 'trashy' (*New York Weekly* 10 April 1876, 4). But often the labor papers promoted the cheap stories, as when the *Labor Leader* recommended a serial running in Norman Munro's *Family Story Paper*, or used them as promotions, as when the *National Labor Tribune* offered dime novels as a bonus for readers who brought in new subscribers.

The place given to sensational fiction in two labor newspapers, the *Workingman's Advocate*, a national weekly 'devoted to the interests of the producing classes', and the *Labor Leader*, a Boston weekly that was close to the Knights of Labor, indicates a complex range of responses by the organizers and leaders of working-class culture and politics to this new commercial cultural form. The two papers not only published dime fiction, particularly of the workingman hero genre, but also published critiques of dime novels and examples of an alternative, 'serious' working-class fiction.

Throughout the 1860s, each issue of the *Workingman's Advocate* would lead the left columns of the front page with a poem and a short tale. Occasionally these tales might be continued over a few issues but none were of novel length. They were not introduced in any way, and often were anonymous contributions. They were basically sketches, exemplary romantic or pathetic incidents. In late 1866, however, the *Workingman's Advocate* editorialized about 'Cheap Literature':

> Every friend of progress and civilization insists upon reading matter being furnished to the people at the lowest possible price. It is by this means that agitation is continued and that knowledge is disseminated.
>
> But there are certain dangers to be guarded against, which result from the very fact that reading matter can be furnished at such a low price. It has brought before the public an immense mass of stuff, which so far from being valuable is enervating and distorts the minds of all those who are in the habit of reading such books. Take for example the ten cent novel: is there anything in one of them that deserves to be remembered? Is there a single picture of human character there that will furnish rational entertainment or thought? Nothing of the kind. A startling picture on the title page is the most attractive feature about the concern and is what sells the book.
>
> Then take the mass of weeklies and monthlies with their doleful stories, their fierce and bloody narratives, their low wit and comic pictures and, not unfrequently, their downright ribaldry; and consider to what extent these foul publications circulate and you will form some conception of the baleful influence which they exert upon the youth of the country, male and female.
>
> We are far from advising against novel reading in the abstract, though certainly it may be carried to a dangerous extent. But we do say that the promiscuous reading of the yellow and the red-backed literature, which load the shelves of our bookstores, are not doing less in the work of ruin than the rum-shop or the house of ill-fame ('Cheap Literature' 1866, 2).

This condemnation of dime novels and story papers is in many ways not too far from those of the genteel critics I will look at in the next chapter. It does avoid the extremes of the genteel critics — that dime novels are meaningless opiates or are read literally and acted out — because it does not attack the readers of dimes, nor cheap reading generally, just the sensational stories themselves. Nevertheless, the cheap stories are doing the 'work of ruin', demoralizing the people and distorting their minds.[9]

However, this editorial was by no means the end of the issue for the *Workingman's Advocate*. Though I have not found any further explicit editorial statements on cheap literature, the shifts in the stories they themselves published is revealing. Soon after the editorial, they announced a series of stories to be published under the title 'Tales of the Borders' which would be a superior alternative to the yellow-back novels. However, a survey of the short tales published shows them to be neither particularly different from their earlier sketches nor from sensational fiction generally, and they were published without much ado, either in terms of introductory comments or bold headlining. This changed with the announcement of a labor story, Martin Foran's *The Other Side*, which was serialized with prominent attention between September 28, 1872 and March 29, 1873, much longer than any previous story. Foran wrote a lengthy preface (1872), published before the story itself began, which 'explains the circumstances under which, and the objects for which' this 'Trades' Union story' was written.

Foran, an organizer and leader of the International Cooper's Union, opens by asserting that 'if the laboring class could be made a *reading* class, their social and political advancement and amelioration would be rapid and certain. ... The men most to be feared by labor, are not its open and avowed enemies, but those of its own ranks, *who do not, will not read.*' Thus for Foran, a central question for the workers movement becomes 'how are we to make the toilers in our fields, workshops and factories, toilers in the vast realm of mind — readers as well as workers?' One answer is to turn to the novel: 'We have long noticed the popular taste among the masses high and low, for fiction — novel-reading. An inherent love for fiction seems implanted in the many, especially in those whose educational advantages were limited, or at least did not include a classical training, and in contemplating this patent fact, we were led to think that much of interest and benefit to labor could be conveyed to the popular mind through this medium.' This explicit overall project for an alternative fiction from the point of view of the laboring classes is also sparked by Foran's immediate desire to respond to the popular anti-labor novel of Charles Reade, *Put Yourself in His Place*. Foran then apologizes for any shortcomings by admitting that he is 'not ... a novel-wright or story writer by trade', and that *The Other Side* 'was not written with the sole design of amusing and pleasing those who might read it. The design of the author was didactic and defensory.'

Foran's novel was serialized prominently over the next six months, but, precisely because he was a union leader not a 'novel-wright', it was a unique intervention. However, immediately after *The Other Side* was completed, another short novel was serialized: *Reuben Dalton's Career; or, A Struggle for the Right. A Story for Workingmen* (C). This was the first of a series of novels written for the *Workingman's Advocate* between 1873 and 1876 by Weldon Cobb Jr., a novel-wright by trade, indeed a prolific writer of dime novels for Beadle & Adams, Street & Smith, and the Chicago-based Nickel Library. Most of Cobb's serials for the *Workingman's Advocate* were not explicitly 'stories for working-men', but were standard sensational fare: *The Fatal Prescription, Under a Spell*, and *A Bold Game* are some of the titles.[10]

The *Labor Leader* also regularly published serial fiction, alternating between stories reprinted from other sources and stories written 'for the *Leader*'. In choosing reprints as in commissioning stories, the *Leader* favored romances of working-class life, particularly the workingman hero genre that I will examine in chapter nine. So they reprinted Charles Bellamy's *The Breton Mills: A Romance of New England Life* (BE) (with an advertisement that commended its portrayal of working-class life, despite its author's distaste for labor politics), and published the work of 'Seyek', their own pseudonymous dime novelist, which included *Ella Inness, A Romance of the Big Lockout; or, How the Knight Won the Prize* (Sa) and *John Behman's Experience; or, A Chapter from the Life of a Union Carpenter* (Sb). Indeed, Frank K. Foster, the editor of the *Labor Leader* and a leading figure in the International Typographical Union, the Knights of Labor, and the early American Federation of Labor, himself turned to fiction late in his career; in 1901 he published *The Evolution of a Trade Unionist*, an autobiography cast as a didactic novel.[11]

So, if the cases of the *Workingman's Advocate* and the *Labor Leader* are at all representative, working-class intellectuals had an ambivalent attitude toward cheap stories. There was a deep suspicion of the commercial culture and of its popularity: as a

Detroit Knight of Labor, testifying before the Senate committee investigating the relations between labor and capital, said, long hours made workers 'incapable of doing anything requiring thought ... They will read trashy novels, or go to a variety theater or a dance, but nothing beyond amusements' (Fink 1983, 10). But there were also attempts to use it, both opportunistically, to sell newspapers, and politically, to encourage cheap stories from the workingman's point of view. The attempts to create an alternative fiction were rare and relatively unsuccessful, in part because the authors of this political fiction were not fiction writers by craft;[12] and, though some professional 'novelwrights' were sympathetic to the workers movement and wrote cheap stories from 'the other side', most were still dependent on the factory-like production and standardization of the dime novel industry.

What then is the relation of dime novels to working-class culture? The evidence suggests that the bulk of the dime novel audience were young workers, often of Irish or German ethnicity, in the cities and mill towns of the North and West; and, that dime novels and story papers made up most of their reading matter. On the other hand, the dime novel was certainly not the self-creation of these craftworkers, factory operatives, laborers, and servants; it was a commercial product of a burgeoning industry employing relatively educated professionals — writers who also worked as journalists, teachers, or clerks. Nor were dime novels limited to working class readers; they were read by clerks, shopkeepers, local professionals, small farmers and their families. Should they, then, be seen as part of a wide and inclusive 'middle-class culture'?

I think not; and a brief look at two central terms in the nineteenth-century rhetoric of class — 'producing classes' and 'middle class' — suggests why not. Neither term refers to a specific class in the nineteenth-century American class structure; rather, both invoke class alliances which had unstable rhetorical and actual existence. 'Producing classes' invoked the union of craftworkers, operatives and laborers with, in the phrase of the Knights of Labor, 'the professional man, the clerk, and the shopkeeper' (Couvares 1984, 74), as well as the small farmer. 'Middle class', on the other hand, invoked a common world shared by manufacturers, bankers, large merchants, and the professional, clerk, shopkeeper, and small farmer.

This distinction is important in understanding the dime novel's public. As a cultural form, dime novels were *not* part of the popular culture of the 'middle class'. The magazines were the key literary form in that cultural universe; its metaphoric centers were the 'self-made' entrepreneur and the 'domestic' household. The dime novels were part of the popular culture of the 'producing classes', a plebian culture whose metaphoric centers of gravity were the 'honest mechanic' and the virtuous 'working-girl'. Indeed, this is how they were seen in that 'middle-class' discourse and practice that sought to reform the culture and reading of the 'lower classes', to which I turn in the next chapter.

4

The Uses of Literacy: Class, Culture, and Dime Novel Controversies

The testimonies of social observers, reformers, labor leaders and workers themselves about the reading of cheap fiction were all to some extent conditioned by an extensive controversy over dime novels and working-class reading. The 'fiction question' — the debates, moral panics, and attempts to regulate cultural production that marked the nineteenth-century reaction to the flood of cheap stories and the marked increase in working-class reading — did not have the material significance of struggles over the eight-hour day, higher wages, workers' control of production processes, or union recognition. Nevertheless, together with struggles over sports and recreations, over drinking and the saloon, over living spaces and public parks, and over the celebration of festivals and public holidays — a set of struggles which historians of working-class leisure and middle-class reform have recently begun to reconstruct and interpret[1] — it marked a social conflict over the relations between the dominant genteel culture, the relatively autonomous and 'foreign' working class cultures, and the new commercial culture, the new 'mass culture'. In this chapter, I want to look briefly at three aspects of the 'fiction question': first, at the debates among librarians and surrounding the public library; second, at the attempts, particularly those of Anthony Comstock, to orchestrate a moral panic about sensational fiction and to use the powers of the state against dime novels; and third, at the attitudes toward cheap stories of leading cultural figures, with particular attention to the mixed attitudes of the *Atlantic Monthly*, a central periodical of the genteel culture. By situating these responses to workers' use of literacy within the larger debates about and changes within working-class culture, I hope to emphasize the separation between genteel and sensational cultures in the nineteenth century, the growing divide between the cultures of America's classes.

The establishment of public libraries in industrial communities throughout the late nineteenth century made the library a contested terrain, a ground on which issues of class access to information and recreation and of class control of that information and recreation were fought out. Recent library history (see particularly Garrison 1979 and Geller 1984) and working-class history have demonstrated the ways the public library was seen by the capitalists who endowed it and the political leaders who subsidized it as a way of extending genteel culture to workers and particularly to the children of workers. 'Every book that the public library circulates helps to make ... railroad rioters impossible,' *Library Journal* editorialized after the 1877 railroad strikes (Garrison 1979, 43). Daniel Walkowitz (1978, 187) notes that as part of the paternalistic culture in the company town of Cohoes, New York, 'management built a reading and lecture room with a "well-selected" library for its operatives'; and Leon Fink (1983, 70) points out that in Rutland, Vermont, 'the list of women library commissioners ... provides as good an index as any to the best families in town.' In Pittsburgh and Homestead, the library was seen as a tool of socialization and social control, shaping habits and values, and regulating reading and recreation. Francis Couvares (1984, 112) cites a characteristic statement of the attitudes of public library boards and library staff: 'If it is proper for the library to furnish books for the people, it is right that they should be good books. If the library has the right to control the character of the reading, it has a right to direct the reader to the desired information.'

This desire to reform and direct working-class reading is a main thread in the discussions of public libraries in the Federal Bureau of Education's 1876 report on public libraries. Arguing for the careful regulation of library selection, J.P. Quincy cites the work of William Kite, a Germantown, Pennsylvania librarian who excluded all fiction. Kite writes, 'As to the question of inducing readers to substitute wholesome reading for fiction, there is no great difficulty about it. It requires a willingness on the part of the caretakers to assume the labor of leading their tastes for a time. A very considerable number of the frequenters of our library are factory girls, the class most disposed to seek amusement in novels and peculiarly liable to be injured by their false pictures of life' (394). William Fletcher, on the other hand, writing on 'public libraries in manufacturing communities', argues that 'in avoiding the Scylla of unlimited trash, the

Charybdis of too high a standard must be equally steered clear of. Those who deprecate the free supply of such fictitious works as the public demands, are generally in favor of the entire exclusion of fiction of a sensational cast, a course which will unavoidably result in alienating from the library the very class most needing its beneficial influence' (410). That class was, of course, factory workers, and like Quincy, Fletcher cites testimony from a factory town librarian, who writes that 'the patrons of the library are mainly operatives, who, after a day of toil, require reading largely of a light character, as a means of relaxation; hence, a large part of our books are of the best class of fiction. The average factory girl takes amazingly to Mary J. Holmes, Marion Harland and the like, while many of the men read Irving, Scott, Dickens and Thackeray' (404n). This struggle between what Dee Garrison has called the 'censorship model' and the 'consumership model' of the library dominates the period, and it is fiction reading that has the most controversial character. I will not go into this fiction debate in any detail; this has been done exhaustively by Esther Jane Carrier (1965). Moreover, all sides of the debate agreed on at least one point: that dime novels, story papers, and the cheap libraries should be excluded from the library. As Samuel Green (1879, 7), the Worcester, Massachusetts librarian who defended the inclusion of popular, that is genteel, fiction in the libraries, said to the American Library Association: 'I presume most of the ladies and gentlemen here present would consider it unnecessary to start the unintelligent reader even, with books of so low a grade. Dime novels be it understood are not immoral. The objection to them is that they are bloody and very exciting.' J.P. Quincy goes further: 'Nobody will deny that an occasional dime novel may be morally harmless to the middle-aged mechanic at the close of his day of honest work. He is amused at the lurid pictures of the every-day world he knows so well, takes care to put the book out of the way of his children, and finds himself none the worse for his laugh over the bloody business of the villain and the impossible amours of the heroine.' However, their effects on young people are demonstrated by Jesse Pomeroy, the boy murderer, who admitted that 'he had always been a great reader of blood and thunder stories, having read probably sixty "dime novels", all treating of scalping and deeds of violence. The boy said that he had no doubt that the reading of those books had a great deal to do with his course, and he would advise all boys to leave them alone.' 'If it is held,' Quincy concludes, 'to be the duty of the State to supply boys and girls with dime novels, and the business of the schools to tax the people that they may be taught to read them, public education is not quite as defensible as many persons have supposed' (U.S. Bureau of Education 1876, 396).

Three points ought to be noted about this controversy. First, as Dee Garrison (1976, 71) has pointed out, the controversy over fiction focused on a moral boundary, not an aesthetic one. No aesthetic ideologies were mobilized against sensational fiction; they were stigmatized either as 'immoral' or as a 'demoralizing' influence. Second, those who favored including fiction in the library were aiming at a reformation of working-class reading, away from sensational fiction and toward the genteel, 'middle-brow' popular reading. And, third, much of the animus directed against dime novels resulted from the fact that they were the direct and successful competitors of the public libraries for the loyalties of workers. As Couvares (1984, 116) notes of Pittsburgh, 'librarians found extension work among mill men frankly discouraging.' Mill workers were suspicious of Carnegie's library, and in 1890, in Allegheny, 'workingmen and their representatives ... raised serious questions about who would control the library which Carnegie had offered the city.' Throughout the period, workers established their own union libraries: an example is the Miner's Union Library established in 1877 in Virginia City, Nevada. It was, according to Richard Lingenfelter (1974, 53), historian of the hardrock miners, 'for many years ... the largest library in the state. The books were selected by a board of five directors elected by the union. They bought only those books that would be widely read — novels, romances, travels, and elementary texts on mechanics and physics.'[2]

Whereas the library debate represented a conflict within the practices of a semi-official but essentially voluntary and non-coercive ideological apparatus, the second struggle over dime novels and workers' reading, the moral panic associated with the name of Anthony Comstock, represented a more immediate and direct involvement of state apparatuses. Anthony Comstock was a young 'reformer' who, with the financial backing of New York patricians, established a Society for the Suppression of Vice, a quasi-legal organization to campaign against immoral and obscene books and materials. It lobbied for the successful enactment of the 1873 'Comstock law' prohibiting the mailing of obscene, indecent and vulgar material; and Comstock himself became a special agent of the Post Office Department to enforce the law. Part of his campaign was directed against dime novels and story papers; he arrested the editor of *Fireside Companion*, a family story paper, for publishing obscene matter in 1872, and 'in the mid-1880s he successfully prosecuted book dealers for selling "criminal story papers" and "stories of bloodshed and crime".'[3] In his 1883 account of his struggles, *Traps for the Young*, he writes that 'the editor of the blood-and-thunder story papers, half-dime novels, and cheap stories of crime ... [is] willingly or unwillingly, [among] Satan's efficient agents to advance his kingdom by destroying the young' (Comstock, 1882, 242). His chapter on half-dime novels and story papers is an account of the boys and girls who have turned to crime as a result of their vicious reading; it is, as Robert Bremner (1967, xv) observes, written in much the same style as the half-dime novels themselves. The atmosphere created by Comstock and his supporters was such as to lead to the introduction of a bill into the New York Assembly in 1883 which would have deemed:

> Any person who shall sell, loan, or give to any minor under sixteen years of age any dime novel or book of fiction, without first obtaining the written consent of the parent or guardian of such minor, ... guilty of a misdemeanor, punishable by imprisonment or by a fine of not exceeding $50 (Carrier 1965, 214).

The bill was not passed, but in 1886 the Massachusetts legislature passed a bill that 'forbade the sale to minors of books or magazines featuring "criminal news, police reports, or accounts of criminal deeds, or pictures and stories of lust and crime"'' (Boyer 1968, 11).

The importance of such sensational incidents can be easily exaggerated, however. That there was a moral panic in the late 1870s and early 1880s about sensational fiction seems clear: Comstock's name has come to symbolize vice crusading. But the precise meaning of this moral panic is less clear: was it an important and symptomatic cultural struggle, or merely a colorful but idiosyncratic incident? The careers of Anthony Comstock and other vice ideologues can not be taken as fully representative of American culture; nevertheless, one should recall that the members and supporters of the vice societies were bastions of patrician and bourgeois culture, and that the vice society campaigns were part of the larger philanthropic activities of genteel reformers (Boyer 1968, 5-15). And though the vice society campaigns were primarily aimed at pornography and crime publications like the *Police Gazette*, its effects were felt by the publishers of sensational fiction both directly, as in the case of the dime novels that heroized outlaws (in part two, I will look at the case of the tales of Jesse and Frank James which Frank Tousey published in his Five Cent Wide Awake Library), and indirectly.

The third aspect of this struggle over dime novels and working class reading is the more properly ideological debate, the statements by traditional intellectuals about this emerging culture industry. As an index to these attitudes, I will look at the responses to cheap literature in the *Atlantic Monthly*, perhaps the leading genteel cultural arbiter. Throughout the late nineteenth century, contributors to the *Atlantic Monthly* treated the issues of dime novel reading and 'lower class' reading interchangeably, as they debated its effects, wondering whether dime novel reading was better than no reading at all.

Just as the *North American Review* had noted the publishing innovation of Beadle's dime books,[4] so the emergence of the cheap libraries in the mid-1870s drew a response from the *Atlantic Monthly*; a correspondent to the 'Contributors' Club' of November 1877 attacked 'this New York literary tramp', Norman Munro, publisher of the *Riverside Library*, for pirating English fiction and inflicting wrongs on English and American authors, reputable American publishers, and the 'general reader' (The Contributors' Club 1877, 619-20). However, in September 1878, another writer for the 'Contributors' Club' defended the libraries for presenting masterpieces of English literature to the 'former habitual readers of the Texas Jack stripe of dime novel'. The writer cited a newsdealer who had noted that 'the oddest thing about the whole business is the number of calls I have for the best novels, in this shape, from men whom I used to think of as wanting only the worst class of publications. ... Such men — women and children, too — can be won from the degrading reading to which they are accustomed only by the substitution for it of good literature, equally attractive and equally cheap.' 'To be sure,' the writer concludes, 'there is still an appalling amount of vicious reading material sold at these same news-stands and periodical stores, but Rome was not built in a day. I am disposed to rejoice over one rift in the clouds, rather than to lament because there are not two' (The Contributors' Club 1878, 370-371). As in the case of the initial reaction to Beadle's dime books, the new format is seen primarily as a possible agent for a change in the content of popular reading.

Within a year of this minor exchange over the format of the cheap libraries, the *Atlantic Monthly* published two more detailed accounts of the cheap stories, both of which I have mentioned in other contexts: W.H. Bishop's article, 'Story-Paper Literature', and Rev. Jonathan Baxter Harrison's reflections in his series of articles later collected as *Certain Dangerous Tendencies in American Life*. Earlier I used these articles for their observations of dime novel readers; now I would like to examine the attitudes of the writers themselves toward this reading. Bishop (1879, 383-393), a novelist, explicitly sets himself against the Comstock hysteria by mocking the tales of boys driven to crime by dime novels. He pays close attention to the situation of the reading, to the stories told, and to the relation of those stories to 'popular movements', the melodramatic stage, and current events. He perceptively notes that there are differences between story papers: some (particularly the *New York Ledger*) publish the same domestic writers who were read in hard covers by the genteel middle class; 'others give away Shakespeare's Sonnets ... for supplements.' 'In general,' he notes, 'in the libraries good literature is beginning to mingle among the bad in a very curious way. Robinson Crusoe, very much mangled, it is true, at half a dime, may be found in the Wide-Awake Library, sandwiched between Bowie Knife Ben and Death Notch the Destroyer.' They are morally unobjectionable and, more importantly, reinforce the genteel domestic code: 'The best of the story papers reward virtue and punish vice. Their dependence upon the family keeps them, as a rule, free of dangerous appeals to the lower passions. ... They encourage a chivalrous devotion to women, though they do not do much towards making her more worthy of it.'

Bishop concludes, then, that the story-papers are 'not an unmixed evil'. The central question for Bishop, as for many of his middle-class contemporaries, was: 'Are they better than nothing?'. His reply is a liberal, humanistic one: 'The taste for reading, however perverted, is connected with something noble, with an interest in things outside of the small domain of the self, with a praiseworthy curiosity about the great planet we inhabit. One is almost ready to say that, rather than not have it at all, it had better be nourished on no better food than story papers.'

Cheap stories were not ostensibly the principal subject of Rev. J.B. Harrison's articles in the *Atlantic Monthly* (1880); they dealt with a range of 'dangerous tendencies' in religion and social life brought on by industrialization and the conflict between capital and labor, the 'labor problem'. As a traditional intellectual,

Harrison expresses the loss of confidence by the directing classes, a loss of the hegemony, the cultural leadership and direction, exercised by the 'middle classes', the 'cultivated men'. Harrison writes that 'my observation of the life and thought of workingmen impresses me with the conviction that the cultivated men of the country are not, in a sufficient degree, in communication with the great body of the laboring people; and that a more direct and vital relation between them would be a great gain to both classes. The things which our best and wisest men are saying to each other should be addressed, and in suitable forms of utterance might be addressed, to the workingmen of the nation' (100-101). However, precisely because Harrison formulates the issue in this way, the question of cheap stories and working class reading occupies a pivotal position in his argument. He writes of the story papers read by young factory operatives:

> I have read some of these stories. They have usually no very distinct educational quality or tendency, good or bad. They are simply stories, — vapid, silly, turgid, and incoherent. As the robber-heroes are mostly grand-looking fellows, and all the ladies have white hands and splendid attire, it may be that some of the readers find hard work more distasteful because of their acquaintance with the gorgeous idlers and thieves, who, in these fictions are always so much more fortunate than the people who are honest and industrious. But usually, as I am convinced by much observation, the only effect of this kind of reading is that it serves 'to pass away the time', by supplying a kind of entertainment, a stimulus or opiate for the mind, and that these people resort to it and feel a necessity for it in much the same way that others feel they must have whisky or opium. The reading is a narcotic, but it is less pernicious than those just named (167).

Harrison's formulation of the common trope that dime novels were an opiate of the people is the other side of the opposition that structures middle-class perceptions of popular fiction: it is either a narcotic escape from daily life with no genuine symbolic meaning or, with Comstock, a symbolic universe so potent as to erase the real world from the minds of readers, leading them to act out the scenes depicted in dime novels. More threatening to Harrison is the reading of the older operatives, the paper 'devoted to the liberation of the working-people of America' whose 'principal literary attraction at this time was a very long serial story of the overthrow of the republic in 1880. . . . The tone and spirit of the paper are indescribably bitter, and expressive of intense hostility against the possessors of property and culture. ... All its teaching is opposed to the spirit and principle of nationality, and tends, so far as it has any effect, to produce social and political disintegration.' Harrison's response to these tendencies is to suggest, not surprisingly, the restoration of a 'direct and vital relation' between 'cultivated men' and working-men through the reform and control of working class reading: 'The capitalists, manufacturers, and cultivated people of every town where there are one thousand operatives should unite in the publication of a small, low-priced newspaper for circulation among the working-people' (198). The irony of Harrison's suggestion lies not only in the objection he himself raises and attempts to answer — that workers would avoid a paper bearing the stamp of capital — but also in the fact that the story papers were the products of 'capitalists' and 'manufacturers', though these new entrepreneurs of the culture industry were largely ignoring the agenda of the 'cultivated people'.

This discouse about mass culture among the contributors to the *Atlantic* differs from both the reform efforts of librarians and the censorship crusades of vice societies; nevertheless, these various attempts by 'cultivated people' to reform, regulate and reflect on dime novels and working-class reading were all provoked not only by the emerging culture industry but by changes in class structure and class awareness in nineteenth-century America. Thus to understand the 'fiction question', we must briefly look at the overall balance of class forces that shaped this period, and then at the dominant classes' changing view of America's workers, and the contradictory forces at play within workers' culture.

In an important synthetic work on American labor and capital, Gordon, Edwards and Reich (1982) argue that there have been a series of long swings in American capitalist development, each the product of a particular social structure of accumulation — the set of economic, political and cultural institutions that organize capital accummulation and make it possible. The breakup of a particular social structure of accummulation, or, in Gramscian terms, of the hegemony of a particular historical bloc, results in a crisis of accummulation and in struggles by other groups and classes to reconstruct the social order. Gordon, Edwards and Reich characterize the period between the 1820s and the 1890s as the stage of 'initial proletarianization'. After a moment of explor-ation and experimentation in the 1820s and 1830s, American capitalism experienced a long boom, and then an extended crisis.

'For a period of some thirty years, say from 1843 to 1873, the US economy and especially the expanding industrial sector in the North showed rapid and more or less continuous growth. ... The long boom (in the North and the West) came to an end with the hard times of the mid-1870s. Starting with the panic in 1873, continuing for more than twenty years, and ending with the "Great Depression" of the 1890s, the US economy experienced the much weaker accumulation possibilities of the new stagnation' (50, 52). The central struggle and key transformation in this period was the creation of 'free labor', of proletarians, both in the emancipation of Black slaves, and in the creation of wage workers by stripping non-capitalist producers of their means of production, driving them to a dependence on wages. This long and contested process meant that for most of the period the wage system was itself in question. The cultural expectation that working for wages was a stage of life rather than a permanent condition persisted, and, as it became a permanent condition for many workers, it was seen as 'wage slavery' (Montgomery 1967, 30-31; Rodgers 1978, 30-35). A bitter conflict developed between capitalists and craftworkers:

> Craft relations underwent continuous change during these years, as the jours and apprentices became increasingly subject to capitalist relations. What was intended by the jours to be temporary employment stretched into long years; what was meant to be a necessary compromise in standards during hard times became impossible to escape even in good ones. 'Prices' gave way to 'wages', a term, Norman Ware reminds us, that had previously applied only to day labor. As a result, craft workers no longer organized their own work; capitalists now did. Despite their skills and extensive control over the immediate processes of production, both of which the craft workers had brought with them into the new relations of production, they were now wage workers (Gordon, Edwards and Reich 1982, 67).

However, precisely because they brought their skills and control over production into wage work, the craft workers remained central to the new capitalist production which, as Gordon, Edwards and Reich point out, 'was based on proletarianized but largely *untransformed* labor. Capitalists hired labor but relied on traditional techniques of production.' Craft workers retained a large measure of autonomy, controlling their own work and directing helpers and laborers (Montgomery 1979, 9-15). When the crisis of the 1870s came, capitalists increasingly attempted to transform and take control of the work process, against the resistance of workers, particularly craft workers. There followed the years of the 'Great Upheavals', from the 1877 national railroad strike to the 1894 Pullman strike, from the organizing of the Knights of Labor to the insurgency of the Populists.

The long struggle that established a permanent and dependent class of wage workers, and transferred control over production processes to owners and managers, was a cultural as well as economic conflict. Richard Slotkin (1985) has noted that the years after the Civil War saw a redefinition of the character of the laboring classes:

> Instead of refurbishing the Jacksonian mystique of a universalized 'producing class', [postwar elites] acknowledge difference and specialization of function, and assign leading roles to the men of capital and organization as against the masses of the laboring classes. Nor do they assert with Lincoln's comprehensiveness the doctrine that each working hand is a potential capitalist: the existence of a permanent proletariat is acknowledged, and regarded as a good and necessary thing ... For the postwar ideology, the vision of the proletarian as contented slave or demented savage became positive doctrine: it justified both the exploitation of the 'dependent' worker and the violent military suppression of the rebellious worker; and it put the blame for exploitation and suppression on the natural 'gifts' of those classes (290-291).

Slotkin shows how the mythologies of the frontier, 'the conception of American history as a heroic-scale Indian war, pitting race against race' (32), entered the rhetoric of class: 'This reversible analogy between workers and savages is the most significant new term in the language of American mythology after the war' (311).

The 'middle class' — another significant new term in the language of American mythology after the war — served both to actively displace the earlier formulation of the 'producing classes', and to distinguish and separate the 'middling interests' of the nation from the worker-savages. From the ranks of this newly-constructed middle class came the efforts to reform and uplift workers and savages alike; from the new picture of a dependent and unruly 'lower class' came the debates over the effects of dime novel reading. Indeed several historians have recently suggested that the organizations and discourses of moral and social reform were a key aspect in the formation of a self-conscious 'middle class' (see Blumin 1985).

Against both the capitalist reorganization of the crafts and these 'middle-class' representations of the American social order, American workers attempted to maintain the vision of a republic of producers, of a cooperative commonwealth, and of the autonomous, independent mechanic. In doing so, they created a working class culture. This culture, often termed a 'producers', 'populist', or 'plebian' culture, was different from and antagonistic to that dominant culture (which was in the process of naming itself 'middle-class'), but it was neither an internally unified, anthropological whole, nor completely independent of the culture of the dominant classes. Each of these three points is worth stressing.

Working-class culture was different from and antagonistic to the culture of the dominant classes. This is not because there are pure, autonomous cultures linked to particular classes. Rather, it is a result of first, material conditions of life, and second, the boundaries drawn between Culture and non-Culture in the exercise of cultural power. Material conditions cannot be overlooked. All cultural activity, whether symphony orchestras or drinking in saloons, depends upon a surplus; and working-class culture was marked by the very small surpluses of time and money available. Nevertheless, though the material conditions of working-class life suggest that working-class cultural activities will differ from those of the more leisured and monied classes, this is not necessary: as nineteenth-century leisure reformers hoped, 'good' books and music and uplifting recreational activities could be 'given' to those who couldn't afford them. The structuring principle that turns the material limits on cultural activity into class-divided cultural formations is the boundary drawn between Culture and non-Culture. As Stuart Hall (1981, 236, 234) has argued in a key essay on popular culture:

> The cultural process — cultural power ... depends, in the first instance, on this drawing of the line, always in each period in a different place, as to what is to be incorporated into the 'great tradition' and what is not. Educational and cultural institutions, along with the many positive things they do, also help to discipline and police this boundary. ... from period to period, the *contents* of each category changes. Popular forms become enhanced in cultural value, go up the cultural escalator — and find themselves on the opposite side. Other things cease to have high cultural value, and are appropriated into the popular, becoming transformed in the process. ... The important fact, then, is not a mere descriptive inventory — which may have the negative effect of freezing popular culture into some timeless descriptive mould — but the relations of power which

are constantly punctuating and dividing the domain of culture into its preferred and its residual categories.

The ideological debates over dime novels and working class reading that I have outlined were precisely such an exercise of cultural power, drawing and policing (literally, in the case of Comstock) a boundary between the *genteel* and the *sensational*. This boundary was a moral as well as aesthetic one, dividing the culture of the 'middle class' from the ways of the 'lower classes', and giving very different inflections to apparently similar stories.[5] Though in its twentieth-century afterlife the dime novel ascends the cultural escalator, becoming a sign of American middle-class boyhood and used to draw a boundary excluding the cultures of Black migrants and the 'new' immigrants, throughout the nineteenth century it is excluded from Culture and gentility.

If the culture of workers was distinguished from the culture of the dominant classes in nineteenth-century America, it was not however a unified, organic whole. Indeed, most of the recent local community studies of nineteenth-century working class life find neither a common world view nor a common set of beliefs. Rather labor historians identify characteristic antinomies, contradictory alternatives growing out of the material conditions and experiences of working class life: the 'rough' and the 'respectable', the world of the saloon and the world of temperance, the bonds of 'mutualism' and the ideal of 'self-improvement'. In the face of these antinomies, Sean Wilentz (1984, 270) has suggested that 'rather than construct two opposing mutually exclusive ideal types — pleasure-seeking benighted "traditionalists", abstemious enlightened "rebels" — it is more useful to consider the republicanism of the Bowery [the plebian world of rough amusement] and the republicanism of the unions as different but at times overlapping expressions of journeymen's fears and aspirations — one focused on the economic and political sources of inequality and exploitation, the other stressing cultural autonomy and manly independence.' This is particularly helpful when looking at the dime novels: for though particular novels can often be aligned with one or another tendency in working-class culture, their characteristic task — indeed the function and purpose of narrative in general — is to offer symbolic resolutions to the antinomies within the culture.

Morever, although in terms of class *structure* this is a working-class culture — a culture with its center of gravity among working-class people, a set of practices, institutions, and symbolic forms used, and sometimes created and shaped, by workers — neither its rhetoric nor its boundaries were strictly of class. David Montgomery (1976, 115-116) writes that 'local shop-keepers and professional men ... shared with the workers elements of a popular culture, in which one never spoke of the "lower classes", but of the "working", "industrious", or "pro-ducing" classes. The praise they bestowed on the "honest mechanics" of their communities echoed through the popular songs and dime-novel literature of the day. ... Although this culture was infused with a populist, rather than a strictly class consciousness, it clearly separated the nation into the "prod-ucers" and the "exploiters".' When the elite, genteel culture remained at a distance, as in small or provincial mill towns, this popular producers' culture often had a kind of local hegemony. In his study of Pittsburgh, Francis Couvares (1984, 31) calls this a 'plebian culture'; it was 'decidedly vernacular' and 'intensely local', 'putting working people and their social equals in the center stage of life in Pittsburgh' (until the emergence of a local elite culture in Pittsburgh in the late 1880s). The dime novel, like the melodramatic theater that Couvares discusses, was a part of this plebian sensational culture, and if its stories opposed them-selves to the genteel elite, they nevertheless often testified to divisions as well as solidarities among the 'people' and the 'producers'.

Finally, this working-class culture is not completely auton-omous. Not only is it intertwined with a commercial culture that is not the self-creation of workers, but it is always subject to the influence and power of the dominant culture. As Stuart Hall (1981, 232-233) argues, 'there is *no* whole, authentic, autonomous "popular culture" which lies outside the field of force of the relations of cultural power and domination. ... There is a con-tinuous and necessarily uneven and unequal struggle, by the dominant culture, constantly to disorganise and reorganise popular culture; to enclose and confine its definitions and forms within a more inclusive range of dominant forms.' The con-troversy over dime novels and working-class reading takes its place in this context. Moreover, this illuminates a key aspect of dime novel production that is often missed in dime novel histor-ies and criticism: that there are two bodies of narratives in this field of fiction, the popular, commercial, sensational stories that captured the reading public, and the genteel, moralistic narratives that attempted to use the dime novel format with varying degrees of success to recapture and reorganize working-class culture. The stories of Horatio Alger, which were published in the story papers and in dime novel formats, are a good example of the latter, though they are often taken as representative dime novels.

However, the imprint of middle-class culture in the dime novels comes not only in these active interventions; it is also found in the appearance in sensational fiction of the codes of the sentimental and the melodramatic. As any literary handbook will say, both of these modes are characterized by an 'excess of emotion', substituting a manipulative appeal to the audience for consistent motivation of the characters and plot. But their differences reveal a more profound kinship than the somewhat snobbish definition as 'excess of emotion'. For both modes translate their social content into a received ethical code: for sentimental fiction, the opposition good/not good, sunshine and shadow, rules all action and character. The 'not good' are victims — the prostitute with the heart of gold, the orphan turned tramp, the noble but dying Indian. All can be pitied and all can be forgiven in the Grand Reunion, as Mary Noel calls it, at the end. For melodrama, on the other hand, the 'not good' pole becomes a positive evil, day and night, and a villain, thoroughly despicable, appears in order to be driven out — the evil Indian, the evil tramp.

Fredric Jameson (1981, 186) has argued that 'these two paradigms, the sentimental and the melodramatic [the way of Dickens and the way of Eugene Sue], which from the standpoint of ideology can be seen as two distinct (but not mutually exclusive) narrative strategies, may be said to be the carrot and the stick of nineteenth-century middle-class moralizing about the lower classes.' It is this legacy that gives the profound sense of moralism to these stories, so thorough that one wonders how they could ever have been attacked for immortality. But these are also the twin temptations that the dime novel, as a contested terrain, a popular form belonging perhaps to the 'people' but not unequivocally to any single class, faces. In part we can read these narratives as attempts to invert these moral dualisms, and even to displace them and restore their social and collective context. They are caught between seeing the city as a mystery or as a place of work, between seeing a tramps' campsite as a den of iniquity or as a utopian community. If, then, these are tales of escape, it is largely the continual story of capture by and escape from the narrative paradigms of middle-class culture.

PART TWO

Cheap Stories of Labor and Capital

5

Reading Dime Novels: The Mechanic Accents of Escapist Fiction

If we have shown, in the first part of this book, that reading cheap stories constituted a part of working-class leisure activity; that, though originating in commercial production, they were taken into working-class cultures; and that there were substantial ideological battles over the reading of sensational fiction; then we are left to account for their significance within those cultures and as an index of those cultures. And for the most part, the consideration of the function and meaning of dime novels can be summed up in one category — escape.[1] Throughout the standard works, these narratives are repeatedly defined as sub-literary — as daydreams, wish fulfillments, narcotics — with no further end than as a brief distraction from a life of work. A labor historian, surveying working-class leisure activities, writes that 'in Germany, where most workers did not even use union libraries, less than ten percent of all books borrowed from their libraries was other than escapist fiction' (Stearns 1975, 8). Is this an adequate conception of this reading? Is the only significant reading the self-improving ten percent, the Bebel and the Kautsky? Are the specific forms and contents of these narratives as little important as the difference between beer and wine, whiskey and opium? To each culture its own poison. I think not.

Nor do I agree with Gareth Stedman Jones (1983, 88-89) who has argued forcefully for a position that would, in the end, see this culture as escapist. 'To study leisure and popular recreation as a distinct subject — particularly if we try to think of it in terms of a polarity between "class expression and social control" — leads to a real danger of overpoliticizing leisure as an arena of struggle.' Stedman Jones insists on the fundamental dissimilarity between struggles over work relations and those over leisure activities. 'The primary point of a holiday is not political. It is to enjoy yourself, for tomorrow you must work. To write into recreations a symbolic form of class conflict — or its reverse, a channeling or diversion of class consciousness — leads precisely to the inrush of theories of incorporation to explain why workers have appeared to accept the capitalization of leisure with apparent passivity.'

Stedman Jones's argument is particularly powerful in that it serves as a self-criticism of his own earlier important essay on music halls and working-class culture. And his warnings against interpreting leisure activities as intentional expressions of resistance (as if they were a strike) or as instruments of social control are well taken and worth keeping in mind. However, his view unintentionally replicates the conclusions of nineteenth-century middle-class moralists: that readers paid no serious attention to these narratives, because they were not worthy of serious attention.

The theorists of an escapist culture give themselves away when they characterize escapist or sensational fiction as dreams, daydreams, or wish fulfillments. For surely what these stories share with these *meaningful* activities are an unconscious, but not uninterpretable, logic. In the case of a daydream which is mediated by the collective and historically specific processes of narrative production and reception, that unconscious is social and political. The contradictions raised and resolved in popular narratives draw their ideological charge from the materials they use, whether or not the individual writer or reader is conscious of this at a particular moment. These materials — genres, conventions, stock characters, uses of language — are all charged with the political content of everyday life.[2] To understand them, we precisely need 'to write into recreations a symbolic form of class conflict.'

'Escapism may indeed be an issue,' Warren Susman (1984, 108) shrewdly wrote, 'but why and how people choose to escape in the particular ways they do — the choices a culture provides — is a much more important question.' Since the dime novel was one of the major choices nineteenth-century American culture offered working people, a history of this culture industry cannot limit itself simply to an account of the mass production and distribution of the commodities; it must consider the nature of the stories narrated and the ways they were interpreted. An economics of the dime novel must be complemented by a poetics of the dime novel.

That is the reason for the detailed analyses of forgotten stories that I offer in part two. In this chapter, after looking at what is perhaps the most important and suggestive discussion of sensational fiction and working-class culture, that of the Italian marxist Antonio Gramsci, I will outline three theoretical models that guide those interpretations of particular dime novels: first, a discussion of allegorical or typological modes of reading; second, an exploration of the figurability of social cleavages, particularly those of class; and, third, a theory of accents, of the multiaccentuality of the figures and conventions of sensational fiction.

Soon after Antonio Gramsci was imprisoned in 1926, he drew up a systematic project of intellectual work. Of its four parts, one was to be 'an essay on serial novels and popular taste in literature'. Serial novels became interesting, he wrote in a letter of 1929, 'if one looked at them from the following angle: why are these books always the most read and the most frequently published? What needs do they satisfy and what aspirations do they fulfill? What emotions and attitudes emerge in this squalid literature, to have such wide appeal?'[3] Unfortunately, Gramsci did not write this essay on serial fiction; rather one finds in his *Prison Notebooks* (1929-1935) a collection of observations, questions, hypotheses and criticisms provoked by his reading of sensational novels and articles about them. Despite their fragmentary form, certain of Gramsci's arguments can be reconstructed.

Gramsci explicitly rejects the 'escapist' explanation of serial fiction. Responding to a critic who sees detective stories as 'a way of escaping from the pettiness of daily life', he notes: 'But this explanation can be applied to all forms of literature, whether popular or artistic, from the chivalric poem ... to the various kinds of serial novels. Is all poetry and literature therefore a narcotic against the banality of everyday life?' (371). He argues that the 'success of a work of commercial literature indicates (and it is often the only indication available) the "philosophy of the age", that is, the mass of feelings and conceptions of the world predominant among the "silent" majority. ... The serial novel takes the place of (and at the same time favors) the fantasizing of the common people; it is a real way of day-dreaming' (349). When another critic claims that 'the serial novel was born because an infinite number of people leading drab restricted lives felt ... the need for illusion', Gramsci writes that 'this can be done for all novels and not only serial ones: one must analyse the *particular illusion* that the serial novel provides the people with and how this illusion changes through historical-political periods' (375-376).

Gramsci's analysis of the *'particular illusions* that the serial novel provides' remains only a beginning, and much of his discussion focuses on the peculiarities of the Italian situation: the fact that the serial novels popular in Italy were not Italian but were imported translations of French *feuilletons*. However, his work offers three perspectives that are crucial to an analysis and history of the *particular illusions* of the dime novel: an attention to their uses in working-class culture; an attempt to sort out the various types of novels; and a concern for the historical meaning of particular narrative patterns and formulaic characters.

Gramsci emphasizes the social context and uses of sensational fiction, noting its role in popular journalism and its place in working-class family life:

> The serial novel is a way of circulating newspapers among the popular classes. ... The man of the people buys only one newspaper, when he buys one. The choice is not even personal, but is often that of the family as a group. The women have a large say in the choice and insist on the 'nice, interesting novel'. (This does not mean that the men do not read the novel too, but it is the women who are particularly interested in it and in items of local news.) This always meant that purely political papers or papers of pure opinion never had a large circulation (except in periods of intense political struggle). They were bought by young people, men and women, without too many family worries, who were keenly interested in the fortunes of their political opinions, and by a small number of families highly compact in their ideas.

This suggests a reason why the story papers in the United States always had larger circulations than the dime novels and cheap libraries; if a family was to buy one story publication a week, the story paper would be the choice since its range of serialized stories accommodated a number of tastes.

Gramsci also calls attention to the importance of the *discussion* of popular fiction at work and in the neighborhood (an activity we will see dramatized in the autobiography of Dorothy Richardson):

> One does not consider that for many readers the 'serial novel' has the same importance as quality 'literature' has for educated people. It

used to be a kind of 'social obligation' for the porters, the courtyard and the people upstairs to know the 'novel' that the *Stampa* was publishing. Each instalment led to 'conversations' sparkling with the logical and psychological intuitions of the 'most distinguished' presences. It can be claimed that the readers of serial novels enthuse about their authors with far more sincerity and a much livelier human interest than was shown in so-called cultured drawing rooms for the novels of D'Annunzio or is shown there now for the works of Pirandello (207-208).

This sense of the social situation of sensational fiction reading is very important; though reading is probably always one of the more private and individual activities, and no doubt many dime novels were read and savored as something private and one's own, the reading of popular fiction in nineteenth-century working-class cultures does have social, familial and communal aspects. The consumption of commercially produced fiction retains aspects of storytelling traditions, even as it supplants those older oral traditions. If the novel has its birthplace in the solitary individual, as Walter Benjamin has said, then these are not yet novels, despite their form.

Gramsci's remark about the existence of an ongoing oral tradition of what might be called 'literary criticism' makes the question of interpretation central. For clearly these stories were interpreted and not merely consumed; and the reading of them was an active process. Thus to understand them and their historical reception we must try to reconstruct these historical interpretations. Our readings of them, as critics and historians in the era of late capitalism, must engage their readings.

Unfortunately the studies of reader response and the aesthetics of reception offer surprisingly little to answer this question, caught as they are between analyses of the implied reader in the text and disputes over the vagaries of individual subjectivist misreadings. In a useful survey of this criticism, Susan Suleiman (1980, 25) notes that, for much of it, 'the reading subject who emerges ... is not a specific, historically situated individual but a transhistorical mind whose activities are, at least formally, everywhere the same.' However, one exception to this is the work of Jacques Leenhardt and Peter Józsa. The results of their investigation of the controlled reading of a French and a Hungarian novel by selected French and Hungarian publics 'prove that the reading process actively involves the reader himself, and is not the area of a terrorist operation in which the text and its meaning are forced upon the reader.' Furthermore, they find that a notion of *the public* as a unified whole cannot be substantiated; nevertheless, the readings did have certain regularities and tendencies. 'Value judgments, reading attitudes, and expectations in the sphere of pleasure appeared to be organically interrelated to such an extent' as to constitute several 'systems of reading', systems which were related to definable *publics* (Leenhardt 1980, 210-214). Though the basic axis of difference they explored was national, and though this work is still relatively undeveloped, the hypothesis that different publics will have different readings, different interpretations, of the same books or stories is central to my argument.

The difficulty lies in establishing those different readings, those different interpretations, when one is left with only the text. Perhaps the most ingenious attempt to solve this problem is Carlo Ginzburg's reconstruction of the culture and cosmos of a sixteenth-century Italian miller. Since this miller, Menocchio, read a limited number of books and testified to the Inquisition about his reading, Ginzburg is able, by juxtaposing the texts with Menocchio's accounts of them, to give some account of the way he read, the way he mobilized aspects of the popular culture and oral tradition in making sense of the print culture. As Ginzburg (1980, xxii) himself poses the issue:

> The almanacs, the songsters, the books of piety, the lives of the saints, the entire pamphlet literature that constituted the bulk of the book trade [we might add, the dime novels], today appear static, inert, and unchanging to us. But how were they read by the public of the day? To what extent did the prevalently oral culture of those readers interject itself in the use of the text, modifying it, reworking it, perhaps to the point of changing its very essence? Menocchio's accounts of his readings provide us with a striking example of the relationship to the text that is totally different from that of today's educated reader. They permit us to measure, at last, the discrepancy that Bolleme quite properly suggested existed between the texts of 'popular' literature and the light in which they appeared to peasants and artisans.

It is precisely in measuring this discrepancy that we face a similar problem regarding dime novels and working-class culture. Thus far I have only found one testimony that lends itself to the sort of analysis Ginzburg undertakes: Dorothy Richardson's account of her workmates telling her the story of Laura Jean Libbey's novel *Little Rosebud's Lovers*, an account which I will look at in some detail in the final chapter.

Nevertheless, there are, I suggest, two forces shaping the system of reading used by nineteenth-century workers: the first is the commodification of reading; the second, the tension between novelistic and allegorical or typological modes of reading. Several cultural historians have argued that the proliferation of cheap, ephemeral publications, advertised and purchased for their novelty and quickly discarded, transformed the activity of reading. Christopher Wilson's (1983) recent analysis of the magazines of the 1890s 'magazine revolution' argues that there was a transformation in the reading process near the turn of the century as ideals of the 'gentle reader', of 'companionate readership', and of reading as a leisurely, contemplative process gave way to a way of reading based on brevity, information, and manipulation of the reader. In a similar vein, Jochen Schulte-Sasse (1983, 100-101) bases his analysis of popular fiction in Germany and the US on an argument that 'the mode in which popular narratives have been read since the eighteenth century has from the beginning revealed distinctly narcissistic traits ... The eighteenth century form of a collective commerce with literature (reading aloud in the family or in a circle of friends with ensuing discussion) disintegrated and, simultaneously, the habit of devouring popular narratives as a means of withdrawing from reality to an isolated phantasy world took over. ... Parallel to this development the intensive moe of reading (few books are read and discussed again and again was replaced by an extensive mode of reading (more and more new stories are consumed and "understood" individually.'

Neither of these analyses is fully adequate to working-class reading (which retains aspects of collectivity), and both of them express a somewhat dubious nostalgia for the older ideals of bourgeois reading. It is worth recalling that the emergence of cheap reading matter in working-class communities not only changes reading but often inaugurates it. The predecessor of cheap reading is less 'companionate readership' than oral storytelling. Nevertheless, these analyses do mark several junctures that are important: the distinction between intensive and extensive reading (which in popular cultures could be marked as the shift from the Bible and *Pilgrim's Progress* as the only books to the proliferation of cheap stories); collective versus solitary modes of reading; and the distinction between reading as a working through of books and reading as a constant absorption of endless printed matter (recall how Bisno learned English from advertisements and signs). A version of this argument that avoids the nostalgia of Wilson and Schulte-Sasse is Fredric Jameson's (1979, 132-133) provocative thoughts on the reification of reading, the way commodified literature leads us to 'read for the ending': 'not only does the *denouement* stand as the reified end in view of which the rest of the narrative is consumed, this reifying structure also reaches down into the very page-by-page detail of the book's composition.' Everything in a narrative is subordinated to the element which provides the 'consumption-satisfaction': the ending in a detective story, the epic 'feeling tone' of the naturalist best-seller. There are similar effects of commodification in the composition and reading of dime novels, ranging from the periodic cliffhangers produced by serialization to the reification of 'genres' and 'characters' in targeting markets and the fetishization of the enticing cover illustration with its caption.

However, if these products of the culture industry do 'program' reading as consumption, subordinating the narrative to a set of catchy 'hooks', there is another force shaping nineteenth-century working-class reading that resists the forms of reification. This is the tension between novelistic and allegorical modes of reading, and specifically the close relation between allegory and popular modes of reading. Allegory is usually taken as a literary genre, an identifiable form of writing, usually deprecated in romantic and modernist criticism (though being revalued in the post-modern shift from consciousness to convention). What I want to suggest is that allegory is a mode of reading as well, that one may read works that do not appear to be allegorical in an allegorical fashion and come up with a kind of reading at odds with what might be expected. To read novelistically, one understands characters neither as existing people (as if it were a 'true story') nor as metaphorical types; one takes them as 'typical' individuals with thoughts, psyches, and motives acting in an everyday world. To read allegorically or typologically, I suggest, the fictional world is less a representation of the real world than a microcosm. Thus the households and families in dime novels that would be interpreted as typical households if read novelistically are interpreted as microcosms of the social world when read allegorically; individual characters are less individuals than figures for social groups. For an allegorical mode of reading to shape a system of reading, there is usually a master plot, or body of narratives, that are shared by a culture; this is clear in the case of Christian allegory. As Janice

Radway (1984, 198) has argued in her persuasive investigation of the reading of popular fiction, 'Although romances are technically novels because each purports to tell a "new" story of unfamiliar characters and as-yet uncompleted events, in fact, they all *retell* a single tale whose final outcome their readers always already know.'

I will suggest, in the interpretations that follow, that such a single tale, a master plot, existed in nineteenth-century working-class culture (though never as deeply lived or widely articulated as earlier Christian plots) and that it shaped allegorical readings of dime novels. This plot was made up of nationalist, class-inflected stories of the American Republic, inter-related, if sometimes contradictory tales of its origins and the threats to it. This narrative of the Republic is a part of a peculiarly artisan variant of republican ideology — the fusion of the emblems and political language of the Republic with the labor relations and social traditions of the crafts — whose emergence in antebellum America has been recently analyzed by Sean Wilentz (1984), and whose persistence in the 'plebian culture' under assault through the panics and upheavals of the last quarter of the nineteenth century has been a dominant chord in the new labor history.[4]

There are several reasons why I would argue that allegorical or typologial modes of reading exist in nineteenth-century working-class culture. To read a *novel*, to understand a story neither as a typological emblem nor as a factual account of a real individual, was a long and complex cultural transformation. The first novel, *Don Quixote*, was largely a reeducation in reading, satirizing both popular and courtly readings through Quixote's literal belief in the romances and his allegorical understanding of the world. Reading novelistically is a relatively new form, a central part of the bourgeois cultural revolution, tied to conceptions of possessive individualism. By the middle of the nineteenth century, novels had re-shaped bourgeois reading fairly thoroughly, and stories began to be told of those 'naive' readers who read novels literally, believing that the characters existed, like those boys held captive by dime novels. But the other form of resistance to bourgeois reading modes, allegorical reading, also persisted. The popular understanding of the sensational plots of the cheap stories drew on the survival of the allegorical modes of popular reading, particularly of *Pilgrim's Progress*, as well as of fairy tales.[5]

Moreover, allegory is a mode characteristic of subordinate

groups. As Alfred Habegger (1982, 111-112) has argued, 'allegory is the literature of exiles, prisoners, captives, or others who have no room to act in their society. ... Allegory is one of many human artifacts expressing a sense of human powerlessness.' So if allegorical modes of reading are in one sense a traditionalist resistance to the novel's individualism, they are also a sign of the powerlessness of working-class readers. The dime novels that elicit allegorical readings in order to make sense of them are novels of disguise: the stories of tramps who are discovered to be heirs, and of working girls who become ladies. All depend on magical transformations to compensate the impossibility of imagining 'realistic' actions by powerful agents. The cheap stories that come closest to novelistic realism — the tales of young craftworkers in small, knowable communities — express the genuine, if eroding, power of the 'craftsmens' empire'.[6]

These hypotheses as to the systems of reading employed by nineteenth-century workers can guide our readings of the dime novels; nevertheless, for the most part, a poetics of the dime novel must begin from the inert and decaying texts themselves. Gramsci (1929-1935, 359), outlining his essay on serial novels, noted that:

A certain variety of types of popular novel exists and it should be noted that, although all of them simultaneously enjoy some degree of success and popularity, one of them nevertheless predominates by far. From this predominance one can identify a change in fundamental tastes, just as from the simultaneous success of the various types one can prove that there exist among the people various cultural levels, different 'masses of feelings' prevalent in one or the other model, various popular 'hero-models'. It is thus important for the present essay to draw up a catalogue of these types and to establish historically their greater or lesser degree of success.

Indeed, most accounts of dime novels, and popular fiction generally, begin with attention to the 'various types', the genres and conventions. Style, the personal mark of a writer, is less salient in popular fiction than rhetoric, the stock of commonplaces that are used to persuade and entertain. And convention and genre are to narrative what rhetoric is to language.

These concepts — rhetoric, convention, genre, formula — are the object of cultural history and cultural criticism generally.[7] To know a culture is to know its conventions and formulas, to know the patterns it places on the world, the stories with which it tells its lives, the maps it makes of its terrain, the names it uses. These conventions and genres stand at the start of cultural study, some already formed and known in the common sense of the culture itself, others part of that culture's image in the histories made by cultures distant in time, space or social world. An account of a culture's conventions can be a tool of critique leading us from the individual texts, the local symbolic acts, to the wider social and historical meanings of cultural production.

A history of cultural conventions would thus use a concept of genre to mediate between individual texts and the social and historical situation. Changes in a genre and shifts from one dominant genre to another can be signs of larger cultural transformations; cultural and political conflict may be read in the struggles between genres and in different inflections of a single genre. However, there are dangers in generic criticism. One difficulty is that there is little consistency in present definitions of genres: some terms are based on subject matter, others on formal attributes. But the temptation to construct abstract and consistent typologies can reify generic categories and lead to a simple pigeonholing of texts. Fredric Jameson (1982, 322) has been particularly aware of this tendency in his insistence on generic discontinuities:

> ... *pure* textual exemplifications of a single genre do not exist; and this, not merely because pure manifestations of anything are rare, but well beyond that, because texts always come into being at the intersection of several genres and emerge from the tensions in the latter's multiple force fields. This discovery does not, however, mean the collapse of genre criticism but rather its renewal: we need the specification of the individual 'genres' today more than ever, not in order to drop specimens into the box bearing those labels, but rather to map our coordinates on the basis of those fixed stars and to triangulate this specific given textual moment.

A similar type of attitude needs to be taken toward the gap between the genres the culture itself understood and the generic terms we employ in reconstructing the culture. To be content with the terms the culture used, with the culture's self-understanding, is to abdicate the historian's task, which is to understand the way a culture's social and political unconscious overdetermines its self-consciousness. On the other hand, a culture's own understanding of its genres is an important part of its rhetoric and must be attended to; any attempt to construct ahistorical, ideal typologies violates the first premises of historical materialism.

With dime novels, there is a good deal of generic consciousness; certain genres, particularly westerns, have been anatomized, and some overall patterns have been noted. Henry Nash Smith built his argument in *Virgin Land* around the shift, indeed the progressive deterioration, in the genre from novels of older frontiersmen based on the genteel code to novels of young cowboys and outlaws cut off from any genteel code: the genre thus lost all social significance in a search for sensation. Daryl Jones's *The Dime Novel Western* (1978) is also an explicitly generic study, defining a western as 'a mode of romance which is set somewhere along the moving frontier at a time when the values of wilderness and civilization are in tension, and which concerns the involvement of a highly stylized protagonist in some form of pursuit' (169). He then tells the history and meanings of the genre in terms of the changes in the setting, the moving frontier, and changes in the protagonist. But both of these works, by focusing on one genre, tend to reify that genre and, though giving an account of its internal relations, lose a sense of its relations to other genres.

The most ambitious attempt to map dime novel genres as a whole is J. Edward Leithead's series of articles in *Dime Novel Round-Up*, 'The Anatomy of Dime Novels' (1965-1971). What the series lacks in depth is made up in range and in bibliographic work as he sketches the lineaments of different types of stories and begins to classify and index particular publications. But his work is only a beginning and remains basically taxonomic.

The difficulty with much of this work lies in an ambiguity in the term 'genre' and an ahistorical use of a contemporary notion of popular fiction genres when looking at dime novels. So while affirming the centrality of categories like formula, convention, and genre to historical materialist cultural studies, it is worth recalling that the present system of 'genre fiction' — the reified categories of 'detective story', 'science fiction', 'gothic romance', and so on — is a relatively recent development, emerging, I would argue, in the pulp magazines of the 1920s and 1930s. Before that the lines between 'genres' were much more permeable: one might take as a symptom of the invention of 'genre fiction' the transition in the pulps between 1910 and 1930 from *All-Story Magazine* to *Detective Story Magazine, Love Story Magazine,* and *Western Story Magazine.* Here John Cawelti's distinction between the concept of 'genre' and that of 'formula' is useful;[8] since the same formulas can appear in different genres, the too quick classification of, say, Deadwood Dick as a 'western' can obscure his relation to other dime novels.

So I am less interested in an encyclopedic catalog of the genres and formulas of nineteenth-century popular fiction, a task which would require a good deal more scholarly work and monographs, than in looking at genres and formulas in a particular way, as enactments of social conflicts and cleavages. Particular formulas enact the conflicts and divisions of the social totality, trying to explain and resolve them; changes in these formulas may mark changes in a culture's view of those conflicts, or indeed in the conflicts themselves.

This approach to popular fiction stems from recent reflections among Marxist theorists and historians about the ruses of ideology, and the renewed recognition that social cleavages, particularly class ones, do not present themselves immediately. This notion is of course based on Marx's own account of the ruses of class representation in *The Eighteenth Brumaire of Louis Napoleon*, where the self-representation of a class (his subject is particularly the various fractions of the bourgeoisie, the petty bourgeoisie and the peasantry) on the political stage is seen to involve a variety of cultural manifestations: a famous example is the way revolutionaries themselves 'conjure up the spirits of the past to help them; they borrow their names, slogans and costumes so as to stage the new world-historical scene in this venerable disguise and borrowed language. Luther put on the mask of the apostle Paul; the Revolution of 1789-1814 draped itself alternately as the Roman republic and the Roman empire' (Marx 1852, 146-147). An example of this that I will look at in detail are the Knights of Labor, who Engels (1887, 494) called 'a truly American paradox, clothing the most modern tendencies in the most medieval mummeries.' If historical struggles do take place in borrowed costumes and assumed accents, if social and economic divisions appear in disguise, then the source for these disguises and the manifestation of these roles lie in the conventional characters of a society, played out in its popular narratives. The figures and characters one sees in dime novels are perhaps not the self-representation of any class, nor are they the class as represented by another; they are a body of representations that are alternately claimed, rejected, and fought over.

This line of thought in Marx and others regarding the ruses of representation, both political and literary, implies, one might think, a notion of a 'true' representation, an accurate self-consciousness, a revolution not fought in disguise, a genuine class consciousness. And there are assertions in *The Eighteenth Brumaire* that the proletarian revolution will not conjure up spirits of the past and will create its poetry from the future. However, it *will* require its own poetry; class consciousness is not immune from rhetoric, and any true/false dichotomy misses the figurative nature of ideas of class. A persuasive version of this argument has been made recently by the political theorist Adam Przeworski (1985, 69-70):

> Classes are not a datum prior to the history of concrete struggles. ... As Marx said, and as Gramsci was fond of repeating, it is in the realm of ideology that people become conscious of social relations. What people come to believe and what they happen to do is an effect of a long-term process of persuasion and organization by political and ideological forces engaged in numerous struggles for the realization of their goals. Social cleavages, the experience of social differentiation, are never given directly to our consciousness. Social differences acquire the status of cleavages as an outcome of ideological and political struggles. ... Is the society composed of classes or of individuals with harmonious interests? Are classes the fundamental source of social cleavage or are they to be placed alongside any other social distinction? Are interests of classes antagonistic or do they encourage cooperation? What are the classes? Which class represents interests more general than its own? Which constitute a majority? Which are capable of leading the entire society? These are the fundamental issues of ideological struggle. The ideological struggle is a struggle *about* class before it is a struggle *among* classes.

I quote this passage at some length because it seems to me that it opens up an important terrain for cultural and ideological history, the analysis of the rhetoric and vocabulary of class and social cleavages.[9] Such an attention to the rhetorical and metaphorical aspects of class ideologies helps recast the concept of ideology itself. Rather than seeing ideology as a system of ideas, a worldview, or a collection of fragmentary opinion — which can be characterized as true or false — one can see ideology as essentially narrative in character, a set of stories one tells oneself to situate oneself in the world, to name the characters and map the terrain of the social world.[10]

Popular narratives play an important role in defining the cleavages in the social order; they can offer new metaphors for those divisions and contest the received and enforced metaphors of the dominant order. In 1879, W.H. Bishop (1879, 389-90) wrote of the story papers and cheap libraries that they are 'written almost exclusively for the use of the lower classes of society', and that 'there are a great many poor persons in the narratives, and the capitalist is occasionally abused, showing that an eye is kept on the popular movements of the day.' Though Bishop's own rhetoric — the use of a term like 'lower classes' — betrays the class stance of the *Atlantic Monthly* and its public, his accurate observation focuses on the aspect of dime novel formulas that I will explore: the way those 'poor persons' and occasional 'capitalists' appear in different genres and formulas, the way social cleavages are figured in a period when the very categories of social cleavage are changing, a change visible in the ambiguities of the term 'producers' and the novelty of the term 'middle classes' (Montgomery 1967, 14). I will argue that new conceptions of class emerged from popular representations of the city in the 1840s, and that, in the subsequent period of prolonged crisis, class conflict, and labor organization, the cheap stories became a terrain of struggle *about* class, about the lineaments of the 'characters' that made up the republic.

At the simplest level, dime novels offered depictions of working class life, and a gallery of working class heroes. This was a marked contrast to genteel fiction; indeed, in 1891, William Dean Howells wrote that, 'The American public does not like to read about the life of toil ... What we like to read about is the life of noblemen or millionaires; ... if our writers were to begin telling us on any extended scale of how mill hands, or miners, or farmers, or iron puddlers really live, we should very soon let them know that we did not care to meet such vulgar and commonplace people' (Rodgers 1978, 68-69). But as David Montgomery (1976, 116) notes, 'for ten cents, workers could find themselves heroically portrayed in stories like *Larry Locke: Man of Iron, Or, A Fight for Fortune, A Story of Labor and Capital*.' From the mysteries of the city of the 1840s, working-class life is central to the cheap stories.[11]

However, as W.H. Bishop also noted, the 'story papers are not accurate pictures' of the life of the 'lower classes'. What we find are less depictions of social classes than figures of social cleavage, less portraits of life in the factory than mythic landscapes of tramps and millionaires. Moreover, the dime novels that seem furthest from working-class life — from the 'legends of the Revolution' to the tales of western outlaws — are often told in accents of mechanics and laborers. So a theory of the figuration of social cleavage requires three distinct levels of analysis: a consideration of the historical conditions for specific figures; an analysis of the displacements and condensations which make up specific figures which are never simple reflections of social and historical realities; and an interpretation of the accents in which those figures are narrated. To conclude this chapter, I will outline some aspects of these three levels.[12]

Figures of social cleavages, particularly those of class, are never 'given'; one can not deduce them simply from an analysis of the class structure of a social formation. Rather, they emerge from the combination of received symbolic forms, continuing experiences of authority and subordination in work, family, and community, and new articulations by the various producers of symbolic forms, from local teachers, preachers, storytellers and singers, to journalists, politicians, labor organizers, and novelists. As Fredric Jameson has written in an essay on class in contemporary popular culture (1977a, 845), 'in order for genuine class consciousness to be possible, we have to begin to sense the abstract truth of class through the tangible medium of daily life in vivid and experiential ways, and to say that class structure is becoming representable means that we now have gone beyond mere abstract understanding and entered that whole area of personal fantasy, collective storytelling, narrative figurability. ... To become figurable — that is to say, visible in the first place, accessible to our imaginations — the classes have to be able to become in some sense characters in their own right.' Thus we must not only identify these figures of social cleavage and interpret their meanings but also explain the social and historical conditions that make possible the particular figure.

The figures that emerged in dime novels were, in the broadest sense, a coming to terms with the expansion and then crisis of capitalist production in the United States. The early serials and pamphlet novels helped constitute the universe of artisan republicanism, and the stories became part of the conflict when battles between workers and capitalists became national events that fractured the culture and challenged the incorporation of the republic — from the miner's 'Long Strike' of 1875 and the national railroad strikes of 1877 to the Homestead Strike of 1892, from the hanging of the Molly Maguires to the hanging of the Haymarket anarchists.[13] But since, as David Montgomery noted, the culture of the 'producing classes, was infused with more a populist than a class consciousness, its producer heroes and accumulator villains appeared in many disguises in the dime novel. The 'producing classes' are 'represented' in all of them, but they may appear as, in Allan Pinkerton's title, striker, communist, tramp or detective.

Thus one finds neither 'representations of workers' in the descriptive, pictorial sense that characterized the ideologies of the emerging 'naturalist' novel, 'muckraking' journalism and 'sociology' of the late nineteenth and early twentieth century, nor chronicles of a 'true', transparent class consciousness, but an unstable economy of formulaic narratives: the 'mystery of the city'; the *bildungsroman* of the 'honest mechanic'; the exploits of celebrated outlaws; the allegorical landscape of tramps and millionaires; the disguised nobleman working in mine or mill; the romance of the orphan working-girl; the workman unjustly accused of a crime; versions of Cinderella and her step-sisters; and the master not of deduction but of disguise, the dime novel detective. These narratives are the dream-work of the social, condensing (compressing a number of dream-thoughts into one image) and displacing (transferring energies invested in one image to another) the wishes, anxieties, and intractable antinomies of social life in a class society. Each of these formulas has its moment of success, when it is able to offer convincing symbolic resolutions to social contradictions, and its historical limits, when the pressure of the real reveals its plots and resolutions to be merely imaginary.

If the 'representative' nature of dime novels is qualified by the fact that their 'representations' of workers are neither accurate nor simple depictions, it is further entangled by a second meaning of 'represent': 'to serve as to the official and authorized delegate or agent for; act as a spokesman for' (*American Heritage Dictionary*, First Edition).

The commercially produced dime novels were a product of a nascent culture industry, not the creation of workers. Whom do they speak for? Whom do they represent? The dime novels were, I suggest, neither the vehicle of workers' self-expression nor the propaganda tools of capitalists; they were a stage on which contradictory stories were produced, with new characters in old costumes, morals that were undermined by the tale, and words that could be spoken in different accents.

Indeed, my title is dime novels *and* working class culture, not dime novels *as* working class culture. One can, I think, say of dime novels what Gareth Stedman Jones (1983, 9-10) said of

British music halls: 'It was certainly never suggested that this culture was the self-conscious creation of workers or that it was confined to workers, only that, by sheer weight of numbers, the preoccupations and predilections of workers imposed a discernible imprint on the shape taken by this culture.' However, if one begins with this very qualified assertion — that by sheer weight of numbers, the preoccupations and predilections of workers, the principal audience of the dime novels, imposed a discernible imprint on the shape taken by dime novels — one can read that imprint, and see how the dime novels attempted to represent, to speak for, their working-class audience.

One can explore the way figures in dime novels speak for their audience by paying close attention to the 'accents' by which they are inflected. I borrow this term from Voloshinov, the Soviet theorist of language (associated with the circle of Mikhail Bakhtin), who maintained that signs are 'multiaccentual'. Voloshinov (1930, 23) argued that:

> Class does not coincide with the sign community, i.e. with the community, which is the totality of users of the same set of signs for ideological communication. Thus various different classes will use one and the same language. As a result, differently oriented accents intersect in every ideological sign. Sign becomes an arena of class struggle.
>
> The social *multiaccentuality* of the ideological sign is a very crucial aspect. ... The very same thing that makes the ideological sign vital and mutable is also, however, that which makes it a refracting and distorting medium. The ruling class strives to impart a supraclass, eternal character to the ideological sign, to extinguish or drive inward the struggle between social value judgments which occurs in it, to make the sign uniaccentual.
>
> In actual fact, each living ideological sign has two faces, like Janus. Any current curse word can become a word of praise, any current truth must inevitably sound to many other people as the greatest lie. This *inner dialectic quality* of the sign comes out fully in the open only in times of social crises or revolutionary changes.

Thus the ideological signs mobilized in dime novels — the characters, particular words and figures, narrative patterns — are not established and univocal. Their ambiguity comes not only from their rhetorical character, their use of metaphor and other figurative devices, but from the different class accents with which they are inflected. These class accents can sometimes be detected in their production, in the way the writer understands the material, but they are equally active in their reception, in the way readers accent their reading. This can be difficult to detect; thus it is essential to begin with an assumption of contradiction, of the multiaccentuality of all ideological signs. Otherwise, the constant attempt of the dominant culture to render them uni-vocal, to make them speak in legitimate accents, will conceal the struggle, and thus the meaning of the ideological document. In what follows I will attempt to hear the conflicting accents of certain signs that are central to both dime novels and to larger political and social discourses. These will include key words, phrases, and names: 'virtue', 'manly', 'knight', 'self-made', 'Molly Maguire', as well as recurring characters: 'outlaw', 'tramp', 'working-girl'. One can detect conflicting accents in formulaic patterns of disguise and revelation, in the represen-tation of speech, and in the happy endings.

Some of the signs originate in the codes of the dominant genteel culture, others derive from residual and emergent alter-native or oppositional cultures. Both sets of signs are fought over: taught, learned, excluded, appropriated, reinterpreted, subverted, coopted. Some of this ideological battle occurs consciously and intentionally; thus, when reading dime novels, close attention need be paid not only to the rhetoric but to the rhetorician. For even if we do not mean to determine the inten-tions of the forgotten, if not anonymous, dime novelist, we must note two crucial forms of the dialogic, what I will call 'ventrilo-quism' and 'impersonation'. The first is throwing one's own voice into the form of another: the reformer who writes dime novels — Horatio Alger, for example — is a characteristic ventriloquist.[14] The second is assuming the voice of another in one's own form, a characteristic stance of the dime novelists who would represent, speak for, their audiences — Ned Buntline, for example. However, in a body of discourses, like a group of popular narratives, many accents are potentially present; by drawing on historians' accounts of nineteenth-century working-class culture, I will try to suggest the 'mechanic accents' that were actualized in workers' reading, consciously and uncon-siously.

It is true that many of the signs mobilized in dime novels are, in Voloshinov's terms, signs 'that have been withdrawn from the pressures of social struggle ... [they] inevitably lose force, degenerating into allegory and [become] the object not of live social intelligibility but of philological comprehension. The historical memory of mankind is full of such worn out ideological signs incapable of serving as arenas for the clash of live social accents.' 'However,' Voloshinov continues, 'inasmuch as they are remembered by the philologist and the historian, they may be said to retain the last glimmers of life.' In the historical and philological readings that follow, I hope to restore to these dime novels their mechanic accents, and perhaps, a glimmer of life.

6

Mysteries and Mechanics of the City

Cheap stories — commercially produced, widely distributed, inexpensive fiction for an audience of artisans and laborers — came into existence in the late 1830s and early 1840s in the wake of the penny press. The early story papers and pamphlet novel publishers competed fiercely, experimenting with various types of fiction in their attempt to capture the new public. The first genre to achieve massive success and to dominate cheap fiction was the 'mysteries of the city'. These novels unveiled the city's mysteries by telling tales of criminal underworlds, urban squalor, and elite luxury and decadence. Eugène Sue's *Les Mystères de Paris*, which was first serialized in Paris' *Journal des Debats* from 9 June 1842 to 15 October 1843, became an international success, translated, pirated, and imitated in Great Britain, Germany and the United States. In the decade that followed, the 'mysteries' proliferated: G.W.M. Reynolds wrote *The Mysteries of London* (1845-1848); F. Thiele, *Die Geheimnisse von Berlin* (1845); and Ned Buntline, *The Mysteries and Miseries of New York* (1848). In the United States, the genre accommodated smaller cities and mill towns, in novels that were often published locally: one could read Osgood Bradbury's *Mysteries of Lowell* (1844), Frank Hazelton's *The Mysteries of Troy* (1847), Harry Spofford's *The Mysteries of Worcester* (1846), and *The Mysteries and Miseries of San Francisco. By a Californian* (1853). The 'mysteries' crossed national boundaries, shadowing the migrations of workers. Not only could German-speaking workers on both sides of the Atlantic read *The Quaker City*, a mystery of Philadelphia by George Lippard (himself a descendent of German immigrants to Pennsylvania), in Friedrich Gerstäcker's Leibzig translation, *Die Quakerstadt und ihre Geheimnisse* (1846), but they could also read German-American 'mysteries of the city' like the anonymous *Die*

Geheimnisse von Philadelphia (1850), Heinrich Börnstein's *Die Geheimnisse von St. Louis* (1851), and Emil Klauprecht's *Cincinnati; oder, Geheimnisse des Westens* (1854-1855).[1]

That these novels were conscious attempts by the new entrepreneurs of fiction to cash in on the success of Sue is hardly surprising; but to see them merely as 'imitations of Sue' is to mistake their significance, both formally and historically. Not all of the 'mysteries of the city' told the same story; the genre encompassed a number of different formulas, some invented by Sue, others developed in a decade of continual translation, adaptation and invention. What emerged in the 1840s was a genre which dominated sensational fiction with its ability to figure the world of the capitalist city to its artisan readers. The power and the limits of this figure led to debates over the ideology of the genre, debates joined in 1845 by the young German communist Karl Marx.

But the politics of the genre went beyond the ideologies of its form; indeed the genre drew Marx's attention because of the politics of its audience and authors. It was the genre of 1848, the sensational reading of Chartists and revolutionaries; and the dreams of the utopian socialists haunt the pages of these mysteries of the city. Moreover, a number of the writers of the mysteries of the city emerged as political figures themselves; Peter Brooks (1984, 152) notes that while Sue

> ... began *Les Mystères de Paris* with the vaguest of ideological orientations — and without knowing at all how the novel's plot and meaning would evolve — Sue emerged from it a declared socialist, a rare case of conversion through one's own work of fiction. He would indeed go on to become a deputy from a working-class district of Paris during the Second Republic, and then figure among the banished after the coup d'etat that ushered in the Second Empire.

Such conversions through one's own fiction were, however, not uncommon among the writers of 'mysteries of the city'. G.M.W. Reynolds became a Chartist in 1848, 'catapulted into active politics by his apparently spontaneous speech at the Chartist demonstration at Trafalgar Square' (Humphreys 1985, 8). In the United States, Ned Buntline entered working class politics, though with nativist rather than socialist tendencies, figuring prominently in the 1849 Astor Place riot. And George Lippard and Augustine J.H. Duganne, author of *The Knights of the Seal; or, The Mysteries of Three Cities* (1846), supported the labor agrarianism of the National Reform Association and the Industrial Congress, the most important antebellum attempt at a national federation of the labor movement; Lippard went on to found a working class secret society, the Brotherhood of the Union. In all these cases, the writer's audience became his constituency, the classes he attempted to represent in fiction became the classes he sought to represent through fiction.

In this chapter I want to look at the contradictory ideology of the 'mysteries of the city', and at the paradoxical union of sensational fiction and radical politics at this moment, by exploring the career and writings of George Lippard, the leading American writer of the 'mysteries of the city' and the most overtly political dime novelist of his or subsequent generations. Lippard is a key figure in the history of the dime novel, mixing the production techniques of the fiction factory with working class ideologies of republicanism and socialism. He was also one of the 'stars', the *auteurs*, of this new culture industry; he is, if you like, the D.W. Griffith of cheap stories: the studio system will follow. And the contradictions that emerge when he attempts to fuse the role of hack novelist with that of labor tribune reveal both the power and the limits of the 'mysteries of the city', and give Lippard's works their continuing peculiar power.

In what follows, I will begin by looking at the emergence of Lippard's mysteries of the city out of the crime stories of the penny press, and will then interpret two central formulas in his mysteries of the city: the figure of Monk-hall, and the continual retelling of a seduction-rape narrative. I will conclude by examining his attempts to incorporate into the 'mysteries of the city' two formulas which would 'represent' — both depict and speak for — the mechanics of the city: the figure of the 'mechanic hero', and a narrative of racial and ethnic riots.

George Lippard, *Godey's Ladies Book* noted in 1849, 'has struck out an entirely new path and stands isolated on a point inaccessible to the mass of writers of the present day. ... He is unquestionably the most popular writer of the day, and his books are sold, edition after edition, thousand after thousand, while those of others accumulate like useless lumber on the shelves of publishers' (De Grazia 1969, 308). His success, however, was tied to the success of Philadelphia's cheap story publishing. Though New York first produced Park Benjamin's innovative weekly story papers, *Brother Jonathan* (1839) and *New World* (1840), and his 'shilling novelettes', Philadelphia was not far behind. The *Saturday Evening Post* and the *Saturday Courier* were weeklies combining news and fiction that predated Park Benjamin's story papers, but it was not until the penny press — the *Public Ledger* (founded 1836) and the *Spirit of the Times* (founded 1837) — took over the news function and the competition of Benjamin's story papers challenged their story function that they became story weeklies. Joined by *Neal's Saturday Gazette*, the three dominated Philadelphia story papers through the 1840s and 1850s. Their circulation was almost double that of the middle-class magazines: Mary Noel (1954, 5) writes that 'when Godey's Lady's Book boasted 40,000, papers like the Philadelphia Courier ... were talking in terms of 70,000 and 75,000.'[2] The production of pamphlet novels, often published in installments, was led by T.B. Peterson & Brothers, a firm founded in 1845 as a bookseller and then publisher of cheap sensational fiction. They became the publishers of Lippard, T.S. Arthur, the temperance novelist, E.D.E.N. Southworth and Ann Stephens, advertising themselves as the 'Cheapest book house in the World'.[3]

Lippard himself began working for a penny paper, the *Spirit of the Times*, in 1841, writing city sketches and courtroom accounts.[4] His first stories and novels were serialized in the *Saturday Evening Post* and in 1843 he became an editor and writer for *Citizen Soldier: A Weekly Newspaper Devoted to the Interests of the Volunteers and Militias of the United States*, turning it into a family story paper, changing its name to the *Home Journal and Citizen Soldier*. Rather than 'a dull, dry, tasteless combination of cast-off military lore, worn-out statistics, and long-winded pieces of declamation', Lippard wrote, 'we wish our paper to go into the heart of the family circle, to be a dweller in the sanctity of the household, a welcome messenger to the country fireside' (De Grazia 1969, 74-75). Lippard's celebrity, however, was the result of his 'mysteries of the city', the best known and most important of the three types of stories that Lippard wrote in his brief but prolific career between the early 1840s and his death in 1854.[5] His first 'mystery of the city' was *The Quaker City; or, The Monks of Monk Hall. A Romance of Philadelphia Life, Mystery and Crime* (LPa), which was published in ten cheap, paper-covered installments in the fall and winter of 1844 and 1845 and reprinted many times in book form by the cheap book publishers, G.B. Zieber & Co. and then T.B. Pewterson & Brothers. His most widely read novel, led to his steady work for the story paper, the *Saturday Courier*, whose circulation he is said to have increased from 30,000 to 70,000 (De Grazia 1969, 184). In 1846, Lippard began to write a sequel, *The Nazarene; or, the Last of the*

Washingtons. A Revelation of Philadelphia, New York and Washington in the Year 1844 (LPb), which was published in shilling (twelve and a half cent) pamphlet installments. He never completed the installments of this novel, though it was published as an incomplete book by Peterson in 1854. In December 1849, Lippard serialized his narrative of the election night riots of October 1849, *The Killers. A Narrative of Real Life in Philadelphia* (LPc), in his own *Quaker City Weekly*. His final major work began as a *Quaker City Weekly* serial, *The Empire City; or, New York by Night and Day* (LPd), in 1849, but its narrative was not completed until the publication of its sequel, *New York: Its Upper Ten and Lower Million* (LPe), in 1853, shortly before his death.

Lippard's mysteries owe much to his training in the penny press. *The Quaker City*, based in part on a celebrated 1843 Philadelphia murder case, is in a way a more elaborate, more revealing version of the humorous sketches of hearings at the Mayor's Police Court that he had written for the *Spirit of the Times* in a column called 'City Police'. We are told that the novel is based on the papers of an old and dying lawyer who tells the narrator: 'They contain a full and terrible development of the Secret Life of Philadelphia. In that pacquet, you will find, records of crimes, that never came to trial, murders that have never been divulged; there you will discover the results of secret examinations, held by official personages, in relation to atrocities almost too horrible for belief' (LPa, 3). Lippard's stance is not that of detective, solving a crime that baffles the police and public with analytic skills, but that of newspaperman, digging up and revealing secret crimes and miscarriages of justice. Though Lippard satirizes the penny press, the '*Daily Black Mail*', when he ends *The Quaker City* with long extracts from a newspaper which, when set against the story we have just read, are revealed as untrue, covering up the crimes and exonerating the guilty elite, his crime stories share both narrative and ideological elements with the crime news of the penny press. Dan Schiller (1981, 54-55) has argued that 'the infusion of crime news into the young commercial papers did not ... merely reflect the hunger for "sensationalized" news that analysts so often attribute to the "mass" public. ... Crime news, embracing police reports from the magistrate's court [the form in which Lippard first got his training], discussion and news of police activities, criminal biographies, and extensive trial coverage of noteworthy cases, dramatized a larger intention: to punish specific infractions of public good. ... Exposure — of dark corners hidden throughout the city, of public vices and private lives — was used to reveal violations of the overarching standard of equal justice.' Lippard, like the penny press, employed the ideological rhetoric of the new public of mechanics, the republican articulation of 'virtue' against 'corruption' and 'luxury', of 'equal rights' and the 'public good' against 'monopoly', defending the Republic and the Revolution against a new 'aristocracy'.

However, the impact of the penny press on Lippard's stories is not limited to his literary apprenticeship to the police court sketch nor even to his use of the narrative of exposure rather than that of detection in structuring his own crime stories: he is truly a *feuilletoniste* in that his novel is structured like a newspaper. Perhaps the most evocative description of Lippard's narrative structure is that of David Reynolds (1982, 44):

> In a curious way, the typical Lippard novel is like Monk Hall, a labyrinthine structure riddled with trap doors that are always opening beneath the reader's feet and sending him tumbling into another dimension. And Lippard is like an ever-present Devil-Bug, sometimes preaching, sometimes praying, sometimes rescuing the poor or virtuous, yet always ready to gloat fiendishly over a decayed corpse or an old woman's brains splattered on the floor.

Reynolds goes on to interpret this structure as a conscious assault on the rational and the linear akin to that of the surrealists, an experiment with 'spatial and temporal disunities ... [which] would be developed in more cerebral, self-conscious fashion by such later writers as Faulkner, Joyce, Virginia Woolf and Nabokov' (48). However, far from being a premature modernism, Lippard's sinusoidal structure is not only dictated by the necessities of serialization, whether in newspapers, story papers, or pamphlet installments,[6] but also replicates the narrative structure of the newspaper. Monk Hall with its labyrinthine rooms and its neighboring but never quite connected stories is not unlike the newspaper itself, which combines stories by sheer juxtaposition.

The key principles of order in the newspaper are the date (as Benedict Anderson [1983, 37-39] notes, 'calendrical coincidence' is the 'essential literary convention of the newspaper') and the city. And it is not surprising that the only unities Lippard keeps, the only structures that hold his mysteries of the city together, are the date and the city: as he writes at one point, 'it is now our task to describe certain scenes which took place in New York, between Nightfall and Midnight, on this 23rd of December, 1844' (LPe, 48). Each of the books of *The Quaker City* is unified by its date; it begins on the night of Wednesday, 21 December 1842, and ends in the evening of December 24. All of Lippard's later mysteries of the city use this form: *The Nazarene* begins on Monday, 1 May 1844 and, though unfinished, was meant to find its climax in the Native American riots of 3 May to 8 May 1844; and *New York: Its Upper Ten and Lower Million* titles each of its parts by date. And the 'mysteries of the city' posited the city as an autonomous and self-contained social whole, despite the fact that the city was losing its autonomy; as Sam Bass Warner (1968, 85) has shown, Philadelphia between 1830 and 1860 was in the process of becoming 'an agglomeration of institutions and activities which were not local but regional and national', with capitalist enterprises and markets leading the way. Though Lippard begins to sense the limits of a single city as an autonomous world in *The Nazarene*, which is a 'revelation of Philadelphia, New York, and Washington', for the most part, the city remains a unifying focus. If Anderson writes that the newspaper is 'an "extreme form" of the book, a book sold on a colossal scale, but of ephemeral popularity. Might we say: one-day best-sellers? ... Reading a newspaper is like reading a novel whose author has abandoned thought of a coherent plot', one might argue that *The Quaker City* is an 'extreme form' of a newspaper, that reading Lippard is like reading a newspaper with a plot; for Lippard's point is that all these disparate stories connected by calendrical and geographical coincidence are part of a secret plot of Philadelphia's elite, one figured by Monk Hall but never resolved into one narrative line or climax.

The heart of *The Quaker City* is Monk Hall, a mansion which stands in the working class district of Southwark. What had been a place of wealth, ease and grandeur now stands in the midst of tenements and manufactories: one finds the 'magnificent mansion of Monk-hall with a printing office on one side and a stereotype foundry on the other, while on the opposite side of the way, a mass of miserable frame houses seemed about to commit suicide and fling themselves madly into the gutter, and in the distance a long line of dwellings, offices, and factories, looming in broken perspective, looked as if they wanted to shake hands across the narrow street' (LPa, 48). It is a sign of the pre-Revolutionary past, though its original wealthy proprietor has been forgotten, and the origin of its name is surrounded with conflicting traditions: 'Could our ancient and ghostly proprietor, glide into the tenements adjoining Monk-hall, and the mechanic or his wife, the printer or the factory man to tell him the story of the strange old building, he would find that the most remarkable ignorance prevailed in regard to the structure, its origin and history. . . . Did our spirit-friend glide over the threshold and enter the chambers of his home, his eye would perhaps, behold scenes that rivalled, in vice and magnificence, anything that legend chronicled of the olden-time of Monk-hall' (LPa, 49). Though Lippard will not tell the story of the origin and history of Monk-hall, he will reveal to the mechanic, his wife and the factory man those scenes of vice and magnificence that take place in the midst of their city. For Monk-hall, with its six floors, three above ground and three underground, and its secret rooms and trap doors, is the scene of the private life of the private citizens of this private city. The Monks are Philadelphia's merchants, professionals and clergy: 'Here too, ruddy and round faced, sate a demure parson, whose white hands and soft words, had made him the idol of his wealthy congregation. Here was a puffy-faced Editor side by side with a Magazine Proprietor; here were sleek-visaged tradesmen, . . . solemn-faced merchants, . . . reputable married men, with grown up children at college, and trustful wives sleeping quietly in their dreamless beds at home' (LPa, 55-56). Their revels range from drunkenness and gambling to incest, rape and murder.

In some ways, Lippard's Monk-hall is characteristic of the fascination with the life of the elite in the 'mysteries of the city', at once reveling in minute depictions of material luxury and denouncing the moral depravity of the 'merchant princes'.[7] But Monk-hall differs from the conventional representations of ornate mansions and fashionable ballrooms in other mysteries of the city, including Lippard's own subsequent ones. For Lippard achieves his figurative energy by appropriating the conventions of the Gothic for the city; Monk-hall emerges as a transformed Gothic castle. Moreover, Monk-hall is not merely a mansion within the Quaker City, one building in the cityscape; it *is* the Quaker City, condensing the social and sexual relations between the 'upper ten and lower million' into a single house.

This figurative reduction of Philadelphia to Monk-hall is one reason modern readers are often disappointed with the 'mysteries of the city' genre. Unlike the popular works of the New York *Tribune* journalist George Foster — *New York in Slices* (1849), *New York by Gas-Light* (1850), and *New York Naked* (1854) — which never free themselves of the conventions of the newspaper sketch, serving as sensational guide books to the city and its low-life (and unlike subsequent realist and naturalist novels of the city), the most powerful mysteries of the city offer very little in the way of urban topography, very little local color; as a historian notes of one novel, 'for all the light it shed on local conditions [it] might as well have been set in Boston or Philadelphia as New York.'[8] The mysteries of the city were not the 'sights' of the city, but the social relations that lay behind closed doors; success in the genre required the creation of a figure — like Monk-hall — which embodied those relations — or a character — like the prostitute — who could move through them. To look in Monk-hall was to 'obtain a few fresh ideas of the nature of the *secret life* of this good Quaker City' (LPa, 23). Monk Hall is thus not merely a caricature of Philadelphia's elite; it figures the city as a whole.

The center of Monk-hall, however, is not simply the depiction of material luxury and moral depravity; it is a particular plot, the seduction-rape story, a crime narrative that is repeated with several variations in *The Quaker City*. In his introduction to *The Quaker City*, Lippard writes that the 'first idea of the Work' was:

> That the seduction of a poor and innocent girl, is a deed altogether as criminal as deliberate murder. It is worse than the murder of the body, for it is the assassination of the soul. If the murderer deserves death by the gallows, then the assassin of chastity and maidenhood is worthy of death by the hands of any man, and in any place.

As he progressed in the work, he then tells us, 'other ideas were added to the original thought. ... I determined to write a book which should describe all the phases of a corrupt social system, as manifested in the city of Philadelphia' (LPa, 2). Nevertheless, the seduction narrative remains the central thread; indeed as Monk Hall comes to figure Philadelphia, so the seduction narrative comes to figure all the phases of its corrupt social system.

The centrality of the seduction-rape plot distinguishes Lippard from other writers of the 'mysteries of the city', who built their narrative around the story of the prostitute: Sue's Fleur-de-Marie in *Les Mystères de Paris*, or Buntline's Big Lize in *The Mysteries and Miseries of New York*. Though a seduction story lies at the origins of these narratives, the narrative proper embodies the city's contradictions in the figure of the prostitute with the heart of gold, and uses her as an entry into the story material of the city's dangerous classes.[9] Lippard, on the other hand, avoids the narrative of the 'fallen woman' by telling the story of the 'fall' — the seduction-rape — over and over again; and by shifting the mysteries of the city from a story about 'criminals' to the story of the 'crime', he escapes, at least partially, the slumming narrative one finds in Sue.

The seduction-rape plot runs through most of Lippard's work; not only are his mysteries of the city the mysteries of abduction and rape but many of his Revolutionary War legends are the tales of virtuous American women pursued by evil British soldiers and rescued by heroic Americans. To understand the popularity and power of Lippard's writings we must understand the way this plot condenses social and political evils into the figure of the seducer. For Lippard and his audience, the 'seduction of a poor and innocent girl' becomes the representative crime narrative, holding within it all other crimes and capable of endless elaboration.

There is nothing particularly novel or unlikely in this: the seduction plot is at the heart of the novel since Samuel Richardson; as Leslie Fiedler (1966, 62) has written, 'the novel proper could not be launched until some author imagined a prose narrative in which the Seducer and the Pure Maiden were brought face to face in a ritual combat destined to end in marriage or death.' And in Richardson and the many novelists who followed his lead, the political meanings of the story were not far from the surface, as it dramatized the class battles between the aristocratic seducer and the virtuous bourgeois woman. It would not be difficult to see Lippard's seduction tale as a minor and belated version of the Clarissa story: despite its origins in the celebrated 1843 Philadelphia murder case where young Singleton Mercer was found innocent of killing the rapist of his sister, *The Quaker City* is another manifestation of a central bourgeois myth, transplanted to America.

But the appearance of this story in the United States of the 1840s is somewhat more complicated. If we consider not the seeming persistence and unchangeability of the archetypal formula but the discontinuities and gaps in its history, we can ask not how the seduction tales of George Lippard in the 1840s and of Laura Jean Libbey in the 1880s and 1890s stand in an unbroken tradition from Richardson to the bodice rippers of the 1970s but how and why they appear at all. For, as Helen Papashvily (1956, 31-32) has noted in her discussion of the popular seduction novels written by American women in the 1790s and 1800s, 'although these novels, Richardson's *Clarissa* and *Pamela,* and many like them continued to attract readers well into the nineteenth century, no more fallen women appeared as popular heroines in American fiction for a century.' The seduction novel gives way almost entirely to domestic fiction, beginning as stories and sketches in the new magazines like *Godey's* and reaching its peak in the tremendous production of domestic novels in the 1850s and 1860s.[10] Nina Baym (1978, 25-26) has also called attention to this shift: 'the women who wrote after 1820 detested Richardsonian fiction and planned their own as an alternative to it ... scarcely any of these novels [by women between 1820 and 1870] are novels of seduction ... the disappearance of the novel of seduction is a crucial event in women's fiction, and perhaps in women's pysche as well.'

This eclipse of the seduction narrative has two sources. First of all, the seduction novel drew much of its force from the class conflict at its heart. As Terry Eagleton (1982, 4) has said of Richardson's novels, they are 'not mere images of conflicts fought out on another terrain, representations of a history which happens elsewhere; they are themselves a material part of those struggles, pitched standards around which battle is joined, instruments which help to constitute social interests rather than lenses which reflect them.' In the United States, the cultural revolution against a feudal aristocracy took place in a displaced form, if at all; the weapons of that conflict were less necessary. Indeed the brief flourishing of the seduction tale in the 1790s and 1800s could be seen as part of the attenuated cultural revolution that followed the battle for independence: the British could be easily cast as aristocratic seducers, a tradition that continues through Lippard's 'legends' of the Revolution and the early dime novels of the Revolution.[11] However, in general, for the American bourgeoisie, the novel was to serve less as a weapon in class conflict than as an organizer of the kinship and sex/gender system. In this role, the domestic novel, the tales of the exchanges of middle class kinship networks, was central.

The eclipse of the seduction novel also marks what Nina Baym calls a change in 'women's psyche' but which might be more exactly interpreted as a transformation in the dominant sex-gender system, the complex of kinship structures and notions of manhood and womanhood by which, in Gayle Rubin's (1975, 159) phrase, 'a society transforms biological sexuality into products of human activity, and in which these transformed sexual needs are satisfied.' These sex/gender systems have a history, changing with shifts in the productive and reproductive processes and with gender struggles.

The anthropologists Edholm, Harris, and Young (1977, 126) have persuasively argued that:

> ... when changes in the productive process bring the sex/gender system into contradiction with the sexual division of labor, when there is no longer congruence between the two, this incompatibility provides a potential for struggle and questioning, for sexual hostility and antagonism. The direction that such a struggle takes, however, cannot be 'read off' in advance.

The changes in the sexual division of labor brought on by industrial capitalism in the decades before the Civil War — isolating some women in the newly 'unproductive' home and bringing others into the new social space of the factory — created disorder and instability in existing sexual and gender ideologies.[12] I will look at the solutions worked out for factory women in the final chapter on the novels of Laura Jean Libbey; here I want to note that the construction of the 'domestic sphere' and of notions of 'true womanhood' in Sarah Josepha Hale's *Godey's Ladies' Book* and the new domestic fiction was, like the emerging woman's rights movement which met in Seneca Falls in 1848, part of a cultural transformation, a struggle over signs and stories, habits and manners, which would create new subjects, a new 'womanhood' and a new 'manhood,' for the capitalist city. The seduction narrative was not, as Papashvily and Baym point out, part of this new culture; it, like the Gothic mode, was a kind of vanishing mediator, linking in a single narrative the two mutually exclusive sex/gender systems — the older, more specifically patriarchal one and the new one organized around separate spheres. Through the intensification of the evil and threat of the past — the aristocratic Lovelaces and the Gothic castles — it served to bring forth the new, and vanished as soon as the new was established.[13]

How, then, are we to understand Lippard's anachronistic seduction tales of the 1840s? First of all, they are an attempt to adapt a tale of class conflict, albeit of the conflict between the aristocracy and bourgeoisie, to the emerging class conflicts between merchants, manufacturers and mechanics, between capital and labor. Lippard indeed spells out the class implications of the seduction tale in *The Quaker City* when he complicates the basic plot — Byrnewood Arlington seeking revenge on Gus Lorrimer for seducing his sister Mary Arlington into a false marriage and rape — by revealing that Byrnewood himself had seduced, impregnated, and abandoned a servant girl: 'In crushing the honor of an unprotected girl, he had only followed out the law which the Lady and Gentleman of Christian Society recognize with tacit reverence. Seduce a *rich* maiden? Wrong the daughter of a *good* family? Oh, this is horrible; it is a crime only paralleled in enormity by the blasphemy of God's name. But a poor girl, a *servant*, a domestic? Oh, no! These are fair game for the gentleman of fashionable society; upon the wrongs of such as these the fine lady looks with a light laugh and supercilious smile' (LPa, 417). This theme is developed at more length in *The Nazarene* where one of the major sections revolves around Nora, the daughter of a handloom weaver who is tempted by the money of Count Waslikow. 'What right have you to be virtuous? Are you not poor?' (LPb, 184), she is asked when she refuses. Clearly at the level of Lippard's declared motives, it is accurate to say, as Larzar Ziff does, that for Lippard 'seduction was a metaphor of economic exploitation.'[14] However, the problem with this interpretation is that, for the most part, Lippard's seduction tales do *not* involve poor girls. Mary Arlington is a merchant's daughter; the origins of Mabel are mysterious but she is introduced as the daughter of a prominent parson and she ends appearing to be the daughter of a merchant; in fact, other than the secondary inset narratives like that of the servant girl Annie, the only poor woman who appears is Dora Livingstone, and she, a cobbler's grand-daughter, far from being a victim of seduction and rape, has raised herself to the 'first circles of the Aristocracy of Philadelphia' as the wife of a wealthy 'Merchant-Prince' (though she would like to rid herself of the 'Merchant' and keep only the 'Prince'). Even in *The Nazarene*, the story of Nora is an inserted sketch; the main lines of the plot follow the daughters of a merchant and a bank president. So the class accent to the seduction plot, though certainly present, does not exhaust it.

Rather the Lippard stories mark a clash between the older narrative pattern and the new ideology of separate spheres. His hostility to the middle class 'aristocracy', the 'merchant princes', is based less on their exploitation of working women than on the perception that, despite the professed belief in feminine 'influence', their 'home' is a paradise of seducers. The manners and gentility of the new sex/gender system are masks for hypocrisy. Monk-hall is a nightmare parody of the bourgeois home. This is why Parson Pyne, the popular anti-Catholic minister who drugs and rapes Mabel, who thinks she is his daughter, is so central. Parson Pyne is the closest to an absolute villain in the book, and, based on the 1844 case of Bishop Onderdonk, defrocked for seducing his parishioners, he stands as a figure for the alliance of ministers, magazinists (Lippard's Sylvester J. Peterkin, editor of *The Ladies' Western Hemisphere and Continental Organ*) and middle class women who served, as Ann Douglas has shown, as the 'organic intellectuals' of the new culture. Thus Lippard's novels are a weird defense, by way of this outdated form, the anti-seduction novel, of women and men against the cultural hegemony of the class of merchants and manufacturers. This can also explain why a later and more politically-seasoned Lippard will become an advocate of women's rights and the publisher of such early feminists as Lucretia Mott and Cora Montgomery in his weekly paper, *Quaker City*.

However, this view of Lippard's seduction/rape tales is complicated by Lippard's own ambivalence toward the seducer. For unlike the seduction novels written by Susanna Rowson and other women writers in the 1790s and 1800s, the focus of the Lippard plot is less on the story of the 'fallen woman' than on the struggle between the good and evil men over that woman; thus he focuses on the struggle between the seducer Lorrimer and the brother Arlington rather than on Mary Arlington herself. Though he will never exculpate the seducer, his doubling of plots allows him to create heroes much like the seducer villains themselves. In *The Quaker City*, whatever relative symmetry and coherence the novel had is disrupted entirely by the sudden appearance in the last third of the novel of Ravoni the Sorcerer, a mysterious foreign scientist-magician, who abducts Mabel into his secret order, his 'new faith'. Though Ravoni is killed, most commentators have rightly noted that Lippard's and the reader's sympathies are mobilized for him; he offers the only alternative to Monk-hall and the corrupt Quaker City. This figure emerges again in *The Nazarene* as the omnipresent Stranger with the features of George Washington, Paul Mount Laurel. Indeed, the ambivalence toward the seducer is highlighted in the story of Nora, mentioned above. For the temptation of Nora, the working girl, by Count Waslikow is delivered by Mount Laurel, who she thinks is her protector. He represents the Count; it is he who asks her 'what right do you have to be virtuous?'. But when she spurns the offer, it is Mount Laurel who turns on the Count, casts him out, and asks her forgiveness. The libertine Paul is revealed as a 'POOR MAN' in disguise; the accomplice of the seducer is Nora's protector. Since *The Nazarene* remained unfinished, there is no resolution of the enigmatic Mount Laurel. However, these supermen are figures of the transition in conceptions of manhood, transferring the energy of the aristocratic seducer to the brotherly protector of the domestic woman.

Lippard's libidinal ambivalence is further manifested in his prose, which is often called pornographic, but is better characterized as voyeuristic. Lippard often characterizes himself as painting a hidden scene in words, and one of his most common scenes is of a woman in partial undress and in partial unconsciousness. The scenes of Mary Arlington swooning before the libertine Lorrimer, of Parson Pyne over the drugged Mabel, and of Livingstone over his sleeping wife and her lover, among others are interrupted by descriptions of the female body: heaving bosoms, unbound hair, flowing and gaping night robes.

> Her head deep sunken in a downy pillow, a beautiful woman, lay wrapt in slumber. By the manner in which the silken folds of the cover-lid were disposed, you might see that her form was full, large and voluptuous. Thick masses of jet black hair fell, glossy and luxuriant, over her round neck and along her uncovered bosom, which swelling with the full ripeness of womanhood, rose gently in the light. ... Her face, appearing amid the tresses of her jet-black hair, like a fair picture half-hidden in sable drapery, was marked by a perfect regularity of feature, a high forehead, arching eyebrows and long dark lashes, resting on the velvet skin of each glowing cheek. Her mouth was open slightly as she slept, the ivory whiteness of her teeth, gleaming through the rich vermilion of her parted lips. She lay on that gorgeous couch, in an attitude of voluptuous ease; a perfect incarnation of the Sensual Woman, who combines the beauty of a mere animal, with an intellect strong and resolute in its every purpose (LPa, 137).

These depictions which fuse the look of the seducer with the look of the protector prompted charges that Lippard was a salacious writer, charges that Lippard always denied, claiming that the writing of *The Quaker City* was 'destitute of any idea of sensualism'. Nevertheless, Lippard's ambivalence toward the seducer and his verbal incarnations of the 'Sensual Woman' subvert the announced intentions of the novel.[15]

The Quaker City divided Philadelphia. Its notoriety led to the cancelling of the stage production because of the possible disruptions (1844 had already seen periods of major rioting in May and July caused by nativist attacks on the city's Irish Catholics). John Bell Bouton, in his 1855 biography of Lippard, wrote that 'the book was the talk of the city. It divided society into two parties, one justifying the *Quaker City*, the other execrating it and the author. The laborers, the mechanics, the great body of the people, were on Lippard's side. The press, by attacks and vindications, kept up the popular excitement' (19). What is striking about Bouton's observation and the unexpected success of Lippard's novel is that the laborers and mechanics adopted Lippard *before* he attempted to represent them — either fictionally or politically.

The early politics of Lippard, though vaguely populist, were hardly developed. In *The Quaker City*, Lippard's sentiments were voiced by Luke Harvey, the poor boy become fashionable young clerk:

> Justice and in the Quaker City! A Strange Monster I trow! One moment it unbolts the doors of the prison, and bids the Bank-Director, who boasts his ten thousand victims, whose ears ring forever with the curses of the Widow and the Orphan, it bids the *honest* Bank-Director, go forth! The next moment it bolts and seals those very prison doors, upon the poor devil, who has stolen a loaf of bread to save himself from starvation! One day it stands grimly smiling while a mob fires a Church [this was written soon after the burning of Catholic churches by nativists in May and July 1844] or sacks a Hall [a reference to the burning of Pennsylvania Hall by an anti-abolition mob in May 1838], the next, ha, ha, ha, it hurries from its impartial throne, and pastes its placards over the walls of a Theatre, stating in pompous words, and big capitals, that THE TRUTH *must not be told in Philadelphia* [a reference to the cancellation of a stage production of *The Quaker City* in November 1844, a production that was arranged before all the installments of the novel had been published] (LPa, 205).

Nevertheless, as late as January 1844, according to his modern biographer, he denounced the striking handloom weavers.[16]

However, as he was taken up by Philadelphia's artisans and laborers, he responded by allying with and speaking for them, working for 'social reform through the medium of popular literature' (quoted in Reynolds 1982, 17). Lippard began to see himself as a political writer, devoting 'his great talents to the cause of the million to the side of Labor when opposed by Capital — to the rights of the people against Monopoly — to the cause of virtue against the black sins of exalted vice' (LPd, i). In an address to the Industrial Congress, a gathering of labor and agrarian reformers in June 1848, Lippard (1848, 186) said:

> I came among you a stranger. I entered this hall, in which you, my friends, the Representatives of the Labor of this wide land, talked

with one another, not of creeds, or theologies, nor yet of barren politics, but of the Elevation of the millions who toil — of the Poor from the shackles of Monopoly — of the perfect freedom of that land, which God has given to the workers, and which Capitalists and Speculators dare no longer take away.

I listened to your discussions, and found that the same thoughts which I had nursed in the loneliness of an author's life, which I had in my isolation rudely endeavoured to embody in my books — I found these same thoughts embodied in this Congress.

This has, no doubt, much of the self-dramatization that characterized Lippard's writings; nevertheless, the sense of finding an organized body of thought that paralleled and extended his work seems accurate. In December 1848, he established his own weekly news and story paper, the *Quaker City*. This was a move towards economic independence; but it was also a vehicle for his political activity as a tribune of the working-man's movement. In a manifesto published in *Quaker City* on 10 February 1849, Lippard announced his labor aesthetic, invoking the European revolutionaries of 1848:

While the authors and poets of England, France, Germany, and Italy are writing and singing in the cause of human advancement, devoting all their energies to the social elevation of the masses, our authors and poets seem to have nothing beter to do than to cut and thrust at one another. (That word 'masses' has become so much a cant phrase of late that we are forced to define what we mean by it. It means, to be very plain, that portion of the human family who are doomed to work and suffer for the benefit of a mere fraction of the whole sum of humanity. By the word *masses* we mean just Nine-Tenths of the human race.) A mere *literary* man, who has no ultimate but fame and no religion but self, is one of the greatest curses that can befall a country. ... We need unity among our authors; the age pulsates with a great Idea, and that Idea is the right of Labor to its fruits, coupled with the re-organization of the social system. ... We would say that our Idea of a National Literature is simply: that a literature that does not work practically, for the advancement of social reform, or which is too dignified or too good to picture the wrongs of the great mass of humanity, is just good for nothing at all. (Reynolds 1986, 280-81)

In a way, Lippard's political development was a typical trajectory, paralleling that of Eugène Sue and G.M.W. Reynolds. Indeed, two other popular contributors to the Philadelphia

Saturday Courier established their own story papers for personal independence and political aims: T.S. Arthur, the temperance novelist, established his *Arthur's Home Gazette*; and Ned Buntline, an organizer of the American party, the 'Know-Nothings,' published *Ned Buntline's Own*.

Moreover, Lippard shares a common rhetoric with other cheap story writers. The author of one of the earliest 'shilling novelettes', Walt Whitman, whose temperance novel, *Franklin Evans*, was issued as a *New World* 'extra' in November 1842, writes in his introduction:

> Can I hope, that my story will do good? I entertain that hope. Issued in the cheap and popular form you see, and wafted by every mail to all parts of this vast republic; the facilities which its publisher possesses, giving him power of diffusing it more widely than any other establishment in the United States; the mighty and deep public opinion which, as a tide bears a ship upon its bosom, ever welcomes anything favorable to Temperance Reform; its being written *for the mass*, though, the writer hopes, not without some claim upon the approval of the more fastidious; and, as much as anything else, the fact that it is as a pioneer in this department of literature — all these will give 'THE INEBRIATE', I feel confident, a more than ordinary share of patronage. ... my book is not written for the critics, but for the PEOPLE (WM, 104-105).

A decade later, Ned Buntline's work was advertised with a similar rhetoric:

> No work ever published in this country created more excitement or met with a more extensive sale than the FAR-FAMED MYSTERIES AND MISERIES OF NEW YORK; and the reason is obvious, — they present in a form easy to be understood, a most STARTLING PICTURE of the VICES and VIRTUES, the MORALS and the MANNERS of the large part of our community who are called the WORKING CLASS; and no man has had more opportunity of becoming acquainted with the details of their life, in all its lights and shades, than Mr Judson, who has been emphatically called the FRIEND OF THE WORKING MAN. ... At the present time, when public attention is strongly turned to the subject, and the working man is rising in his might to shake off the chains that weigh him to the earth, and to demand a just equivalent for his labor, this book [Buntline's *The G'Hals of New York*] ... is calculated not only to give the laboring man a just appreciation of his rights, but also for the employer, that he may see the justice of the maxim — 'the Laborer is worthy of his hire.' It is, in fact, *the book for the people*.[17]

All of these dime novelists shared the vocabulary and rhetoric of an artisan republicanism; in an ideological universe that continued to be shaped by battles over the meaning of republicanism and the legacy of the revolution, the urban craftworkers had given a peculiar mechanic accent to the discourses, rituals and icono-graphy of the Republic. Building on the traditional republican vision of an independent and virtuous citizenry subordinating self-interests to the public good — the commonwealth, journey-men emphasized the centrality of equal rights and the corrupting influence of large inequalities of wealth; the labor theory of value and, as Lippard puts it, the 'right of Labor to its fruits'; and a craft pride which envisioned a productive social order based on cooperative and independent workshops, where wage labor was merely a stage toward the artisan's competence.[18]

How are we to interpret the politics of these popular novelists? Are these novelists like politicians and the editors of the penny press, merely mouthing populist and labor rhetoric, in order to attract support, sensation and sales? Indeed, just as many social-ists mistrusted Sue, many Chartists thought G.M.W. Reynolds a charlatan.[19] As for Buntline, one could scarcely say either that his fiction served to promote his politics or that his politics pro-moted his fiction; as Peter Buckley (1984) has shown, populist politics and popular fiction both served in the production of 'Ned Buntline', the fictional persona of E.Z.C. Judson. On the other hand, there is little doubt about Lippard's political sincerity; his activities as founder, organizer, and leader of the workingman's secret society, the Brotherhood of the Union, ruined him finan-cially and led him largely to give up fiction writing and to abandon the *Quaker City* weekly; his final publishing project was the unsuccessful attempt at a journal of the Brotherhood, *The White Banner.*[20]

However, since popular novelists are neither professional politicians nor political thinkers, questions about the sincerity of their purported beliefs or the adequacy of their political pro-posals are less interesting than questions about the narrative embodiment of their political ideologies. What is the relation between the 'mysteries of the city' and this artisan republican-ism? Was the genre adequate to the ideologies of its practi-tioners, to the ideologies of its readers? Does the popularity of the genre clarify those ideologies? These were the questions raised by Karl Marx in 1845, when he, living in Paris, became involved in a critical controversy over Eugène Sue's *Les Mystères de Paris*. In response to the acclaim given Sue's novel in a German literary journal, Marx devoted a large portion of *The Holy Family* to a critique of Sue's *feuilleton* and of the interpretation of it by the German critic, 'Szeliga'.[21] In one of the most detailed treatments of a literary subject in all of his work, Marx both recognizes the significance of the new commercial fiction and its popularity among working people, and examines and criticizes the mysteries of the city genre.

In analyzing Sue's novel, Marx considers its narrative stance, its fictional world, and its protagonist. All three aspects are relevant to the genre as a whole, and to Lippard in particular. First, Marx notes that the narrator's stance is that of an implied bourgeois public. Workers are represented through bourgeois eyes, Marx argues, as passive victims or active villains, to be moralized or punished. The point of the story is to call the attention of the rich to the plight of the poor: 'Sue commits an *anachronism* out of courtesy to the French bourgeoisie when he puts the motto of the burghers of Louis XIV's time "Ah! si le roi le savait!" in a modified form: "Ah! si le riche le savait!" into the mouth of the working man Morel' (Marx and Engels 1845, 56). Though Lippard tries to avoid this, by inverting Sue and revealing the crimes of the elite to 'the mechanic or his wife', the seduction plot reinforces this narrative stance. Sue, like the Lippard of *The Quaker City*, has his characters reflect on the seduction/rape of poor women; however, as Marx points out, 'Rodolphe's [Sue's hero] reflections do not go so far as to make the *servants' condition* the object of his most gracious Criticism. Being a *petty* ruler, he is a *great* patronizer of servants' conditions. Still less does he go so far as to understand that the general position of women in modern society is inhuman. ... He deplores only that there is no *law which punishes* a seducer.' This is precisely the position of Lippard's novel, despite his efforts to avoid a narrative of slumming.

Second, Marx notes Sue's representation of the city as a peculiar combination of the criminal underworld and the elite: 'after leading us through the lowest strata of society, for example through the criminals' tavern, Eugène Sue transports us to "*haute volee*", to a ball in the Quartier Saint-Germain. ... The disguises of Rodolphe, Prince of Geroldstein, give him entry into the lower strata of society as his title gives him access to the highest circles.' Lippard's Monk-hall also embodies this trope of a society constituted by merchant princes and the 'outcasts of the Quaker City', who occupy the lowest level of Monk Hall: 'in the day-time, vagabond man and woman and child, lay quiet and snug, in the underground recesses of Monk-Hall; in the night they stole forth from the secret passage thro' the pawnbroker's shop in the adjoining street, and prowled over the city, to beg, to rob, or perchance to murder' (LPa, 477-478). It is a figure with some power; Lippard sees the anti-abolitionist mobs as the result of this unholy alliance (LPa, 277, 482), and, indeed, Marx's own understanding of the coup of Louis Napoleon invokes an alliance of the lumpen proletariat and the aristocrats. Nevertheless, the mysteries of the city exclude the city's working masses: there is no place for mechanics in Monk Hall.

Finally, Marx criticized Sue's hero, Rodolphe, the nobleman in disguise, who acts as Providence in the novel, punishing evil characters, and bringing the victims into a moral, Christian universe. 'The whole of Rodolphe's character', Marx writes, 'is finally summed up in the "pure" hypocrisy by which he manages to see and make others see the *outbursts of his evil passions* as *outbursts against the passions of the wicked*' (Marx and Engels 1845, 206). So the superman, who rescues the poor and the virtuous, who imagines utopian reforms, is driven by a vengeance and resentment against the objects of his reform. We have seen this fascination with the superman in Lippard as well — the magician-scientist Ravoni in *The Quaker City* and the enigmatic Paul Mount Laurel in *The Nazarene* — and it seems a product of both a guilty admiration for his seducer villains, and the sign of an inability to imagine a resolution to the serial mysteries of the city, a force that could counter the crimes of Monk-hall.[22]

Together, these aspects of the genre produce a narrative that, one might conclude, not only fails to embody but actually contradicts the ideology of artisan republicanism. However, the apparent contradiction between narrative and ideology is further complicated by a discrepancy between the implied reader and the actual audience. For if the implied reader of the mysteries of the city is often the bourgeois public (note how the advertisement for Buntline says that he presents to 'our community' a picture of 'their [working class] life'), the actual readers were the working people of the city; and the mysteries of the city, including the novels of Sue, remained, as Nina Baym has noted (1984, 213), a scandal to the middle class reading public.

The curious union of the mysteries of the city and artisan republicanism could be resolved by appealing to the deceptive logic of the culture industry. The mysteries of the city was a form imposed upon its mechanic readers, not a species of working class fiction; and the artisan republican rhetoric of the novelists is belied by the formulas of their fiction.[23] However, the relation between popular narrative and popular ideology is more complex than this solution suggests. For the convergences and disjunctures between the mysteries of the city and artisan republicanism reveal not only the contradictions within popular culture but the various attempts to resolve those contradictions.

In his contribution to the theory of ideology, Göran Therborn (1980, 25-28) has argued that since class ideologies are positional ideologies, which subject one to and qualify one for a particular position in the world, they consist in both ego-ideologies, conceptions of one's own position, and alter-ideologies, perceptions of the Other and of one's relation to it. This is a useful distinction for us, for it is in the delineation of an alter-ideology that the mysteries of the city and artisan republicanism converge, and in the search for an ego-ideology that they diverge. As I noted earlier, they share a narrative and rhetoric of exposure: the republic's virtue is upheld by revealing the luxury, decadence, and corruption of its seducers. The seducers include immoral clergymen, parasitic lawyers, and corrupt politicians; but they come together in the figure of the 'merchant prince', a condensation of artisan suspicion of the unproductive commercial capitalism with republican disdain for aristocracy.

The tensions between and within the mysteries of the city and artisan republicanism surface in the elaboration of an ego-ideology, in the place of a mechanic hero. Though the figure of the honest, independent mechanic is at the center of the vocabulary of artisan republicanism, no such protagonist appears in the mysteries of the city. The advertisement for Ned Buntline's work that I quoted earlier states that *The Mysteries and Miseries of New York* presents a 'PICTURE of the VICES and the VIRTUES, the MORALS and MANNERS ... of the WORKING CLASS'; however, as Peter Buckley (1984, 444-445) has noted, 'in the 147 named characters in the *Mysteries*, there is only one person who may qualify as an honest mechanic.' The narrative elements Marx identified in Sue — the depiction of workers as passive victims, a world made up of the elite and the lumpen, and the quasi-aristocratic supermen heroes — prevent the emergence of an active working class protagonist, a mechanic hero. Despite the labor sympathies of the writers and the working class public of the genre, the paradox persisted.

Lippard's attempt to represent in fiction the mechanics he sought to represent politically highlights the contradictions of the genre. He begins by telling the stories Luke Harvey had only alluded to: stories of poor men cheated by bankers. Thus in one of the later installments of *The Quaker City* he inserted an episode as 'a pleasing illustration of that Justice, which in the Quaker City, unbars the jail to Great Swindlers, while it sends the honest Poor Man into the grave of the Suicide' (LPa, 404). In this allegorical sketch, the Mechanic, John Davis, is refused his money by the Bank President, Job Joneson, because the bank has failed. Though the bank failure has not affected Joneson's 'visage redolent of venison steaks and turtle soup' nor his 'large mansion in one of the most aristocratic squares of the city', it leaves the Mechanic destitute. His wife and child die and he commits suicide.

In the sequel to *The Quaker City, The Nazarene; or, The Last of the Washingtons. A Revelation of Philadelphia, New York, and Washington, in the Year 1844,* Lippard sets out not only to 'depict the lineaments of Fraud, which has crawled up into high places', but to represent Philadelphia's workers, to 'portray ... the untiring energy, the patient virtue of that class of the sex, who serve their task-masters for a pittance per day ... THE WHITE SLAVES OF PHILADELPHIA.' Though *The Nazarene* was left unfinished, the episode entitled 'Nora' does attempt to depict the city's workers. Inset within a more sensational narrative, it is a brief tale of a Kensington handloom weaver who is on strike; three children are dead of smallpox, and his wife is dying. It opens with a characteristic Lippard diorama:

> Let us wander into the northern districts of the city. ... Do you see that huge building lifting its enormous walls, high over the surrounding structures, which seem dwindled into nothing by comparison with a red glare, flashing from each of its thousand windows? Do you hear the sounds that groan and thunder, from the cellar of this mammoth edifice to the roof? Perhaps it is a great festival hall, where an army of revellers feast with wine and music? Wherefore this sound, this light, this motion? Look through those windows, rendered almost opaque by foul air, look by the glare of the red lights, and the mystery is explained.
>
> There you may see an army, but such an army never crouched beneath the lash of the Slave-Driver in the cotton-fields of the south! While the Steam Engine growls his unceasing thunder, here in rooms, filled with an atmosphere as dense and deadly as the blast of an unclosed charnel, you may see men and women and children bending down over their labor, which begins with the sun, and ceases not when the night comes on. ... This is a Factory.

> Let the Mammoth Factory blaze with its thousand lights, but we
> must hurry on. . . . Here we behold a house of time-worn brick, there
> a toppling frame; on every side the crash of looms, urged by weary
> hands even at this hour, disturbs the silence of the night (LPb, 166-
> 168).

This is only a brief selection from the extended tour of Kensington on which Lippard leads his reader and which ends in the
tenement of an Irish handloom weaver and his daughter Nora.
The mysterious building is no longer a private club for the elite;
Monk Hall, as it were, is revealed as a factory. And he explicitly
addresses 'you, Mechanic and Laborer'. Nevertheless, it remains
an essentially static picture, a pathetic diorama.[24] The tale that
follows is not unlike the John Davis tale of *The Quaker City*, an
exemplary tale of the victimized handloom weaver, driven
almost to crime (but saved by the generous stranger, Paul Mount
Laurel), and his virtuous daughter.

Lippard was more successful in imagining a mechanic hero
set in the past; and one of his most popular lectures was entitled
'The Mechanic Hero of Brandywine', a short tale of a heroic
blacksmith at the Battle of Brandywine, which was collected into
Blanche of Brandywine. In a way, Lippard's 'legends' of the
American Revolution (sixty-two of which were published in the
Saturday Courier between 1846 and 1848) were a form more
adaptable to the accents of artisan republicanism than the
mysteries of the city. Lippard was able to depict the mechanic as
an autonomous and heroic agent in his tales of the Revolution;
the contemporary city seemed to eradicate the mechanic's
autonomy, leaving only a passive and defeated victim. In an
illuminating comment, John Bell Bouton (1855, 19), an associate
of Lippard in the 1850s and probably a member of his Brotherhood of the Union, writes: 'It must be borne in mind that the
Quaker City was written to depict the dark side of Philadelphia
life; its mission was to be the stern and unsparing foe of vice. . . .
We like it the least of all Lippard's writings on this account. We
prefer those in which he speaks more hopefully and cheerily of
mankind.' The more hopeful and cheerful writings are those set
in the past, defending and appropriating the legacy of the
Revolution.

A mechanic hero does appear in Lippard's later mysteries of
the city when he replaces the seduction plot with an inheritance
plot. Both types of plot co-exist in all of Lippard's fiction;
however, in the later novels the inheritance plot becomes

dominant, providing an overall structure that allows for Lippard's shoemaker heroes, Elijah Watson and Arthur Dermoyne. In *The Killers. A Narrative of Real Life in Philadelphia* (1849), Lippard's short novel of the election night riots, the riots (to which I will return) serve as the culmination of the story of Jacob D.Z. Hicks, 'that embodiment of inimitable energy, and grasping meanness, which in modern days is called a "business man"' (LPc, 11), and his two sons: the profligate Yale student Cromwell Hicks, disinherited for preferring 'the race course, the bar room and the brothel' to the 'counting room'; and the shoe-maker Elijah Watson, raised, unknown to his father, in a tenement. Elijah is revealed as Hicks's true son, and Cromwell as the illegitimate son of a count; nevertheless, when the violence of the riots brings father and sons together, Elijah rejects his father and defends his adopted sister — 'We ain't brother and sister by blood; we are brother and sister by the years of poverty and starvation we've passed together' (LPc, 41) — before they all perish in a fire. In a surprise denouement, however, we learn that Elijah and his sister did not die, but escaped to Panama by blackmailing Philadelphia merchants with evidence of their transactions in the African slave trade. As this magical escape suggests, Lippard's story of Elijah Watson remains only a sketch of an artisan solution to the mysteries of the city.

In his final 'mystery of the city', his mystery of New York, we see Lippard working through the contradictions of a mechanic hero in the character of Arthur Dermoyne. The story began as *The Empire City; Or New York by Night and Day. Its Aristocracy and its Dollars*, serialized in *Quaker City* weekly in 1849, and published as a book in 1850. This volume sets up the tale of the 1823 will of the wealthy Gulian Van Huyden, who commits suicide when he discovers his wife and his brother are lovers. The estate is to be divided among seven descendants of '"Our Ancestor," who landed on this shore in 1620, "penniless, a beggar, and a vagabond"' (LPd, 28) on Christmas Day 1844. The rest of the volume introduces us to the seven — including a corrupt statesman, Gabriel Godlike, a satirical amalgam of Webster, Clay and Calhoun; a lecherous minister, Herman Barnhurst; the financier Israel Yorke; the merchant prince Evelyn Somers; the southern slaveholder Harry Royalton; and the dandy Beverly Barron — a typical pantheon of Lippard villains. The seventh is Arthur Dermoyne, a minor character who is said to be a reformer, a deist, and given to quoting Eugène Sue. When he appears, he is tracking the seducer of the innocent Alice Burney.

Lippard brings *The Empire City* to an abrupt close, never really completing any of the multiple plots, and not even reaching the climatic Christmas Day of 1844. Arthur Dermoyne is married off to a daughter of Van Huyden in the last paragraph, and shares in the estate.

But the story of the Van Huyden estate, a story of the battle over the legacy of the Republic itself, continued to haunt Lippard in the early 1850s, a period when his lecturing for the Brotherhood of the Union, his declining health and finances, and the death of his wife and son, interrupted his writing of fiction. And in late 1853, a few months before his death, Lippard published *New York: Its Upper Ten and Lower Million*, which took up the story of the Van Huyden will and completed it, summarizing the action and characters of the first volume while ignoring its peremptory ending. When Arthur Dermoyne appears, the minister asks:

> By-the-bye, you spoke of your profession. A merchant, I suppose?'
> 'No, sir.'
> 'A lawyer?'
> 'No, sir.'
> 'A medical gentleman?'
> 'No, sir.'
> 'You are then—'
> 'A shoemaker.'
> 'A WHAT,' ejaculated Herman jumping from his chair.
> 'A shoemaker,' repeated Arthur Dermoyne. 'I gain my bread by the work of my hands, and by the hardest of all kinds of work. I am not only a mechanic, but a shoemaker (LPe, 107).

In the elaborate speech to the minister that follows, Dermoyne tells his story and defends his trade; that narrative and the rhetoric of his defense will become common in the dime novels after the Civil War, as the mechanic hero flourishes.

Dermoyne's defense begins with a specifically literary point, refuting the convention by which the worker is always a low comic figure, by appealing to the type of Christ: 'On the stage no joke is so piquant as the one which is leveled at the "tailor" or the "cobbler"; in literature, the attempt of an unknown to elevate himself, is matter for a brutal laugh; and even grave men like you, when addressed by a man who, like myself, confesses that he is a — shoemaker! you burst into laughter, as though the master you profess to serve, was not himself, one day, a workman at the carpenter's bench' (LPe, 108-109).

Second, Dermoyne plays with the meanings of nobility and gentility, at once ironically claiming noble descent — 'So you see, I am *nobly* descended. ... Not a single idler or vagabond in our family, — all workers, like their Savior, — all men who eat the bread of honest labor' (LPe, 109) — and then refusing polite society — 'Mr Burney did me wrong; for while I was a shoemaker, he persisted ... in thinking me — *a gentleman!* the labor of honest men' (LPe, 109).

Dermoyne's story has three moments which will becom key formulas: the past history of fraud; self-improvement combined with the refusal to rise; and righteous revenge. First, Dermoyne's father was the victim of the perjury and forgery of a rich merchant; thus he has been cheated of his rightful inheritance. Furthermore, Dermoyne is one of the seven heirs to the Van Huyden estate. These inheritance plots thus serve as an allegory of the Republic itself, and part of Lippard's story will be to restore the mechanic to his rightful part of the Revolutionary legacy. This is done, however, without transforming Dermoyne into a member of the elite; despite his self-education, he refuses to 'enter one of those professions called learned' and separate himself 'from that nine-tenths of the human family, who seem to have been only born to work and die — die in mind as well as body — in order to support the idle tenth with superfluities' (LPe, 108). Finally, Dermoyne joins earlier Lippard supermen with his 'almost superhuman strength. ... a kind of trust, given to me by Providence. ... To punish those criminals whom the law does not punish; to protect those victims whom the law does not protect' (LPe, 111).

Lippard's Arthur Dermoyne has the lineaments of the producer hero, the honest mechanic of working class republicanism, lineaments that will appear in various disguises and formulas in the dime novels that follow. But he does not dominate Lippard's novel; as we shall see, the story of the slave's inheritance moves to the foreground, as it did in the nation as a whole. Dermoyne does, however, get the last scene; but whereas *The Empire City* ended with the now wealthy Dermoyne living happily ever after with his new bride, *New York* ends with 'three hundred emigrants, mechanics, their wives and little ones, who have left the savage civilization of the Atlantic cities, for a free home beyond the Rocky Mountains' led by 'a man in the prime of young manhood, dressed in the garb of a hunter, with a rifle on his shoulder. ... the Socialist, — Arthur Dermoyne' (LPe,

284). Lippard combines the various elements of artisan republicanism, labor agarianism, and utopian socialism with the hero
of the dime novel western. It was not an uncommon move; the
German-language mysteries of the city often ended with a move
to the west, and of course Ned Buntline created a second career
for himself when he abandoned the mysteries of the city for the
dime novels of Buffalo Bill.[25]

If the absence (and arduous creation) of a mechanic hero
marked the tensions between the mysteries of the city and
artisan republicanism, the riots that erupted at regular intervals
in the Atlantic cities of the 1830s and 1840s marked the limits of
both genre and ideology, throwing both ego-ideologies and alter-
ideologies into disarray. In Philadelphia during the 1830s and
1840s, crowd actions included anti-Catholic nativist riots, attacks
on blacks and abolitionists by white Philadelphians, and battles
between police and striking handloom weavers.[26] In *The Quaker
City*, Lippard denounced the riots in passing; but in his subsequent fiction he attempted to narrate them, to reveal the
mysteries behind the violence: what emerged were contradictory
tales of ethnic and racial confrontation that fractured the world
of artisan republicanism.

In 1846, Lippard announced that the depiction of the May
1844 nativist riots in Kensington was to be the central event of
his new installment novel, *The Nazarene*. In his introduction,
Lippard writes that his object is 'to portray the scenes of two
successive riots, when all that is barbarous in religious war, all
that is horrible in arson or murder, all that is terrible in the
spectacle of graves torn open, living men shot down like dogs,
churches laid in ashes, was enacted in Philadelphia' (LPb, v).
However, he never fulfills his promise, never realizes the project.
The Nazarene becomes an assembly of fragments, eventually
abandoned.

There are both formal and historical reasons for Lippard's
failure 'not only to picture crime, but also its remedy; not only to
portray the scenes of Kensington and Southwark, where fanati-
cism raised the torch of civil war, but also to record the deeds of
a noble band, who young, generous, enthusiastic, went forth,
into the arena of blood and flame, determined to assert the
divine principles of Love and Charity, even in the face of
frenzied rioters, even by the glare of burning churches' (LPb, vi).
The formal difficulty is betrayed by the existing installments of
The Nazarene: their central concern is the plotting of the riots by
secret societies, and, behind them, by the bank president, Calvin

Wolfe. Wolfe is the leader of the nativist Holy Protestant League as well as the secret anti-papist brotherhood, the G.O.O.L.P.O.; he is also responsible for inciting the Irish weavers to take up arms. But beyond this powerful, if inaccurate, explanation of the riots as a ploy by capitalists to divide the workers,[27] these scenes take the riots out of the streets and put them in underground vaults and covert conspiracies, back in Monk Hall, so to speak. The figurative reduction of urban life to the secrets behind closed doors that we noted earlier as a central trope of the mysteries of the city endlessly displaces and defers the representation of urban violence. Indeed in a convergence of formal convention and ideology, Lippard's narrative of secret conspiracies produces and reproduces his conception of history as the actions of secret societies. Thus as the narrative agents of his novel become Protestant and Catholic secret societies, so his political activity, announced in the introduction to the novel — 'In one word, it will be my object to illustrate this principle: *The immense good which may be accomplished, by a Brotherhood, who, rejecting all sectarian dogmas, take for their rule of action, those great truths of Christ our Saviour, on which all sects agree*' (LPb, vi) — becomes the organizing of the Brotherhood of the Union, a secret society that combined the rituals and fellowship of the Masons and Odd Fellows with a commitment to the cause of labor.

To go into the details of Lippard's Brotherhood and its relation to the flourishing of secret societies, mutual aid organizations and utopian communities is well beyond my scope here. However, it is worth noting that Lippard's major project for the Brotherhood, the writing of a volume of rituals, was a continuation of his attempt at social reform through popular literature. As he wrote, 'many persons, who cannot receive ideas through the means of Books, or oral lessons, may be instructed by means of rites and symbols' (quoted in De Grazia 1969, 405).

A second reason for his failure to depict the riots is a historical one. At the same time that Lippard was entering labor politics, the politics of class were being eclipsed by the politics of ethnicity. Philadelphia's remarkable working-class solidarity in the 1830s had eroded by the time of the defeat of the weaver's strike in the early 1840s, a defeat that was caused, as David Montgomery (1972, 50-51) has shown, by 'the fact that they were no longer supported by the other workmen of Philadelphia. Quite the contrary; their final defeat had come in the wake of actual physical assault by other workers, for the most part native-born Protestant artisans.' The rise of anti-Catholic nativism fractured the ideological universe of artisan republican-ism: as Bruce Laurie (1980, 168-177) has argued, the success of the Philadelphia nativists was due in large part to their ability to rearticulate the artisan republican rhetoric in nativist accents, to combine the praises of mechanics with attacks on non-producers and immigrants. Far more successful than Lippard's Brotherhood of the Union was the nativist Order of United American Mechanics.

Unwilling to scapegoat the Irish Catholic victims of the riots as the Other, Lippard found the explanation systems of both his sensational genre and his mechanic politics inadequate to the narrative of the nativist riots. For the most part, he condemned the nativism that led to the riots, vehemently satirizing anti-Catholic sentiments in both *The Quaker City* and *The Nazarene*, and sympathetically portraying the Irish weavers in *The Nazar-ene*. However, by *The Empire City* and *New York*, Lippard's sense of the role of the Papacy in the defeat of the revolutions of 1848 led him to a elaborate narrative of two Catholic Churches, an absolutist one plotting to establish an anti-republican empire in North America and, within it, 'another Church of Rome, composed of men, who, when the hour strikes, will sacrifice everything to the cause of humanity and God' (LPe, 73). The difficulty of maintaining an anti-nativist stance is indicated by the careers of two other dime novelists, 'Ned Buntline' and A.J.H. Duganne. Buntline was a key figure in articulating an artisan nativism through his story paper, *Ned Buntline's Own*, and took part in New York's 1849 Astor Place Riot. Duganne, on the other hand, had been associated with Fourierist utopian socialism, and, like Lippard, had supported the National Reform Association and the Industrial Congress; indeed Lippard had dedicated the first edition of *The Quaker City* to him. Despite this background, he joined Buntline as an organizer of the Know-Nothing Party in the 1850s.[28]

Curiously Lippard was more successful in narrating Phila-delphia's racial confrontations that he had been with its ethnic battles. For in December 1849, he began serializing *The Killers. A Narrative of Real Life in Philadelphia* in the *Quaker City* — 'In which', the title page tells us, 'the deeds of the Killers, and the great Riot of election night, October 10, 1849, are minutely described. Also the adventures of three notorious individuals, who took part in that Riot, to wit: Cromwell D.Z. Hicks, the Leader of the Killers, Don Jorge, one of the Leaders of the Cuban Expedition, and "The Bulgine", the celebrated Negro Desparado of Moyamensing.' The relatively short novel that follows does indeed include a depiction of the riot, ignited by the burning of an Afro-American tavern, the California House, by a white street gang, the Killers; moreover, it successfully tied the development of its plot to the riot, which serves as an apocalyptic conflagration destroying all the characters (although, as noted earlier, the mechanic Elijah Watson and his sister are magically resurrected in the denouement).

There are three reasons why *The Killers* succeeds in creating the narrative Lippard had failed to deliver three years earlier in *The Nazarene*. First, the actual existence of the Killers, one of the gangs which grew out of 'bar and street-corner cliques, militia units returning from the Mexican War, and work groups that already involved gang labor on the waterfront and rivers' (Laurie 1980, 151), allowed Lippard to use his formulas of secret societies and their subterranean meeting places with a degree of verisimilitude he previously had not achieved. Second, he is able to use the local confrontation as a figure for a national and international plot. Though nativist writers saw the Catholic-Protestant clashes in Philadelphia — whether in the streets or over the use of the Bible in public schools — as signs of a great Jesuit plot to conquer America, Lippard could neither fully accept nor contest this story. However, in *The Killers*, he ties the white attack on the Black community in Philadelphia to the threat of the extension of the slave empire. The leaders of the Killers are sons of wealth — Cromwell Hicks, the son of a Philadelphia merchant, and Don Jorge, the son of a Cuban slave trader; they plan to follow the election night riot — 'the Mexican Campaign of the ensuing night' — with a filibustering expedition of 'the most desperate devils ... in Moyamensing' to Cuba, a fictional version of the several mercenary attempts in the decade after the Mexican War to extend America's empire and slavery in the Caribbean and Central America. Though this is dubious history, it is successful myth, fusing local racial tensions with the national trauma surrounding slavery and expansion.[29]

Finally, Lippard produces two protagonists that match his villains in narrative energy without becoming mere doubles of those villains. The first, the mechanic Elijah Watson, I have discussed; the second is 'Black Andy, or the "Bulgine" in the more familiar dialect of Moyamensing', the Negro proprietor of a groggery. Beaten by the Killers in the riot, he recovers and kills Cromwell Hicks, the leader of the Killers and the false brother of Elijah; he is last seen attempting to rescue Kate Watson from the fire. Black Andy is one of several active Black protagonists in Lippard's work, including the Revolutionary War hero, Ben Sampson, in *Blanche of Brandywine*, and Royal Bill, the escaped slave in *The Empire City* and *New York*, who cites Biblical authority for slave resistance (LPd, 105-107) and presides over the Black Senate while it tries and executes the fugitive slave catcher Bloodhound (LPe, 116-122).

Indeed the intricate machinations of the inheritance plot in Lippard's final mysteries of the city revolve largely around the story of a slave's inheritance. Harry and Randolph Royalton are half-brothers, the one of a white mother, the other of a Black slave mother. Both have a claim on the Van Huyden inheritance, and Harry has hired the slave catcher to abduct Randolph and his sister to the South to enslave them. To this elaborate plot, Lippard adds the revelation that Randolph's slave mother was the daughter of a great statesman and 'leader of the American people' — Washington some critics suggest, but perhaps Jefferson. The story of Jefferson's Black slave daughters was well-known, and William Wells Brown used it in his *Clotel, or The President's Daughter*, first published in 1853, the same year as Lippard's *New York*. If for Brown (BR, 123) the story was one of white America's failure — 'Jefferson is not the only American statesman who has spoken high-sounding words in favour of freedom, and then left his own children to die slaves' — for Lippard it is an allegorical assertion of the Black Randolph's rightful share in the inheritance of the Republic, a story paralleling that of the mechanic Arthur Dermoyne. Neither receive their inheritance; at the end Dermoyne heads west with the emigrant mechanics, and Randolph Royalton, like Brown's George Green, escapes America's racial structure by going to Europe.

Although Lippard shared with large segments of the antebellum labor movement both the racist notion of 'white egalitarianism', which saw Blacks and Indians as degraded and dependent races, and an anti-slavery sentiment, based not on abolitionism but on the common metaphorical equation of slavery and wage labor — 'the slaves of the city, white and black, ... of the cotton Lord and the factory Prince', as Lippard puts it (PLa, 389) — his story of Randolph Royalton suggests how the inheritance narrative within the mysteries of the city allowed Lippard to work through, and to some degree transcend, these contradictions within the ideology of artisan republicanism surrounding race and slavery.[30]

Though Lippard's attempt to fuse popular fiction and popular politics was not unusual among the writers of the mysteries of the city, it becomes increasingly rare as the fiction factory develops and rationalizes. In the years after the Civil War, there are few figures like Lippard who consciously try to articulate a mechanic voice. Lippard's legacy was less his working-class politics than his mechanic formulas; those formulas — the republican plots of inheritance, the secret brotherhood of workers, and the 'mechanic hero' that he labored to develop — give the later dime novels and story papers their mechanic accents.

7

The Molly Maguires and the Detectives

In March and April of 1876, three leading story papers — *The Fireside Companion*, the *New York Weekly*, and the *Saturday Journal* — began serial novels about the Molly Maguires, who were the focus of a series of trials then taking place in the anthracite coal country of Pennsylvania. It was certainly not unusual for the story papers and pamphlet novels to take their subjects from celebrated crimes and trials; as we have seen, Lippard's *The Killers* began appearing less than two months after the election night riots it depicted. Cheap fiction often served as a kind of journalism, casting contemporary events into popular formulas. These crime stories inform, titillate, moralize and entertain; but as they do so they also form the heart of an ideological conflict over the meaning of the crime, and over different conceptions of justice. Writing of eighteenth-century criminal broadsheets, Michel Foucault (1978, 67-68) has suggested that:

> Perhaps we should see this literature of crime, which proliferated around a few exemplary figures, neither as a spontaneous form of 'popular expression', nor as a concerted programme of propaganda and moralization from above; it was a locus in which two investments of penal practice met — a sort of battleground around the crime, its punishment, and its memory. If these accounts were allowed to be printed and circulated, it was because they were expected to have the effect of an ideological control. ... But if these true stories of everyday history were received so avidly, if they formed part of the basic reading of the lower classes, it was because people found in them not only memories, but also precedents; the interest of 'curiosity' is also a political interest. Thus these texts may be read as two-sided discourses, in the facts that they relate, in the effects they give to these facts and in the glory they confer on those 'illustrious' criminals, and no doubt in the very words they use.

The stories of the Molly Maguires — the twenty Irish coal miners who were hanged in the late 1870s for an assortment of murders supposedly committed by them as members of a secret society called the Molly Maguires — are indeed 'a battleground around the crime, its punishment, and its memory'. Not only do different stories narrate the deeds of the Molly Maguires with different formulas and different accents; each story itself becomes a 'two-sided discourse' as contradictory formulas jostle each other, their very conventionality highlighting the moments their conventions fail.

Indeed, one of these stories, Allan Pinkerton's *The Mollie Maguires and the Detectives*, published in late 1877 as the sixth in his series of 'Detective Stories', and telling of the infiltration of the Molly Maguires by the Pinkerton agent, James McParland, based on his courtroom testimony, has dominated most subsequent accounts of the Molly Maguires, though it has been regularly challenged over the last century by claims that McParland was an *agent provocateur*, that the hiring of the Pinkerton agents by the president of the Philadelphia and Reading Railroad, Franklin Gowen, was part of a long campaign to break the miner's unions and fraternal associations, that there was no connection between individual terrorism and either the miners' union or the Irish fraternal organization, the Ancient Order of Hibernians, and that the so-called Molly Maguires never existed. Indeed the historiographic situation is so murky that Harold Aurand and William Gudelunas (1982, 101) have recently concluded, after reviewing the most prominent interpretations, that the only statements that can be made with any certainty are:

1. Numerous murders were perpetrated in Schuylkill County between 1861 and 1875.

2. The Philadelphia and Reading Companies financed a private investigation into a reputed secret criminal society.

3. As a result of that investigation twenty men were executed for allegedly committing some of those murders.

It is not my intention to re-assess the historiography;[1] indeed I have some sympathy for Herbert Gutman's (1963, 38) criticism of the overemphasis on the case: 'excessive interest in the Haymarket riot, the "Molly Maguires", the great strikes of 1877, the Homestead lockout, the Pullman strike, and close attention to the violence and disorder attending them has obscured the deeper and more important currents of which these things were only symptoms. ... Surely it is time to broaden the approach into a study of labor in the society of the time as a whole.' Nevertheless, I return to the Molly Maguires (and to the 1877 strikes in the next chapter) first, because the two decades since Gutman's criticism have seen a 'new labor history' which has followed his advice, enabling us to see these cases as symptoms of a wider working class history rather than as the whole, and second, because the central issue of the Molly Maguire case for *cultural history* has not been addressed; the question not of the actual events in the anthracite counties, nor of the guilt or innocence of the men hanged, nor even of the existence of the 'Molly Maguires', but of the meaning of the case in that set of collective stories we call ideology. In a way, Aurand and Gudelunas (1982, 91, 103) come closest to this when they claim that 'the real significance of the Molly Maguire episode lies in its mythical qualities'; however they tend to see myth as identical with falseness and criticize the 'myths' of various historians: 'many schools of thought can use "Molly Maguire" to justify their ideological positions or validify a particular belief.' But in many ways these uses of the Molly Maguires — the retellings of their story — are of greater historical significance in American culture than the actual events in Schuylkill County. So rather than judging the accuracy of the stories historians have told about the Molly Maguires, I will look at the stories that dime novelists told at the time, particularly the stories that were told before the 'authoritative' Pinkerton novel was published, to reconsider the 'mythical qualities' of the Molly Maguires.

In many ways, the story papers allowed a more complex response to cases like the Molly Maguires than did the newspapers. Whereas the newspapers, both commercial and labor, were caught within the conventions of crime reporting and the narrow, if vital, issue of guilt and innocence, the story papers could weave elements of the court testimony into a wider narrative of the mining community. Thus, the commercial papers quickly made the Mollies villains; indeed the Pottsville *Miner's Journal* and the Philadelphia papers had been printing stories of Molly Maguire outrages for fifteen years (Broehl 1964, 157). The New York *World* and New York *Herald* consistently linked the Molly Maguires to Indian 'savagery' (Slotkin 1985, 369, 442, 463, 468). The labor papers tread carefully, all too aware of the attempts to link the 'Molly Maguire' crimes with the labor

movement; the *National Labor Tribune* (3 June 1876) attacked the
Molly Maguires, and accepted McParland's testimony. The *Irish
World* was at first principally anxious to dissociate the Mollies
from the Irish fraternal organization, the Ancient Order of
Hibernians (20 May 1876), though later it attacked the press
coverage of the case and suggested that the secret society was a
myth (Bimba 1932, 10).

In the story papers, the Mollies are neither simple heroes nor
absolute villains; they become a narrative center around which to
construct a plot, a plot that can account for the relation of the
Mollies to the miners in general, to the Irish, to the miners'
organizations, and to the social and production relations of the
mining community. As one would expect, the stories draw on
the narrative of underground secret societies that we saw in
Lippard's mysteries of the city; but they are also shaped by
several other formulas — the nobleman in disguise, the honest
workman unjustly accused, the strike narrative, and the detective
story.

I will look at six dime novels about the Molly Maguires, as
well as at Pinkerton's novel. Three of them — Albert Aiken's *The
Molly Maguires: or, The Black Diamond of Hazelton. A Story of the
Great Strike in the Coal Region* (AI), Daniel Doyle's *Molly Maguire,
The Terror of the Coal Fields* (Da), and William Mason Turner's *The
Masked Miner; or, The Iron Merchant's Daughter. A Tale of
Pittsburgh* (T) — were serialized almost simultaneously between
March and July of 1876 in three major, competing story papers:
Aiken in George Munro's *The Fireside Companion*, Doyle in Street
& Smith's *New York Weekly*, and Turner in Beadle & Adams'
Saturday Journal.

One of the others — Tony Pastor's *Down in a Coal Mine; or, The
Mystery of the Fire Damp* (PA) — was published in *The Fireside
Companion* in 1873. Though it does not mention the Molly
Maguires by name, it does treat a 'secret brotherhood' and was
reprinted in the Old Sleuth Weekly, a cheap library, as late as
1909 with the revised title *Foiled by Love; or, The Molly Maguire's
Last Stand*. The other two are detective tales that were published
in the decade after the events: Sergeant O'Donnell's *Coal-Mine
Tom; or, Fighting the Molly Maguires* (OD) published in 1884 in
Frank Tousey's Five Cent Wide Awake Library; and *The Molly
Maguire Detective: or, A Vidocq's Adventures Among the Miners* (U),
written by 'A U.S. Detective' in Frank Tousey's New York
Detective Library in 1886. I hope to show that the dime novels
written about the Molly Maguires before, during and after the

trials crystalize conflicts within the culture of the 'producing classes', conflicts over ethnicity, over strikes and union militance, and over the lineaments of a mechanic hero. The earliest stories displace attention from the trial of the Molly Maguires to the trial of an honest workingman, using narratives of disguise to reveal a mechanic hero; but the later stories set the Molly Maguires against a character who will come to dominate the dime novel, the detective, a master of disguise who may or may not be a mechanic hero.

Down in a Coal Mine, serialized in *The Fireside Companion* in 1873, is not one of the richest of these stories, but, since it was written before the Molly Maguire trials (yet after a decade of rumors and allegations of secret criminal societies in the anthracite towns), it establishes several formulas and conventions which the later stories, written with the details of the trials in mind, use and modify. First, the history of its publication and purported authorship figures the emergence of the dime novel detective. The story was originally 'authored' by Tony Pastor, a popular stage and music hall star whose song, 'Down in a Coal Mine', gave the story its first title and, when the hero sings it, its theatrical ending.[2] However, when the story was reprinted in the Old Sleuth Library (1890) and Old Sleuth Weekly (1909) after Pastor's star had dimmed, it was credited to 'Old Sleuth' himself.

Second, the story itself is an example of a curious and contradictory formula in which the workman proves to be a noble in disguise. Sandie Carmichael comes to the mines with a mysterious and possibly criminal past; at the end, after a mine explosion and his daring rescue of the trapped miners, he is revealed to be Lord Osmond. Though there is no explanation of why he became a miner, he is always proud of being a miner — 'I am only a miner, and I see no reason to be ashamed of my vocation' (PA, 20) — claiming that his 'record as a miner is the proudest and best of [his] whole career' (PA, 39). Early in the story, when the mine manager's daughter tells her aunt that a gentleman has called, her aunt replies, 'where is the gentleman? I don't see him. ... Why, dear, that's only a miner!' To which Miss Gertie says, 'Can't a miner be a gentleman, pray?' (PA, 2). In some ways, the story proves that a miner can be a gentleman, first figuratively and then literally.

Third, the story's 'secret brotherhood' draws on newspaper reports of 'Molly Maguire terror', and in turn will shape the later stories explicitly about the Molly Maguires. When Sandie Carmichael overhears a plot to murder the mine manager and informs him, it provokes a confrontation between Sandie and this 'secret brotherhood'. In a striking contrast to the later tales of the Molly Maguires, however, the miners and their 'secret brotherhood' in this story are not Irish; they are 'men and Britons'. The only Irish character, 'Mike the Irishman', is not a miner but a servant in the mine manager's house. There is also a complicated relationship between the plots of the brotherhood and labor conflict. The 'brotherhood' acts not out of personal revenge or evil but from dissatisfaction on the job. Though no strike occurs, it looms in the background. The narrative's equivocal stance toward the miner's demands is indicated in the account of Thumping Brad's speech, a speech that leads to the crowd burning the mine manager's house:

> 'Thus perish all traitors! And now, comrades, the night grows apace, let's away to the village; there's more work to be done yet, and we're the jolly boys to do it, too!' . . .
>
> 'Ay, ay, Brad. . . . Tut, comrades, are we not men, and haven't we the same right to make war for our rights as one king against another?' . . .
>
> 'We want only what is right and just; we have tried fair means to gain our just rights, and we have been met with insults and derision; we have been laughed at when we should have been treated with respect. If a miner don't earn his pay, tell me, lads, who does? . . . Isn't the demon of the fire-damp always lurking in hidden crevices, ready at any moment to spring forth and smother us? . . . And then, what cares the capitalist what becomes of us as long as he gets his dividends.'
>
> And, alas! the miner's words were but too true, although he was a bad man himself, and only used the facts to inflame the miners so as to bring them to favor his own evil designs (PA, 5).

The justness of their cause is asserted without question, but the extremity of their actions is displaced on the bully and scape-goat, Thumping Brad; it is the same distinction that Sandie will make on the witness stand when he testifies against Brad but refuses to implicate any other miner. But Brad shares one charac-teristic with the other miners, including Sandie: his speech.

As often happens in dime novels, the miners speak in dialect, in a form distinguished from the narrative discourse by spelling, punctuation, and word order. In many cases, this is a reproduc-tion of the codes of genteel fiction where, as Alan Trachtenberg (1982, 189) has pointed out, 'with few exceptions, dialect either appeared within a grammatical framework or otherwise made clear it was intended for a grammatically proper reader. .... it is unmistakably recognized as "low", as culturally inferior to the *writing* of the narrator ..., subordinated by plot and other devices of social designation to what can be called a discourse of respectability — a mode of writing which takes as its own the speech and social perspective of its "grammatical characters".' In a way Sandie is a 'grammatical character', as the issue of dialect is called to the readers' attention in the very first scene when Sandie is suspected of a mysterious past 'when [he] who has all along used the slang of the miner, suddenly speaks in as fine English as a gentleman' (PA, 1). However, the irony of the 'miner's slang' is that it is a version of Elizabethan English, and, far from making the miners seem low, ignorant and inferior — as in the case of the dialect given to the American Indian character — it gives a dignity and color not only to Thumping Brad's speech quoted above but also to his curses: 'Ay, and dost thou threaten a man like me, thou spoony offspring o' a strumpet!' The unknown hack who wrote the serial used the accents of the popular Shakespeare, and, consciously or not, disrupted the condescension implied by the genteel levels of style.

Finally, it is worth noting several plot formulas which recur regularly, and to which I will return: the central place accorded the trial narrative; the romantic plot which on the one hand is simply a narrative of abduction and rescue but is also a romance of a reunited community of producers, since Sandie's sweetheart is the mine manager's daughter; the centrality of the 'fistic duel' as a narrative event; and the character of Injun Joe (who rescues Gertie and kills Thumping Brad) who together with Sandie form an instance of the common white American narrative of a white hero with a man of color as a faithful sidekick.

The 'Tony Pastor' serial was published in the fall of 1873, just as the Pinkerton agent, James McParland, began his infiltration of the miners' community; the first Molly Maguire trial began more than two years later, on 18 January 1876. Michael J. Doyle had been accused, with two others who would be tried separately, of the murder of John Jones, a mine superintendent, in September 1875. He was found guilty on 1 February and sentenced to be hanged. At some point in late January or early February, the second accused man, Jimmy Kerrigan, turned informer. More arrests followed, and by the middle of February, the newspapers, at first local and then national, began to speculate on the events and the arrests. As one historian sums up the situation in March and April, 'no official testimony of

Kerrigan had been made public, but the newspapers were now dangerously close to trying the case in the press' (Broehl 1964, 294). The existence and testimony of the Pinkerton agent McParland was not public until May. It was in this context that the story papers began serializing their Molly Maguire tales.

The most detailed and complex of the story paper serials was *Molly Maguire, The Terror of the Coal Fields* by 'Daniel Doyle, A Mine Boss', which *The New York Weekly* issued in seventeen installments running from 13 March 1876 to 3 July 1876. The readers were told that Doyle 'is now, and has been for the past six months, a "mine boss" in the coal region, although there known under another name. He understands his subject thoroughly, and has painted his scenes and characters from observation.' The front page quotes the Scranton *Republican* about the confession of one of the 'Molly Maguires' (that is, Kerrigan) and the arrests that have been made. On page four, where new and future serials are introduced, the editors write:

> This story is from the pen of a PRACTICAL MINER, who assumes the *nom de plume* 'Daniel Doyle', to shield his life from the misguided men who might misinterpret his motives. He draws most of his scenes from real life, and gives some powerful portrayals of Poverty and Crime in Pennsylvania. He strikes with an unsparing hand the vice that like a leprosy has spread itself over the rich region of the anthracite belt; points out the TERRIBLE TYRANNY OF MONOPO-LISTS AND MILLIONAIRES, and the awful struggles that agitate the working classes in the 'black battle of life' underground. ... The writer does not identify honorable Irish societies of any kind with this worse than Communistic combination, which has been repeatedly Denounced by the Catholic Church, and he draws his heroes from all classes and creeds that play a part in mining pursuits.

The story evoked a strong response from readers, a response which can be gauged both by the front page and from the miscellaneous items on page four. In general, story paper serials were featured on the front page for the first two or three installments; then a new story was featured and the final six to ten installments would be on the inside pages. Doyle's story did drop from the front page to the inside pages in the third week; but it then returned to the front page for three more weeks in April. The continued interest can also be seen in the columns of page four which are filled with an unusual number of letters, responses and related Molly Maguire items throughout the spring.

Doyle's *Molly Maguire* consists of three different plots, not superimposed and moving toward a single denouement, but one after another. Twice the story seems about to conclude when another plot begins. The first plot employs the formula of the honest workman who is unjustly arrested; the second is essentially a strike novel, a relatively rare formula in 1876; and the third is a murder mystery. Though the three plots overlap and share characters and locale, their concerns are very different, the response of readers varies, and the explanatory systems that situate the Molly Maguires change.

The first plot is the story of Harry Morgan, mine boss, *versus* the Molly Maguires. It opens with the killing of a miner, Miles Murphy, by Molly Maguire assassins who thought they were killing Morgan. Nevertheless, they turn the mistaken murder to their benefit by getting Morgan arrested for it. After a series of complications, the most striking being the attempted assassination of a priest in the midst of a sermon denouncing the Molly Maguires, there is an inquest at which the testimony of a boy slatepicker and of Harry's honorable rival in love clear Harry: he is released from prison. The real murderers are arrested, but, just as the story could be wrapped up, they kill the arresting constable and escape. This first plot, which has lasted for five weekly installments, is a straightforward murder mystery, with an honest mechanic unjustly accused and then cleared; the Molly Maguires add a bit of topicality along with the device of the 'coffin notice', hand-written threatening letters with drawings of coffins, revolvers, and skull and bones, which are reproduced in 'fac-simile' on the front page of the *New York Weekly*. The question of miners organizing in unions or mutual assistance societies is not raised; the reason for the attempted murder and then frame-up of Harry Morgan is simply the personal vengeance of the previous mine boss, Dan Davis, who has been dismissed for drunkenness and replaced by Morgan.

The second plot, which begins when the serial returns to the front page with the sixth installment, is quite different, opening with a ten-percent wage cut and a strike. Dan Davis, previously the drunken former mine boss with a grudge against Harry Morgan, is revealed as the president of the 'Miners' and Laborers' Society', which calls the strike. But, as soon as the strike begins, Davis betrays his fellows and leads a group of blacklegs into the mine; he is restored as mine boss, and Harry, who refuses to work with the blacklegs, is dismissed. This sudden turnabout is followed by scenes of violence between the crowd of striking miners and Davis and his blacklegs, culminating in a pitched gunbattle inside the mine between the Molly Maguires, fighting for the strikers, and the blacklegs. In this scene, the reader's sympathy is entirely with the Mollies fighting against the dastardly Davis who had betrayed his fellow miners, shot a miner's wife in the confrontation between strikers and blacklegs, and, of course, been the villain of the first plot, trying to kill the hero. Indeed, the sympathy with the Mollies in their battle against the blacklegs is so thorough that the only way to end this plot without making them the heroes is catastrophe: a fire begins in the breaker, engulfs the mine, and, in a dramatic scene, kills both Mollies and blacklegs. The company is at fault for failing to provide a second exit, and this plot ends with the community's general grief; even Harry Morgan is on the brink of death. Unlike the first plot, where the Molly Maguires were a murderous group of villains attacking a popular mine boss and a popular priest, in this second plot, now situated in the midst of a struggle between miners and the company, the Mollies become an effective and necessary, though never entirely sanctioned, arm of the miners.

The third plot begins with the tenth installment, in the week of May 15. McParland, the Pinkerton agent, had shocked everyone with his testimony of infiltrating the 'Molly Maguires' when he took the stand on May 6 to 9 in the trial of five men — three miners, a mine engineer, and a tavern owner — for the murder of a policeman, Yost, the previous summer. And the third plot in Doyle's serial begins to rely heavily on the trial. But whereas the major national papers immediately linked the so-called Molly Maguires to union and strike activity — the New York *Herald* called striking New Jersey laborers Molly Maguires that week, while the New York *Times*, the Pittsburgh *Gazette* and the Philadelphia *Inquirer* all accused the Molly Maguires of fomenting or enforcing strikes in articles of that second week in May[3] — the Doyle serial told a distinctively different story. The scene shifts to another town, as Harry Morgan finds work as a miner elsewhere after recovering from the mine disaster. There are two more murders, one of a mine superintendent and one of a lawyer, by the Molly Maguires, and a further attempt on Morgan's life. But the central action is the formation of a 'vigilance committee' by the town elite (led by Harrison Cole, whose name is a distinct contrast to Harry Morgan, Neal Nolan and Charlie Blake, the heroes). The vigilance committee wants to track down the Mollies, but they are so misguided that they mistake the priest, Father O'Neill (who recovered from the assassination attempt), for a Molly. Their fumbling turns to tragedy when they attack a house they suspect of harboring Mollies (the reader knows it doesn't), and apparently kill the innocent sister (though she too recovers in the final paragraphs of the story) of one of the heroic characters. This leads him to join the Mollies, against the pleadings of the priest, and he is unjustly implicated by the informer and imprisoned at the end. Though the guilty Mollies are hanged at the end of the story, the vigilantes are never caught.

Thus Doyle's fictionalization of the vigilante Wiggins Patch murders of December 1875 shifts attention away from the acts of the Mollies themselves; without exonerating the Mollies, he succeeds in making the vigilantes the villains. Moreover, Doyle satirized the newspapers' accounts of the events. In his story, the newspapers report, inaccurately, that the burning of the breaker was an act of the Molly Maguires, and Carl Cash, a reporter for the New York *Herald*, comes to Shanty Hill to find out about the Molly Maguires. He is a naive fool, entirely wrapped up in his own sensational fantasies, unable to distinguish Welsh from Irish, and expecting to see every citizen 'bristling with bowie knives and revolvers'. He comes across Thady Hooligan, a comic character, and interviews him, continually ignoring his name and calling him 'Mr Molly Maguire'. Thady, much insulted, responds in kind by calling the reporter Mr Hard Money, since he is willing to pay for any kind of information, accurate or not.

The third plot also recasts and then wraps up the romantic narrative, the story of Harry Morgan, mine boss, and Ellen Sefton, the daughter of the storekeeper. They were to be married at the beginning when the arrest of Harry upset the idyllic opening; nevertheless, after many complications they are married at the end. However, there are several interesting aspects to this romance. At first, the romantic story has little tension or conflict because there is no class distinction between Harry and Ellen; indeed the absence of this conventional complication, which we saw in *Down in a Coal Mine* and which we will see in other tales, is so strongly felt that Ellen's father suddenly becomes affluent two-thirds of the way into the story and sends Ellen to a Philadelphia academy. After that the romance becomes more problematic.

Nevertheless, Harry does *not* turn out to be a nobleman. He becomes worthy of Ellen when he is promoted to mine superintendent at the end. In general, one of the remarkable aspects of

Doyle's story is that, while depicting 'the terrible tyranny of monopolists and millionaires', there are no depictions of monopolists and millionaires themselves. As Doyle writes, in a digression to explain the occurrence of 'Molly Maguirism':

> Some of the poor men, who never saw the real owners of the mine in their lives, ... naturally attributed all their misery to those with whom they came in contact. The superintendent and the mine boss were blamed for what was planned by the mine monopolist at his office in the great city, and these frequently had to suffer the consequences of his tyranny.
>
> This is what first introduced Molly Maguirism into the coal regions. It is a notorious fact that in no other portion of the United States, and in connection with no other pursuit than coal mining, has the society a footing. Men who felt themselves persecuted, and found that they were continually descending in the scale of degradation, attributed their condition to the petty masters, the mine bosses, who had immediate charge of them, and on these they sought to wreak, and have often wreaked, vengeance for wrongs which they were powerless to prevent (Da, 20).

So Doyle depicts not the monopolists but the mine bosses and mine superintendents.

There is, however, an important distinction between mine bosses and mine superintendents, a distinction that a number of historians miss,[4] but one that each of the dime novels makes in delineating their mechanic heroes. The mine boss, or inside foreman, directs the work of the miners in the mines. As Anthony Bimba (1932, 32-33) writes, 'the mine bosses were usually workers taken out of the ranks. They were given a fairly high wage and no manual work was required of them. They also had, and exerted, the privilege of petty graft at the expense of those who worked under them — they sold jobs and collected bribes for keeping them.' The mine superintendent was on another occupational and social level entirely: 'The mine managers and superintendents, who stood above the bosses, were the representatives of absentee owners at the mines. They were well paid and comfortably off — so long as their operations produced profits.' The heroes of the dime novels are very often mine bosses: not only are both Doyle's hero, Harry Morgan, and villain, Dan Davis, mine bosses, but 'Daniel Doyle' himself is purportedly a mine boss. The superintendent, however, is never a hero, and rarely a prominent character. Harry Morgan is from the ranks; 'frugal, temperate, and thrifty', he has worked his way up from slate picker, to mule driver, to laborer, to miner, to mine boss. Doyle's superintendent Carr, on the other hand, has the nicest house in town, a home and family that embodies the genteel domestic ideal, and receives visits from the Episcopal minister and, to return to our romantic plot, from the Seftons: 'their recently acquired wealth lifted them to be the equals of the Carr family' (Da, 32). So the end of the story does see a kind of upward mobility for Harry Morgan; though not a nobleman, his promotion from mine boss to superintendent and his marriage to Ellen Sefton puts him in the town's elite.

Doyle's serial was accompanied by a number of editorial statements and generated a range of responses in the pages of the *New York Weekly*. These statements and responses are not only part of the ideological battle over the Molly Maguire case, but are also a clue to the ways that the function and workings of popular fiction were understood by readers, authors and editors. I want to look briefly at three aspects of these texts which were part of the experience of reading the serial: the stance of the *New York Weekly* and the issue of the 'motive' and 'truthfulness' of Doyle's story; the relation of the Molly Maguires to the Irish, and in particular to the Ancient Order of Hibernians; and the relation of the Mollies to the 'monopolists and millionaires'.

The *New York Weekly* dramatized their own publication of the Doyle novel. In the issue containing the third installment, they inform the readers that their agent in Hazelton, Pennsylvania was warned against posting the story paper; if he did he would be a 'marked man' (27 March 1876, 4). They also reproduce a graphic 'coffin notice' from 'Molly Maguire' warning Street and Smith not to show any secrets of the society in their story. Several weeks later, they note that 'threatening letters still pour in upon us ... these threats have no terrors for us, and we shall publish the story to its end, regardless of the desparadoes whom we have made tremble by giving publicity to their iniquitous proceedings' (24 April 1876, 4). Indeed, they eventually take credit for 'putting relentless justice upon the trail of the assas-sins. ... Many persons at first thought the astounding revelations of Daniel Doyle were mere fiction ... but no one can now deny, since the press in all parts of the country has followed the lead of the NEW YORK WEEKLY in discussing this subject, that our story of "Molly Maguire" is based on startling facts' (5 June 1876, 4).

The confidence and sensationalism of these editorial state-ments are tempered not only by the novel itself but also by the letters published in the *New York Weekly*. But the issue of the 'motive' and 'truthfulness' of Doyle's account is maintained throughout:

> Here is seen the good work which can be effected by a writer who labors earnestly for the public welfare. Daniel Doyle had a *motive* in writing his history of the 'Molly Maguires'; for although it appears in the form of a story, nevertheless it is *history*. His motive was the dispersion of the banded bullies of the anthracite regions, and success crowned his effort (26 June 1876, 4).

As we have seen, the actual plots of the novel exhibit a more contradictory stance than the tendentiousness implied by the editors. But if his *motive* was more complex (both broader and narrower: one part of Doyle's story explicitly seeks to aid the passage of a law requiring mines to have two exits; nevertheless our ignorance of who 'Daniel Doyle' was makes it difficult to judge his motives more exactly), clearly this kind of 'labor for the public welfare' was a common stance in popular fiction, whether the issue was temperance, child labor, or the exploitation of needlewomen.

What is even more clear is the sense of the story as *history*. Several months after the story was completed, the editors defend Doyle's depiction of the Mollies shooting a priest, a scene which some 'supersensitive readers' objected to, by quoting an informer's testimony that the Mollies were to have killed three priests. But they are also proud of the 'graphic descriptions of the various duties of the miners' that Doyle includes. In one issue, they print a letter from a Pennsylvania miner congratulating Doyle and writing: 'The readers of the *New York Weekly* can rely on the truthful foundation of Mr Doyle's story. As a miner I would recommend this story for everybody's perusal. Those people who never had an opportunity to visit a coal field will be delighted with the descriptions from Mr Doyle's pen' (17 April 1876, 4). Indeed the narrative does extensively describe the work of the miners and the activities of the mine. One of the major descriptive digressions is straightforward; the narrative voice just begins telling the reader about the mine: 'There were employed in the mine and coal-breaker of the Black Diamond shaft four hundred men and boys, and as the day advanced, and the works were fairly under way, the scene was a busy one indeed.' And a lengthy description of the physical surroundings and the varieties of jobs follows. There is particular attention to the work of the boy slatepickers; the issue of child labor is important to Doyle, and his next serial for the *New York Weekly* will be *The Slate-Picker; or, The Slave of the Coal-Shaft* (Db).[5] One also sees that Doyle's *motive* is not merely the exposure of the Molly Maguires. In the midst of this descriptive passage, he writes of a child labor law: 'But what do the Pennsylvania coal operators care about such a law? Wherever their personal interests or their purses were concerned they were fully as selfish, exacting and tyrannical — though perhaps not as sanguinary — as the Molly Maguires. Yet even this statement will not bear qualification. If the nature of mine accidents is taken into account, and the horrible catalogues of murder caused by disasters that could be averted by employers did they but comply with the law, it will be seen that they are guilty of even more deaths than the society that has made itself the terror of the coal fields' (Da, 14).

How are we to understand these passsages of observation, description, and moral/political assessment? This story is not meant for coal miners in the way that their own oral storytelling is; it assumes an audience that has never seen a coal mine. But does this imply a middle class, sentimental public? I think not, and this is suggested by the device of the other major passage of 'graphic description', which takes place inside the mine and shows the miners at work. Here, rather than direct narrative address, there is a representative of the reader in the story. But it is not a reporter, a mine inspector, a detective, or a mine owner's daughter (we find the last example in the Aiken tale) being taken on a tour; it is a 'greenhorn', the young Irish immigrant Neal Nolan who, when told in the opening scene that his uncle 'is workin' on the night-shift', asks, 'The night-shift did ye say? . . . Is my uncle turned a samesthress or a tailor, or are ye makin' game out o' me?' (Da, 1). The miner's work is described to the reader when Neal, about to start work as a laborer, is taken down in the mine for the first time. So the reader is placed in the position not of the middle class observer but of the inexperienced laborer.

The second issue that emerges in the authorial, editorial, and reader statements about the story is the relation of the Molly Maguires to the Irish. In the opening advertisement, the *New York Weekly* explicitly stated that the story does not identify the Molly Maguires with 'honorable Irish societies of any kind', so as not to alienate Irish-American readers. And though the hero, Harry Morgan, is Welsh, the story is careful to show, as one Irish character says, 'that although there may be some mean, mis-guided Irishmen, we are not all as black as some would paint us' (Da, 9). The central narrative agency in this is the Catholic priest; the story takes advantage of several actual denunciations of the Molly Maguires by Catholic bishops and clergy. They also publish a letter from a Scranton Irish person who writes that the Mollies are 'composed of two classes of members, first Saloone keepers and a few Store keepers. . . . The Second Class are all the outcasts, villains, and drunkards', and concludes 'Hopin the Publick at Large will not think that all Irishmen belongs to them' (27 March 1876, 4). Several weeks later, a Toronto 'Exile of Erin' asks whether 'there is no other people but Irish connected with those societies' and concludes that 'no matter where my country-men turn to earn an honest living, they will find someone to oppose them.' The *New York Weekly* answers this letter at length, saying that, though the Molly Maguires are Irish, this should be no stigma on the Irish race: 'There are plenty of honorable Irish societies all over the land to which men can belong, and where they may work in a fraternal spirit for their mutual advance-ment.' Furthermore, the author, Doyle, needs be thanked for 'his vindication of all that is pure and good in the Irish character as evinced in his portrayal of Father John O'Neill, the Blake family, and Neal Nolan' (1 May 1876, 4). Indeed the care taken to emphasize this point may well indicate a substantial Irish reader-ship of the story paper, a possibility supported by the use in the story of a number of Irish words and phrases without any explanation or translation.

This issue became even more pointed when the prosecution, none other than railroad president Franklin Gowen, the Pinker-ton agent, several Catholic priests, and the major urban news-papers maintained that the Molly Maguires, in the words of the *New York Times*, 'are carried on under a charter granted by the Ancient Order of Hibernians', the largest Irish fraternal organ-ization in the nation (Broehl 1964, 294). This attack on the AOH drew a letter from Daniel Doyle himself, who writes that the impression that the Molly Maguires and the Ancient Order of Hibernians are one and the same organization is 'utterly false. The Ancient Order of Hibernians is one of the most honorable, influential and intelligent societies of Irishmen in the United States' (3 April 1876, 4). This is a position that the story paper will always maintain.

The third issue that concerned the readers of Doyle's serial was the relation between the Molly Maguires, the miners' union and the monopolists. As I have shown, Doyle often compares the crimes of the Mollies and those of the mine owners, and finds the latter the more grievous. Though he says that a strike is 'one of the greatest evils of the coal fields, whether precipitated by employer or employed', a position that many working-class leaders also held (including miners' leader John Siney), he devotes a long chapter to justify and explain the strike: 'when the news goes out that the men in the mines have struck for higher wages, let it be remembered that it is often the monopolist and millionaire who have precipitated such a calamity, in their great greed for riches, and their sordid desire to conquer "other worlds" with the ammunition wrung from the brow and the heart of the Pennsylvania miner' (Da, 20). These sentiments drew a favorable response from readers: two issues later a letter from an Ohio miner is published defending the Mollies: 'I joined an Order similar to that of the Molly Maguires, and believed then, and do now, that I was right in becoming a member of the Union. Those organizations are not for the commission of crime, but for the protection of the miners from the monopolies of the operators.' This letter is answered by the editor who says that there are no objections to trades organizations: 'no effective opposition can be made by workmen against capital unless by union.' However, he does object to combinations that use 'force and brutality' (17 April 1876, 4). The defense of the miners is taken up again in a letter from an old English miner who writes of Doyle's 'truthful and graphic delineation of life in coal regions ... showing the greedy selfishness of the corporations in their dealings with the miners' (10 July 1876, 4). For these readers, the second plot, the story of the Long Strike of 1875, had more salience than the murder mysteries that bracketed it.

Doyle's *Molly Maguire* is a remarkable achievement; its three overlapping and sometimes contradictory plots attempted to shift the reader's attention from the trials and crimes of the Molly Maguires — the events that frame it — to the trial of an honest miner, the crimes of vigilantes, and the story of a strike. Combining a vindication of the Irish miners' organizations, a 'truthful and graphic delineation of life in coal regions', and an almost week by week fictionalization of courtroom testimony, Doyle's story embodies the contradictory attitudes of his working class readers toward the case of the Molly Maguires; in his stories and the reader's letters it elicited one can hear the mechanic accents of the dime novel.

While Doyle's *Molly Maguire* was running in the *New York Weekly, The Fireside Companion* was serializing Albert Aiken's *The Molly Maguires; Or, The Black Diamond of Hazelton. A Story of the Great Strike in the Coal Region*, in fourteen installments. Aiken, from a family of actors, was a prolific writer of dime novels and serials, a playwright for the melodramatic theater, and an actor. Indeed, within a month of the completion of the serial, *The Molly Maguires* was produced as a play; Aiken himself played the role of the hero, Harry Audenried.[6]

It is easy to see how Aiken adapted the tale to the stage; unlike Doyle's serial, it has both the extravagances and the unities of melodrama. The millionaires are present, both in the relatively benign figure of Marinus Duychinck, the mine president and 'of the good old Patroon stock of New York', and in the evil figures of Zibeon and Nathan Lyfford, 'specimens of Connecticut hardware', proud of being 'self-made men'. The Molly Maguires are villains, tied to 'enforcing' strikes; since they are not only Irish but include Britons and Welshmen, they are a miners' organization, not an Irish one. The hero, Harry Audenried, is a mine engineer, a 'common workman', with a mysterious past. All come together in a melodramatic plot where the capitalists, the 'self-made men', use the Molly Maguires to foment a strike that will destroy the mine owner, and allow them to take over the mine and the mine owner's daughter. The hero, the engineer Harry Audenried, refuses to strike, defeats the Molly Maguires and the evil millionaires, saves the mine owner, and wins his daughter. Harry, like Pastor's Sandie Carmichael, then turns out to be the son of an English earl.

If Doyle's story struggled to find a plot which was adequate both to the realities of working class life and to the details of the courtroom testimony, Aiken's story for the most part sets the Molly Maguires within a conventional plot; its ideological tenor may be gauged by its curious anti-strike rhetoric. This is not simply the objection to a particular tactic that one found in Doyle; Aiken vehemently attacks any sort of militant resistance by the miners, and equates the strike leaders, who find their best support 'among the ignorant and reckless men', with the Molly Maguires. Harry Audenried refuses steadfastly to join the strike, except for one brief moment toward the end. That moment, however, reveals much of the specific ideology of this narrative, which is not one of the stories of workers as savages told by genteel bourgeois society in novels like John Hay's *The Breadwinners*. Harry decides to strike when he is led to believe, wrongly, that Nathan Lyfford, the villainous millionaire, has taken over the mine. When he is told by the mine owner's daughter that this is not true, and that Lyfford wants to foment a strike in order to drive her father into bankruptcy, Harry persuades the men out of the strike. The point of view of Harry and of the story is consistently that of the town and its unity. If a strike will divide the town, it is wrong. If the town is threatened from outside forces, then a strike against the external threat is legitimate. So it is not surprising that when Aiken discusses strikes in a digression, he sympathizes not with the mine owners nor with the miners but with the 'storekeepers — literally the men in the gap ... they in their hearts cursed both men and bosses.' Thus Albert Aiken's story, though written by a New York dime novelist and actor about a small coal town in Pennsylvania, seems caught in the middle just as those shopkeepers were: managing to praise the handsome engineer while distancing itself from the miners' battles, opposing strikes that would divide the community, but supporting ones aimed at outside capitalists, defending the republican community against the greed of 'self-made men'. Here we can see that if the story papers were 'of the people', they were not an expression of any one class so much as a terrain of negotiation and conflict over the proper accents of the popular. This popular culture — a 'producer's', 'populist', or 'plebian' culture — was shared by shopkeepers, local professionals, and workers, particularly in small cities and mill towns.[7]

Nevertheless, the story is unable to keep this plot fully under control as contradictory formulas appear and alternative accents can be heard. First, several installments before Harry Audenried, the mine engineer, is revealed as a lord, the narrator notes that Nathan Lyfford, the villain, 'began to fear that the engineer was going to turn out to be a great man in disguise, after all, just as the heroes in novels generally do — thanks to a sort of depraved taste common to the average reader, who enjoys that sort of thing' (AI, 16). It is unclear whether this should be taken as a little self-conscious game with the reader, gently mocking the conventions of the form, or as a vicious aside by a hack author with contempt for his audience and his occupation, or as a genuine desire to avoid 'that sort of thing', a desire that is foiled by the conventions of the genre or the demands of the story paper editor. In any case, it self-consciously raises the question of this 'depraved taste' for the 'great man in disguise', a question I will return to at the end of this chapter.

The second ambiguity in this tale of the Molly Maguires lies in a name. For one of the heroines of the tale is a miner's daughter named Mary 'Molly' Maguire. Nothing is made of this coincidence until Harry Audenried has to straighten out the confusion of the mine owner's daughter. After explaining that the Molly Maguire of whom she had heard was not the girl but a 'secret league of desperate men', Harry says that 'there is no connection between the two, except in the similarity of names; it is a coincidence, that is all' (AI, 20). And though the matter is left there, it remains a remarkable coincidence. It is as if Aiken knew, consciously or not, that the power of the name Molly Maguire in the popular imagination was such that it was necessary to invent a 'good' Molly to counterpose to the 'bad' Mollies. Unable to redeem the secret society from the condemnation of the press and 'respectable' society by making them heroes, he would displace the name onto a heroine, giving it the accents of 'a true type of Irish beauty', the 'brogue of the "dear old Emerald isle"'. At the beginning of the story, all signs point toward a romance between Molly Maguire and the engineer Harry Audenried: he has rescued her from a drunken admirer; she warns him that the Molly Maguires are after him when she overhears her father mention it; and her father is opposed to any match between them. But this romantic plot goes nowhere, and at the end she is married off to a nephew of the priest. Aiken's story is thus haunted by an absent plot in which Harry is just a 'common workman', and, after a set of adventures, marries Molly Maguire; unable or unwilling to tell that story, Aiken makes Harry a 'great man in disguise' and marries him to Diana Duychinck, the mine owner's daughter, 'just as the heroes in novels generally do'. It leaves a curiously divided tale.

A month after the Doyle and Aiken serials began, the *Saturday Journal*, the somewhat less successful Beadle's story paper, entered the competition by reprinting William Mason Turner's *The Masked Miner; Or, The Iron Merchant's Daughter. A Tale of Pittsburgh*, which had originally been serialized in 1870.[8] Though this not only has nothing to do with the Molly Maguires but is set not in the anthracite fields but in Pittsburgh, I will look at it briefly for two reasons. First, Turner was a prolific and representative writer of working-man and working-girl dime novels. Second, his serial was clearly intended to compete with the Molly Maguire tales. When they reprinted the second installment in the 22 April 1876 issue, the editors noted that 'While Dr Turner, in his "Masked Miner", does not specially treat of the

"Molly Maguire" ruffians, his romance opens up the underground world and its strange character so successfully that
succeeding romancists have made the Doctor's "Black Diamond
Mine" the locale of their stories. The Doctor can stand this
"poaching on his preserves", no doubt.' Indeed it is true that
both Aiken and Doyle set their tales in the 'Black Diamond
Mine'; and in the 22 May 1876 issue of the *New York Weekly*,
there is even an account of two 'practical miners' who have built
and are exhibiting in Scranton a miniature working mine and
breaker, 'a marvel of mechanism', which they call the 'Black
Diamond Breaker'. The *New York Weekly* takes credit for the
fictional name, even saying that the use of the name testifies to
the 'truthfulness' of Doyle's account.

Turner's tale of the Black Diamond Mine is a populist tale
where 'Lordly Wealth and honest Poverty stood face to face'.
Like the first third of Daniel Doyle's serial, it uses the formula of
the honest worker unjustly arrested and forced to clear himself.
Tom Worth, 'a common laborer in the Black Diamond Mine', is
at first a hero for rescuing the daughter of a millionaire from a
runaway carriage, but then finds himself accused of abducting
her. The story of her abduction, captivity and rescue dominates
the action, as Tom discovers that his double has been black-
mailed into the employ of the villain, the rich young man about
town, Farleigh Somerville; hence the mistaken identification that
led to Tom's arrest. At the end, Tom Worth is revealed as a
nobleman, marries the millionaire's daughter, saves their
mansion from the clutches of Somerville, and takes evēryone,
including the loyal old Cornish miner, Ben, back to England. His
double, not really a villainous man, is forgiven and goes on to
live an exemplary life; the villainous Somerville manages to bury
himself alive. There are only a couple of brief mentions of a
secret society, the 'Great Allegheny'; the rich villain Somerville
tries to blackmail Tom and Ben into it but they refuse. However,
as the story progresses, it is forgotten: the display of Tom's
'worth' is central.

All in all, then, the first dime novels of the Molly Maguires
are stories of honest mechanics — mine bosses, handsome
engineers, and worthy laborers — involved in mysteries of
murder and abduction against the drama of the Long Strike
of 1875. The strike is viewed ambivalently, as well it might
after the miners' disastrous loss. And the Molly Maguires remain
a multiaccentual sign, at one time the vengeful arm of the
miners, at another time a criminal organization for the personal

vengeance of the villains, at yet another time in league with millionaires and monopolists. Indeed the trial of the Molly Maguires is often displaced by the trial of the honest mechanic himself. Dan Schiller (1981, 55-56) has argued persuasively that 'the crucial political basis' of crime news, including the 'extensive trial coverage of noteworthy cases', was 'that the trial of one man's rights not figuratively but *literally* brought the entire political nation to the bar of justice.' And we see this in the trials of the unjustly accused Harry Morgan and Tom Worth in the dime novels of the Black Diamond Mines. These dime novels are thus a locus of competing notions of justice — that of the hangman and that of the coffin notice, that of the mechanic and that of the shopkeeper, that of union and that of incorporation.

However, this 'battleground around the crime, its punishment, and its memory' becomes more complex when a new figure, the detective, enters. The figure of the detective emerges in American popular fiction as a common and recurring character in the 1870s and 1880s; the first successful detective character was Old Sleuth who appeared in the pages of *The Fireside Companion* in 1872, and the first dime detective 'libraries' were the New York Detective Library (beginning in 1882 and featuring Old King Brady) and the Old Cap Collier Library (beginning 1883). These early detectives were often based on and influenced by the semi-fictional narratives of actual detectives which were published at the same time, among them the memoirs of George McWatters (1871), John Warren (1874), and Allan Pinkerton (whose successful series began in 1874).[9] This new prominence of the detective can be measured by looking at Dan Schiller's important study of the meaning of crime news for the working class readers of the *National Police Gazette* in the 1840s, where there is no mention of the detective; the character that Edgar Allan Poe had idiosyncratically fashioned from the Gothic superman had not yet come to dominate crime narratives, fictional or not.

The detective made his first appearance in the dime novels of the Molly Maguires when Albert Aiken's *The Molly Maguires* introduced a Pinkerton operative on the streets of Hazelton, Pennsylvania two months before the existence and testimony of the actual Pinkerton operative, James McParland, became public. Sly Dick Johnson, the 'famous human bloodhound', a member of Allan Pinkerton's Chicago detective force, enters the story on the trail of Harry Audenried as the first installment ends. However, as it turns out, the human bloodhound is not on the trail of the

Molly Maguires and indeed does not even know why his employer, an Englishman (who turns out to be Harry's nobleman father), has hired him to find Audenried. The detective finally fades out of the story and there is no mention of McParland in subsequent installments.

Despite his relative insignificance in the plot, the account of the detective that we see in Aiken's serial is illuminating. Far from being the extraordinary figure that Old Sleuth and his progeny were, he is 'a coarse, common fellow, to whom all the finer instincts of humanity were strangers'. He is consistently rude to the honest engineer who he has been tracking. He is 'of the stuff that our popular demagogues were made of — the men that boast that they are of the people, work for the people, and finally end their careers by fleeing to some foreign country with a pocketful of ill gotten gains belonging to the people' (AI, 14). After the Pinkerton operative invents an entirely false tale about Audenried, the narrator remarks on 'that exact regard for truth which is so eminently a feature of detective life' (AI, 41): the irony of this line may well have been reinforced by its appearance in the issue of May 15, just a week after McParland's first testimony in the Yost trial. In general, the attitude of this narrative to the detective is summed up in a one sentence paragraph: 'The modern detective is a dreadfully overrated creature' (AI, 26).[10]

Overrated he may have been, but the detective became central to the story of the Molly Maguires in 1877, shortly after the first hangings, when Allan Pinkerton published his narrative of the case, *The Mollie Maguires and the Detectives*. This was not simply another of the group of books published about the case by supporters of the prosecution — books like the 1877 *The Molly Maguires* by the Pottsville lawyer, Franklin Dewees, and the pamphlet publication of Franklin Gowen's final summation. This 'factual' account of the case was also one of the series of 'Allan Pinkerton's Great Detective Stories', written by a team of ghost writers, and published by G.W. Carleton & Co., who, though not a dime novel publisher, aimed principally at a mass audience.[11] Since the Pinkerton tale is thus not only a narrative of the Molly Maguires, but also holds an important place in the history of the detective story, rather than assess its accuracy or reliability as a history of the events I will consider the meaning of its narration, its myth.

'The settings of Pinkerton's adventures', John Reilly (1976, 159-160) has written, 'are growing, prosperous cities (Oakland,

Michigan; Montgomery, Alabama; Geneva, New York; Mariola, Illinois), cities into whose harmonious pattern of expansion a criminal aberration enters, the removal of which enables the city to continue with its inevitable and blessed process of economic expansion.' And this is the way that Pinkerton presents Potts-ville, Pennsylvania:

> A visitor's impressions of Pottsville, when first beholding its spires of churches and evidences of industry and thrift, from the heights above, cannot well be other than pleasing ... to one unaccustomed to see cities perched upon steep mountainsides, the sight is well calcu-lated to evolve surprise. Having some twelve thousand inhabitants, there is in it much enlightenment and great wealth. Abundantly provided with handsome and elegant churches and school-houses, imposing business structures and beautiful residences ... Pottsville is the concentrating point for an extended radius of rich mining country, and the depot of supplies for an equally wide circle (PI, 62).

This is a remarkable contrast to the setting the dime novelist Albert Aiken depicts — 'all nature seemed to smile, even in the Hazel valley, where man's destructive hand has ruined the looks of half the pleasant valley at least, by covering the green turf with the black refuse of the mines' (AI, 17). For the dime novel-ists, the mine with its breaker and railroads in the midst of a sublime landscape lent itself to the pervasive trope of the inter-rupted idyll, the 'machine in the garden' that Leo Marx has mapped. Moreover, the dime novelists saw the mining towns, east and west, as a frontier locale; Hazelton and Pottsville, no less than Deadwood and Virginia City, were on the border of civilization and wilderness, and were described in the dime novels as 'wild and barren', 'one of the wildest regions of Pennsylvania'.

So if the dime novelists told a story of a landscape disturbed by the lawlessness of a frontier mining town, in Pinkerton's story, it is the Molly Maguires who have upset a peaceful and prosperous community: 'Why is not this a hive of industry, and the chosen seat of the investment of capital? ... Why is it that a curse and a blight has rested for so long upon this country? Because, fostered and protected here in the mountains of this country, was a band of assassins and murderers.' When they are exposed and hanged at the end, progress resumes: 'Now all are safe in this country; come here with your money; come here with your enterprises' (PI, 536). The irony of this passage is that it is spoken by Franklin Gowen, the president of the Philadelphia and Reading Railway, the monopolist who was acquiring large tracts of mining land, and the object of the attack of an Anti-Monopoly Convention in Harrisburg: but here he speaks as a local Pottsville lawyer (which he had been).

Pinkerton's Pottsville is a town not unlike the small industrial cities which fostered middle class anti-monopoly sentiments; and his tales not only portray these cities but actively intervene in shaping the popular consciousness of the shopkeepers, clerks and professionals of these cities. Thus Pinkerton's story has two heroes, not only the Irish detective James McParland, who infiltrates the Molly Maguires disguised as 'James McKenna,' but also the Irish prosecutor, Franklin Gowen, the president of the Philadelphia and Reading. McParland's tale takes up most of the volume. It is a tale of elaborate and painstaking disguise, an underground life for more than two years. McParland/McKenna is the vehicle of the reader — the 'uninitiated reader' (PI, 372) — as he or she gets a view of a violent, secret world with its signs and 'goods' (secret passwords), its 'habits and customs' which are 'mostly novel to the average American reader' (PI, 172). It is a world clearly subordinated to the 'grammatical': as Pinkerton writes in the preface 'all endeavor to express themselves in Anglo-Saxon, but their foreign idioms and native eccentricities will, spite of themselves, occasionally crop out' (PI, x). So we see taverns and shebeens, dogfights and cockfights, Polish marriages and Irish wakes. Despite the book's avowed purposes, there is as much violence against the Molly Maguires at the hands of rival gangs, the Modocs and Sheet Irons, as there is by the Mollies. McParland finds himself in situations like the 'yellow-covered romances of the blood-and-thunder style of literature' (PI, 443). His central and repeated dilemma lies in maintaining his disguise as a prominent Molly without engaging in their violent deeds. For the Mollies are no scapegoat villains; despite occasional protestations about good citizens, they are the heart of the wretched community McParland enters. They are identified with the Ancient Order of Hibernians, who are 'from root to branch ... rotten and corrupt'. Furthermore, 'the Laborers' Union and the Mollies had made common cause': the strikers are a 'mob' of 'communists'. Eventually the task gets too difficult. As suspicion of him grows and violence escalates, he escapes to take the witness stand.

At this point the other hero takes over, and Pinkerton includes chunks not of McParland's testimony as we might expect but of Gowen's speeches. The railroad president gets to interpret the action of the drama. He speaks of himself as 'the hero of romance', bringing to a close a 'contest' which began 'when I was District Attorney of this county, a young man' (PI, 537, 511). Against the attorney for the defense, Gowen maintains that this is not 'the old story of capital against labor'. The Molly Maguires are not 'the representatives of the laboring people of Schuylkill County'; rather 'I now stand here on behalf of the laboring people of this county' (PI, 535). Gowen himself begins to speak in mechanic accents:

> I yield to no man living in the respect and admiration that I pay to the workingman. Let him who will erect an altar to the genius of labor, and, abject as an eastern devotee, I worship at its shrine,
>
> 'Gathering from the pavement crevice, as a floweret
>   from the soil,
> The nobility of labor, the long pedigree of toil.'
>
> ... I stand here as the champion of the rights of labor — as the advocate of those who desire to work and who have been prevented from doing so.

If the final clause betrays the rhetoric of those 'champions of the rights of labor' who gave us 'right-to-work' laws, the passage as a whole makes clear the limits of rhetorical analysis: one must note the rhetorician as well as the rhetoric. For the multiaccentuality of the sign works both ways; not only can the popular classes, the 'subaltern classes' in Gramsci's phrase, transform the meanings of the signs of a dominant culture, but the dominant culture can repossess the signs of the 'people'. Gowen's efforts at repossessing a mechanic rhetoric in his courtroom summation is made more powerful and convincing as the climax of Pinkerton's narrative: the tale of McParland's impersonation of character, disguising himself as a miner and a Molly Maguire, provides the basis for Gowen's rhetorical impersonation.

Indeed it is the very success of McParland's disguise that causes the prosecution and the Pinkerton narrative the most trouble. Both have to repeatedly deny that McParland himself instigated and committed the crimes he recounts, that the man who was 'the most eccentric and savage appearing Mollie Maguire' (PI, 332) was not in deed the most savage. The narrator spends a good deal of time addressing these accusations, and maintaining that the detective is a 'professional' not a criminal.

But it was this very ambiguity that gave the detective his interest and his ideological uncertainty.

The combination of the Pinkerton narrative and the general emergence of this dime novel detective brought the detective and the Molly Maguires together in the final two stories I will look at: *The Molly Maguire Detective; Or, A Vidocq's Adventures Among the Miners*, by a 'U.S. Detective'; and Sergeant O'Donnell's *Coal-Mine Tom; Or, Fighting the Molly Maguires.*[11] Both were published in Frank Tousey's cheap libraries in the middle 1880s. Though I have argued that the constant reprinting of the same stories in different formats — in story papers, cheap libraries, dime novels, and installment novels — means that in general they can all be treated as parts of a single body of cheap stories, nevertheless changes in format had some effects on the fiction. The stories written especially for the cheap libraries, the weekly series of complete novels published as pamphlets, tended to be much less wordy and more telegraphic in style than the serials in the story papers that would continue as long as an audience could be held. The library tales had much more dialogue and more single-sentence paragraphs. Thus the kind of descriptive detail and plot complication that one finds in the serials of Aiken, Doyle and even Turner is not found in the Tousey detective tales. Though this clearly reduces the 'realism' of the stories, it should not be taken as simply a sign of deterioration. Though in this particular case neither of the tales is as interesting as the Doyle serial, the cheap libraries in general have a freer and more imaginative use of the vernacular than the story papers; the reduction of the narrative to dialogue begins to break the hold of genteel codes of fiction on the cheap stories, a development that will find fuller flower in the pulp magazines of the early twentieth century.

The Molly Maguire Detective; Or, A Vidocq's Adventures Among the Miners, credited to 'A U.S. Detective', one of Tousey's house writers, was published in the New York Detective Library in May of 1886, where it appeared among the adventures of Old King Brady, the major detective of the library, and, a couple of months later, a story dealing with the contemporary events of Haymarket: *The Red Flag; Or, The Anarchists of Chicago*. Unlike the earlier stories, this is not a telling of a contemporary tale, but a retelling of old legends: the story takes place 'during the great Pennsylvania coal strikes' when 'the Molly Maguires are terrorizing the entire country'. And it is a dime novel version of Pinkerton's narrative (the detective may have been called a 'Vidocq' rather than a 'Pinkerton' to avoid legal battles at a time when there were a number of contests over the ownership of trade names). A detective disguises himself as a miner to hunt the Molly Maguires, the 'terrible banditti', who have abducted and apparently killed a miner. He infiltrates the secret order, whose aims are 'money and revenge'. His most difficult challenge comes when he is ordered to kill the miner's daughter, Maggie Gilder; however, he concocts a charade with an effigy of her and is fully accepted into the order. After a couple of fights, and a humorous scene when two inept detectives try to catch him, he leads the police to the Mollies' hideout and they are all captured.

This relatively straightforward version of the dime novel detective formula is unable to situate the striking miners that make up the background of the story: at first there is a note of sympathy for 'hard-fisted miners ... crushed by the oppression of capital until they could endure that oppression no longer'; on the other hand, the miners in the foreground work for Mr Blight, who 'was lenient with his employees, paying them fair wages and working them like human beings rather than animals or mere machines' (U, 2). Blight's miners do not strike, raising the wrath of the Molly Maguires; he hires the Vidocq. Later it appears that the strikers, 'the poor half-starved, ill-paid, over-worked miners', are not Mollies at all. The Mollies are a 'mere gang of outlaws'. A chapter later, however, the strikers are a 'race of madmen'. These inconsistencies are largely the result of combining the populist rhetoric of the workingman dime novel with the Pinkerton plot; there is a villain in the Molly Maguires but there is no mechanic hero to pose against them. This absence is felt most fully in the romantic plot; Maggie Gilder is married off to the detective at the end, but this is entirely unconvincing not only because there has been no romance between them but because the figure of the detective, a professional outsider, does not lend itself to the dime novel romance.

The other detective story, Sergeant O'Donnell's *Coal-Mine Tom; Or, Fighting the Molly Maguires*, published in the Five Cent Wide Awake Library in July 1884, manages to unite the detective and the mechanic hero. A much less complicated story since it is aimed at boys, it is a brief tale of Luke Mullen, the son of a mine foreman who is shot by the Molly Maguires, and a young stranger from New York looking for his father's murderer, teaming up with Coal-Mine Tom, a mine inspector who is secretly a detective, against the Molly Maguires. The story focuses mainly on the abduction and rescue of Luke's sister and his sweetheart, and when the dust settles, we find that the suspected miner, Jack Dawson, is not really guilty: the villains are Dawson's prodigal brother and the son of the mine owner. In effect, 'Molly Maguire' is merely a convenient label for a band of villains in a mining town setting. The story itself is a typical populist detective tale with the son of the miner defeating the son of the mine owner, and it is the latter who is the Molly Maguire.

This story is an instructive contrast to William Mason Turner's *The Masked Miner*, the earliest of these tales, first published in 1870. In many ways the tales of Tom Worth and Luke Mullen are very similar: the honest young miner, the abduction and rescue of a young woman, the rich young villain, and little actual connection to the story of the Molly Maguires. But whereas the 1870 tale focuses on Tom Worth's unjust arrest and subsequent attempt to clear himself, the 1884 tale introduces the master detective, the mine inspector, to help the young man. But there is another difference; neither Luke Mullen nor his friend from New York turn out to be noblemen, like Tom Worth. The mysterious *deus ex machina* of the worker-nobleman, so characteristic of the earlier stories, is replaced by the detective. The relatively stable disguise that said, 'the worker is a gentleman', gives way to a proliferation of disguises: the detective, a mysterious man, impersonates anyone.

How are we to understand these and other disguises which are so central to the narratives of dime novels? The pervasiveness of the narrative of disguise would seem to have a particular significance for our more general interest in the figurability of class, in the ruses of the representation of social cleavages. Contemporary theorists of narrative have had little to say about the way disguise works. The novel, a central part of the construction of a 'possessive individualism' in the bourgeois cultural revolution, in general works on a law of self-identity: x is x, or, since, this describes 'flat' rather than 'round' characters, in the novel of development, x is x, becoming x. By this logic, if x is revealed to be y, one assumes that x is not x, x only pretended to be x. The hermeneutic code of the narrative, in Roland Barthes' (1974, 76) useful term, constructs an enigma which creates an expectation and desire for a solution: 'truth, these narratives tell us, is what lies *at the end* of expectation.' Recognition, in the Aristotelian sense, is a move from ignorance to knowledge.

However, this is not how disguise and recognition work in the sensational stories. Here disguise is the narrative equivalent of metaphor, working synchronically rather than diachronically, vertically rather than horizontally. To say that x is y does not mean that x is not x; x is y *and* x is x. Or to invest these terms with their present content: to reveal that the mechanic is a nobleman is not to deny that he is a mechanic; the characters all continue to insist on their character as mechanics. This is why so little narrative time and energy is spent on explaining why the nobleman is pretending to be a mechanic in the first place: the metaphoric juxtaposition of mechanic and noble is what is important, not the story of the noble's pretense. The conclusion of Tony Pastor's *Down in the Coal Mine* is archetypal: his new wife reminds Sandie,

> 'You once told me that you had never worked at any other occupation but that of a miner.'
> 'Dear one, I told you truly ... that was my first and only occupation, and thus far, my record as a miner is the proudest and the best of my whole career.'
> 'My husband, what drove you to become a miner?'
> 'Gertie darling, you have always trusted me; you pledged your troth when you thought me poor and humble and a workman; not until the day preceding our marriage did I tell you the secret of my birth. Dear one, you must trust me once more, but the day will come when you shall learn why Sandie Carmichael toiled in the depths of the mine.'
> 'Sandie, I am willing to wait.'

We the readers are also willing to wait for an explanation that will never come. Sandie is not a noble who was driven to become a miner; he is a miner who *is*, the 'is' of metaphor, a noble.

The detective, the master of disguise, shifts this somewhat. He can be anyone; anyone can turn out to be the detective in disguise. Here the sense of pretending and acting a role is stronger; Pinkerton's McParland pretends to be a miner, in order to succeed as a detective not as a miner. Nevertheless in the dime detective tales there is a strong sense that the detective is merely an effect of his different disguises. The early detectives were ciphers, a 'Pinkerton', a 'Vidocq', an 'Old Sleuth', with almost magical abilities to move through society and to assume any character. As George McWatters (1871, 653) wrote, 'everywhere throughout a great city, in the horse cars, in Wall Street, in all the great stores, at the churches on Sundays, in the lager-beer gardens, on the steamboats at the wharves, throughout the large manufactories, around various dens of iniquity, at the

148

theatres, etc., the detective is at his work. To-day he perhaps personates one character; to-morrow, another.' The dime novels are filled not only with the successful series detectives — Old Sleuth and Young Sleuth, Old Cap Collier, and Old and Young King Brady — but also with innumerable others: the Irish Detective; Black Tom, the Negro Detective; Lady Kate, the Dashing Female Detective.

Though the dime novel detective is usually omitted from histories of the detective story which pass from Poe and Vidocq to Conan Doyle and Anna Katherine Green, we should be wary of simply inserting Old Sleuth into a great tradition between Dupin and Sherlock Holmes, and thereby miss both the discontinuities of popular fiction history and the several levels and audiences of 'popular' fiction. Arthur Bartlett Maurice, writing in *The Bookman* in 1902, contrasted the detectives in fiction by 'social scale': 'Old Rafferty, Old Sleuth, Butts, and all of that ilk may be designated as the *canaille*, the proletarians; Poe's Dupin, Gaboriau's Lecoq and Père Tirauclair, and Dr Doyle's Sherlock Holmes are the patricians; ... between these extremes are the detectives who belong to the *bourgeoisie* of detection. ... An excellent type of this middle class is the Mr Gryce of the stories of Anna Katherine Green' (234). The 'proletarian' detective does not rely on exercises of rational deduction or ploys of the least likely suspect; indeed their stories often seem not to be detective stories at all with their reliance on disguise, physical strength, and melodramatic villains. But these proletarians of detection are extremely successful through the nickel and dime libraries of the 1880s and 1890s; and, in the next chapter, I will examine how this populist detective story becomes entwined with two other figures of class and masters of disguise that emerged out of the depression and class conflict of the 1870s, the tramp and the outlaw.

8

Tramps, Outlaws ...: Figures of the Great Strike

> The strike of the trainmen on the Baltimore & Ohio Railroad was the serving of a notice upon the people of this nation that wages could not be further reduced, — a protest against robbery, a rebellion against starvation. The trainmen were under despotic control. To leave their employ was to become tramps, outlaws ...
>
> George E. McNeill, 1886

As Daniel Doyle's serial, *Molly Maguire*, was reaching its end in the *New York Weekly*, a new serial by Horatio Alger, *Tony, the Tramp* (AL), began. Alger, whose 'Ragged Dick' series of 1867-1870 had made him a well-known writer of stories for children, began writing serials for the *New York Weekly* in 1871 (Scharnhorst 1980, 44), and *Tony, the Tramp* is introduced as 'a story for old and young ... parents and guardians will read it, and recommend it to their children, because in many cases it will revive recollections of their own early struggles ... each boy ... will fancy himself the hero, and of course feel his blood pulse sympathetically as he "puts himself in his place"' (*New York Weekly* 19 June 1876, 4). But what is particularly interesting about this Alger serial is that it is one of the earliest appearances of the tramp in fiction.

The 'tramp' is no myth or symbol in the 'American mind', no eternal archetype of 'America'.[1] It was a category constructed in the wake of the 1873 depression and the 1877 railroad strikes to designate migratory and unemployed workers; indeed it was ideological naming of the new phenomenon of unemployment. The very success of the establishment of a work force dependent on wages meant that 'the slump of the 1870s ... created for the first time a national specter of huge groups of workers deprived of their means of livelihood' (Gordon, Edwards & Reich 1982,

53). So the 'tramp' became a category of law in anti-tramp legis-
lation (first in New Jersey in 1876), of social science, of charity
and relief discourses, even of biology: in the late 1870s it was
argued that pauperism and crime connected to tramping was an
inherited trait. The tramp became a character in middle class
fiction in Lee Harris' *The Man Who Tramps: A Story of Today* (1878)
where the tramps move to Pittsburgh to aid in the 'railroad riots'
of 1877. Rewriting history, Harris has the riots crushed and the
tramp leader killed.[2]

As the number of tramps increased, newspapers sensationally
reported crimes by tramps and attacked the 'tramp evil'; anti-
tramp vigilance committees were formed to prosecute a 'war on
the tramps' (Bruce 1959, 20-22, 68-69). The tramp became an
increasingly visible character in the next twenty years, often
replacing the Indian as a figure of savagery in the collective
stories of the dominant ideology. At a meeting of the American
Social Science Association in 1877, the Dean of the Yale Law
School, speaking less as a social scientist or lawyer than as a
novelist, said, 'as we utter the word *Tramp* there arises straight-
away before us the spectacle of a lazy, incorrigible, cowardly,
utterly depraved savage.'[3]

The tramp was not, however, a univocal figure and it could be
turned against itself: Herbert Gutman (1976, 96) has pointed out
instances of labor newspapers identifying tramps with Christ in
the mid-1870s, and Michael Davis (1984, 147) notes recurring
analogies in labor papers between tramp 'armies' and Lincoln's
Grand Army of the Republic. Even Allan Pinkerton (1878, 31-33),
perhaps betraying his Chartist background, wrote that 'Jesus
Christ was himself a tramp ... I do not agree with Professor
Wayland [who had attributed the 1877 riots to "our great
standing army of professional tramps"] and others as to the
universal villainy and ferocity of the tramp ... While wishing it
thoroughly known that I deplore and condemn the vicious
features of the fraternity, I am quite as willing to have it known
that I have a kind word to say for thousands of them who have
become homeless wretches and wandering outcasts.'

The dime novel also became an arena of this ideological
struggle over the tramp. Alger's *Tony, the Tramp*, one of the
earliest stories of tramps, preceding the 1877 upheaval, is the
story of an orphan boy tramp who does not like his life on the
road but is held captive by his evil tramp 'uncle'. Tony goes
through a series of escapes from and recaptures by the evil
tramp, but eventually makes his way in the world with the help

of a rich young man whom he rescues from a thief. Tony, who is repeatedly told that being a tramp is his 'misfortune' not his 'fault', eventually discovers that he is heir to an English fortune. The revelation displaces entirely his life as a tramp; and indeed Tony's position as tramp is further repressed when Alger reprints the novel as *Tony, the Hero* in 1880. Apparently this was Alger's own title; it was the *New York Weekly*, aware of the interest in and controversy over tramps, that gave it the title *Tony, the Tramp*.[4]

A more complex dime novel about tramps was serialized in Beadle & Adams' *Saturday Journal* in 1881: Frederick Whittaker's *Nemo, King of the Tramps; or, The Romany Girl's Vengeance. A Story of the Great Railroad Riots* (WTa). *Nemo* is an excellent example of dime novel disguises. Its multiple, interwoven plots in a relatively short novel are filled with what seem to the modern reader like absurd coincidences, implausible disguises and misrecognitions, and byzantine family relationships (orphans revealed as heirs, men revealed as women, secret and forgotten marriages, etc.).

To simplify matters slightly, *Nemo* consists of two stories that take place in the hot summer of 1877. One of the stories concerns the wealthy Calvert family of Pennsylvania — the Senator, his nephew Oliver, the president of the Air Line Road, and Helen Chester, the Senator's ward, who continually rebuffs Oliver's attentions. The other story concerns a tramp retreat in a nearby woods consisting largely of gypsies and led by Nemo, king of the tramps, a 'monarch of tatters'. Into this wooded retreat comes a boy, Jack. Both the Calverts and the tramps move to Pittsburgh where the railroad strike has occurred (and Oliver has telegraphed: 'Mow the rascals down . . . no quarter to communists'). There is a detailed depiction of the Pittsburgh riots: of the Philadelphia militia (sent in by the state on the railroad's request) firing on the crowd; then of the siege of the roundhouse (where the militia had retreated) by the combined forces of railroaders, tramps, and citizens; and finally of the burning of the railroad yards.

Just before these scenes comes a theatrical 'riot', a play within a play produced by Nemo — now Trevlac (a mirror of Calvert), the theatrical agent — and his troop of gypsy actors, at the Pittsburgh Opera House the night before the riots. The play, *The Gipsy's Vengeance* (whose audience includes Oliver Calvert, the railroad president), features an actor, made up to look exactly like Calvert, who is beaten by the gipsies and then killed by the gipsy queen:

... the railroad magnate had the mortification of seeing himself caricatured before his eyes as a pompous bully and coward, while all the spectators enjoyed it immensely. The way in which the joke was received satisfied him that he was not so popular as he had thought, which was indeed the case. Pittsburgh, being a railway center, was largely under the influence of railroad men, who in 1877 almost universally sympathized with the strikers (WTa, 8).

This story of the gipsies' melodrama allows Whittaker to depict a symbolic action, the killing of the railroad president, which parallels the crowd's actions in the climax of the riots, the burning of the roundhouse.[5]

In the intricate machinations that make up the last third of the story, Nemo is revealed to be the wrongly disowned son of Senator Calvert, having been framed by Oliver, and Jack proves to be the betrayed wife of Oliver. Nemo, now Harvey, is taken back into the family and marries Helen; Oliver is cast out and becomes a tramp. One way to read this, and other tales of orphans revealed to be heirs, is to see it as a return to bourgeois conventions; the hero or heroine cannot *really* be 'lower class'. But this is to read it as a novel, a story of individuals and of an individual family. Read thus, the fact that the Senator fails to recognize his son seems absurd. Rather it is necessary to read the story as an allegory, a way of reading that has long been a part of popular culture, for it to make sense. Read in this way, the Senator, the patriarch of Calverton, widely respected and well-liked at the beginning of the story, is a figure of the Republic, deceived and betrayed by the railroad president, Oliver. The restoration of Nemo/Harvey is not a denial of his status as tramp; unlike Alger's Tony who had said in the first scene that he didn't want to be a tramp and that he was ashamed of being one, and whose his evil 'uncle' had lied when he told Tony his parents were tramps, Nemo is from beginning to end proud of his title, king of the tramps, though, as he tells Jack: 'These gentlemen are not *tramps* at all. That is a vulgar word used by a vulgar world, and quite out of place here ... We are all wanderers; not tramps' (WTa, 2). Rather it is an affirmation that the disinherited tramp is the rightful heir of the republic.

Furthermore, Nemo/Harvey regains his rightful place with the help of the 'gipsies', a synecdoche for immigrant workers, perhaps even for the new and still exotic immigrants from eastern and southern Europe who were beginning to be visible. The 'gipsies' are seen in the noblest light; much attention is paid to their 'Romany' language (which Nemo speaks), with phrases and songs translated in footnotes. Their idyllic campsite is a utopian image set against the violence at the Calverts' mansion and the militia marching into Pittsburgh. And it is the gipsies who go and rescue Senator Calvert from the roundhouse where the militia are besieged. They take him to the city — a strange rescue considering that the Senator is an 'enemy' of the gipsies, but an important one in that it is at that moment when the militia are fighting the citizens that the Senator, in his symbolic role, must move spatially from the roundhouse to the city, and, as father, from Oliver the railroad president to Nemo the tramp.

This allegorical reading, I have suggested, is a characteristically working class way of reading in the nineteenth century, and it enables us to make sense of the typological plots of sensational fiction. It is perhaps most characteristically embodied in the use of disguise as a narrative equivalent of metaphor rather than as the sign of an enigma to be solved.

This allegorical mode of reading depends upon the existence of a master plot by which to read the disguises; and that master plot was in working class cultures of the nineteenth century the story of the Republic itself. The stories of individuals and of individual families become types of the citizens of the republic, both in utopian images of its fulfillment as the cooperative commonwealth and in the stories of its betrayal, as it becomes a land of tramps and millionaires.

For Whittaker's *Nemo* is not directly a story of labor and capital; despite its focus on the railroad strikes, no striker or railroad worker appears as a character. It is a story of tramps and millionaires, a figure of social cleavage that was to find wide resonance in the 1880s and 1890s. Perhaps the most striking occurrence came in the preamble of the 1892 Omaha platform of the People's Party, a preamble written by a popular novelist, Ignatius Donnelly:

> ... we meet in the midst of a nation brought to the verge of moral, political, and material ruin. ... our homes are covered with mortgages; labor impoverished; and the land concentrating in the hands of the capitalists. ... The fruits of the toil of millions are boldly stolen to build up colossal fortunes for the few, unprecedented in the history of mankind; and the possessors of these, in turn, despise the republic and endanger liberty. From the same prolific womb of governmental injustice we breed the two great classes — tramps and millionaires (Hicks 1931, 439).

One hears similar accents from a Knights of Labor lecturer in Rutland, Vermont in 1887: 'We [the Knights] stand today as the conservators of society. We have watched the growth of a privileged class and of a vast army of tramps. If these extremes come together there will be a crash. We are building between them a platform upon which all men may stand on an equality' (Fink 1983, 94). In the next chapter, I will look at how the Knights of Labor formed not only a platform upon which all men could stand equal, but a metaphor that, for a brief period, could replace the rhetoric of tramps and millionaires in the dime novel. But before turning to those dime novel knights of labor, I want to look briefly at two dime novels of tramps and millionaires from the 1890s, when the 'vast army of tramps' materialized in several 'tramp armies', the most famous of which was Coxey's industrial army, which marched to Washington in the spring of 1894. One of the stories, published in the Old Cap Collier Library on May 30, 1894, explicitly deals with Coxey's Army: *On to Washington; Or, Old Cap Collier with the Coxey Army* (OLb). The other story, published in 1895 in the Young Sleuth Library, juxtaposes the two characters in the title: *Young Sleuth and the Millionaire Tramp; Or, Diamonds Under Rags* (Y).

The two tales reflect the same shifts in the cheap stories that we noted with the Molly Maguire tales. Both of these stories are ostensibly detective stories, unlike the Alger and Whittaker tales of tramps. Neither has a named author; they are ascribed to 'The Author of' Young Sleuth and to Old Cap Collier. Whereas the Alger and Whittaker stories were first written for serialization in the story papers, these are written for the cheap libraries where they appear in their entirety the week of their publication, to be supplanted by another adventure of their heroes the following week. Nevertheless they show as great an ideological range as the earlier stories.

On to Washington; Or, Old Cap Collier with the Coxey Army is a topical story, published within a month of Coxey's arrest in Washington after leading thousands of unemployed workers to the capital to offer a 'petition in boots'. And this dime novel Coxey is cast in the mold of Nemo, King of the Tramps: when a man says to him, 'The papers call us tramps', Coxey replies:

> Call us tramps, do they? Many of us look like tramps, it is true; but what has brought us to this condition? What has thrown us out of employment? What has caused our mills and work shops to shut down? What has brought many of us to starvation? These men in

Congress — the men who have control of the machinery of government — these men, I say, the majority of whom are the slaves of the corporations and trusts, who sell their souls for the flesh-pots of Egypt, who shut their ears to the cry of the starving (OLb, 1).

The story itself opens with a rumor in the ranks of the Commonweal Army that a government spy, 'one of the greatest detectives in the world', Old Cap Collier, is in the camp. When Coxey hears of this, he tells the men: 'we are not conspirators, and we have nothing to fear even if a thousand detectives are sent to watch us.' The rumor is true, Old Cap Collier is present, and two story lines dominate the rest of the dime novel.

The first is Old Cap Collier's story. Called by the chief of the Secret Service to 'join Coxey's army and keep the government thoroughly informed of the movements of that body of tramps', Collier objects to the term and sides with the Commonweal Army. Collier is described as a 'plain man', a favorite epithet of the populists, and is contrasted to the pompous, overbearing chief (OLb, 2). He accepts the engagement, though 'all of his sympathies were with the movement' (OLb, 3), in order to prevent trouble. He disguises himself first as Abel Browne, a Wisconsin farmer, and later as Tom Green, a Cincinnati carriage painter, and most of the story consists of his ferreting out a group of criminals who mean to disrupt the Commonweal Army; by the end, Collier has 'learned that General Coxey had formed no conspiracy of any kind against the government, and that his movement was a peaceful one' (OLb, 23). His original sympathies are vindicated.

However, a second intertwined plot casts a shadow over the populist detective. It is the story of one of Coxey's main advisors, known only as the 'Unknown'. For most of the tale he remains an enigma, but at the end it is revealed that he is in love with the daughter of a judge who has refused his consent to the marriage because the Unknown is involved with the Commonweal Army. Finally, he chooses love over politics and leaves the Army concluding that 'nothing can be gained for the laboring people and unemployed in this way. The only way to accomplish anything is through the ballot-box' (OLb, 24). The populist detective story ends with an incongruous marriage of a Coxeyite and a judge's daughter and this civics lesson.

The Young Sleuth tale, *Young Sleuth and the Millionaire Tramp; Or, Diamonds Under Rags*, published in 1895, is actually a detective story in the classic sense: the detective uses a variety of clues to solve a murder which baffles the police, and captures the murderer. The murdered man is a wealthy New York diamond dealer at his country house; the discovery of a tramp sign nearby throws suspicion on a neighboring tramp encampment. Young Sleuth goes 'to spy upon the miserable gang of social outcasts who were assembled there' and notices two suspicious tramps, Ross, who looks like a German professor, and Gentleman Nick, who looks as if he had been a gentleman at one time. Young Sleuth goes underground, disguising himself as a tramp, complete with dirt, rags and tramp slang. After a variety of adventures, he discovers that Gentleman Nick had been wrongly found guilty of a similar, previous murder: Gentleman Nick is actually Dudley Pembrooke, a 'millionaire tramp', who keeps his property in the form of diamonds, hidden under his rags. Ross, actually Hubert Rossvitch, a German Socialist machinist who has invented a 'wonderful weapon', a percussion rifle, is guilty of both murders, avenging his murderer brother. The evil German is captured along with his marvelous weapon, and the story ends with Dudley restored to his 'rightful place in society'. If one were to argue for the essentially conservative nature of the detective tale, protecting property and maintaining order, this story would be solid evidence, with its good millionaires and evil tramps. Whereas Old Cap Collier was in a genuine dilemma that had to be explained away — spying for the government on a movement with which he sympathized — Young Sleuth has no question about his loyalties: the story opens with him enjoying the hospitality of the millionaire.

Nevertheless, the structure of the tale is not unlike that of the Whittaker and Old Cap Collier tales. All three are built around the two poles, millionaires and tramps. This opposition structures not only the characters but also the landscape of the stories, which is a landscape of mansions and tramp encampments. In the Young Sleuth story, this becomes a static opposition. The murder is at the mansion, the murderer is in the tramp camp, the murderer is caught by infiltrating the tramp camp, and the mansion is protected. Both of the other stories begin with the same opposition. Whittaker's *Nemo* begins with the Calvert mansion and the tramp's retreat. There is an attack on the Calverts, and they are about to go on a 'tramp-killing bee', when the strike news from Pittsburgh interrupts the story and moves both parties, tramps and millionaires, to Pittsburgh. The confrontation between tramps and millionaires is displaced from a murder mystery to the railroad riots of 1877. A similar displacement of the narrative occurs in the Old Cap Collier story. The Ohio encampment of the Commonweal Army is set against the mansion of 'Judge Morse, one of the wealthiest men in the state.' But before this opposition emerges into a full plot, the Army and the story's characters are marching to Washington. The Judge Morse plot reenters at the very end, but the confrontation of tramps and millionaires takes place not so much in the romantic entanglement of a Coxeyite and a judge's daughter (which is resolved, more or less) but in the confrontation with the police in front of the Capitol.

The Young Sleuth story does not find any way to a political or historical terrain; it remains simply a murder mystery. The tramp as a utopian figure, an image of an ideal egalitarian community or of a free life on the road, is not present, as it is so powerfully in Whittaker's Nemo and his gipsies and Old Cap Collier's Coxey and his army. The only resolution that is left is the violent juxtaposition of the title which remains more ambiguous than the plot itself: diamonds under rags, the millionaire tramp.

If the depression of the 1870s produced a figure of a nation divided into tramps and millionaires, the year of the national railroad strike, 1877, saw the appearance of another figure of class conflict, a figure that was to cause more controversy than any other dime novel character: the road agent, the outlaw. 'Grim and uncommunicative, there roams through the country of gold a youth in black, at the head of a bold lawless gang of road-riders, who, from his unequaled daring, has won and rightly deserves the name — Deadwood Dick, Prince of the Road.' So concludes the first of Edward L. Wheeler's Deadwood Dick stories, the first issue of Beadle's Half Dime Library, one of the cheap nickel and dime libraries that emerged in 1877.[6] The novelty of Deadwood Dick is accurately gauged by Daryl Jones (1978, 81) in his study of the dime novel western: 'Never before had a Western hero openly defied the law. Never before had a Western hero reacted against social restraint so violently as to waylay stages and rob banks.' And he was to become one of the most popular heroes of the cheap stories. Wheeler wrote 33 stories of his adventures; and after Wheeler's death, other writers wrote 97 more stories about Deadwood Dick Jr (Johann-sen 1950, 1: 60). Deadwood Dick has also been the subject of some critical discussion because of his place in the dime novel western, and, though I am not dealing at any length with dime novel westerns in this book, I want to briefly look at the criticism of Deadwood Dick and the western outlaw to see whether the general perspective of this book might change our view of Deadwood Dick. Put another way, what happens if instead of thinking the trajectory of the dime novel as 'from Seth Jones to Deadwood Dick',[7] we think of it as 'from Molly Maguire to Deadwood Dick'?

Henry Nash Smith's discussion of Deadwood Dick is set within a larger discussion of 'the western hero in the dime novel', and that, of course, is set within a wider and justly classic interpretation of the impact of the American West as a myth and symbol in American consciousness, literature and social thought. Nevertheless, Deadwood Dick holds a strategic place in the argument as a whole; Smith's conclusions about Deadwood Dick are the conclusion to the middle section of the book, 'The Sons of Leatherstocking'. Smith (1950, 100-102, 119) draws three general conclusions from his description of the Deadwood Dick saga. First, Deadwood Dick with his humble origins and his heroic skills 'embodies the popular ideal of the self-made man.' Second, he 'exhibits a concern with social problems that is, as far as my knowledge extends, unique in the dime novels.' And third, he, and his partner Calamity Jane, mark an abandonment of the code of gentility which, though a necessary step for American litera-ture, reveals 'a progressive deterioration in the Western story as a genre ... the Western story lost whatever chance it might once have had to develop social significance ... [Deadwood Dick's] fame reflects the kind of sensationalism that increased so markedly in the later 1870s.'

Though Smith is right to note the break with codes of gentil-ity, he misjudges the meaning and consequences of that break. First, the break with gentility is better seen synchronically than diachronically. As several interpreters of the narratives of Kit Carson have shown,[8] Carson's life had different meanings for different audiences. In the sensational dime novels about Carson, as Richard Slotkin (1985) notes, 'conflict and conquest, not patient labor and steady rise in status, are the dream story of success purveyed in the dime novel: it is the underclass's dream of success, not that of the established bourgeois' (206); on the other hand, Slotkin sees 'the genteel tradition in Carsonian mythology ["propagated in polite (or politer) fiction and bio-graphy, published between hard covers and designed for more 'respectable' sectors of the reading public" (203)] as systemat-ically linking the "myth of the hunter" to the success ethic and the myth of the self-made man and entrepreneur' (204). Thus

Deadwood Dick's break from the codes of gentility marks a break from the ideology of the self-made man. He is closer to the traditional highwayman than to a self-made man. Deadwood Dick has been unjustly dispossessed of his father's fortune, and his life as a road agent was originally an attempt to protect himself from the villains (the law being no help as the villain 'was a man of great influence') and to seek revenge.

Moreover, Deadwood Dick's 'concern with social problems', which, as this book has tried to show, is by no means unique in the dime novel, is not extrinsic to the character and plot but is central to the stories. Indeed to characterize Deadwood Dick's involvement with a miners' union as a 'concern with social problems' is, I will argue, to misread the character. Far from being a kind of 'sensationalism', never developing a 'social significance', Deadwood Dick becomes a popular and contested figure precisely because of his social significance. And this significance comes not primarily from his character as a Western hero but from his character as an outlaw, a bandit. It is symptomatic that Smith hardly mentions Deadwood Dick as outlaw, and his account of the western hero in the dime novel passes over the James Brothers.

Daryl Jones (1978), in his recent discussion of Deadwood Dick, begins from the 'phenomenal' popularity of the outlaw over three decades (roughly 1877 to 1903). He focuses on the contradictions raised by the appearance of the heroic outlaw in the dime novel. His analysis of the narrative formula of persecution and revenge, and his argument that 'it is nearly impossible to overestimate the importance of conventional persecution and revenge as a means of justifying the outlaw's rebellion against established social and legal codes' (96), are convincing. The outlaw tales are built not around the education and success of a self-made man nor around an interclass romance but around the persecution of the hero or of a defenseless person which forces the hero into a justifiable though illegal revenge. Jones demonstrates the way that this plot emerged in the tales of other bandits: Joseph Badger's series of dime novels about Joaquin Murieta began in 1871 with Murieta as a minor character, a 'demon incarnate'; by the late 1870s and early 1880s, the emergence of the outlaws allows Murieta to become the central character whose violence is justified by his early persecution (91-94).

Indeed the outlaw story became so widespread and popular in the years after the appearance of Deadwood Dick in 1877 that the

Postmaster General apparently forced the dime novel publisher Frank Tousey to withdraw his outlaw tales in August 1883. The outlaw tales dealing with the Jesse James Gang returned to the market in 1889 when both Street & Smith and Frank Tousey began publishing them, and they remained popular until another public outcry led to the suspension of the stories in 1903. It is the first of these periods — 1877 to 1883 — that I am primarily interested in. Though the exact agent and cause of the 'cleanup' remains unclear, certain reasons for it can be suggested.[9] First of all, the outlaw stories that were attacked appeared in nickel libraries that were aimed at boys. Tousey's Five Cent Wide Awake Library, which replaced over sixty outlaw stories including the eighteen 'original' Jesse James stories and at least twenty five Claude Duval stories (since back issues of the libraries were kept in stock, Tousey not only ceased publishing the outlaw and highwayman tales but had to replace the ones already published with substitute titles), was considered a 'boys' weekly', as was Beadle's Half-Dime Library which carried the Deadwood Dick stories. Second, the James Brothers stories, as well as other 'real-life' bandit stories, were published while the outlaws were still at large. The moral panic seems to have come in the wake of the shooting of Jesse James in April 1882, which made him a martyr. The last of the Tousey stories appeared on 22 August 1883; the immediate cause of the cessation may well have been the opening of the trial of Frank James on 21 August 1883, a trial at which he was acquitted. But clearly the major reason lay in the stories themselves: as dime novelist Eugene Sawyer noted in 1902, in dime novels 'virtue must triumph, vice and crime must not only be defeated, but must be painted in colours so strong and vivid that there is no mistake about it. The stories of the James boys are the only exceptions I know; but, after all, they came to grief at last' (Burgess 1902, 530). For a short period between 1877 and 1883, outlaws defied the law and got away with it, escaping the moral universe of both genteel and sensational fiction.

In the best treatment of the James Brothers dime novels to date, James Deutsch (1976) looks at the depiction of the outlaws in a variety of stories and concludes that the 'Jesse James tales neither wholly glorified nor defamed the bandits, but reflected the societal ambivalence to the outlaw hero figure ... In these publications, Jesse might be a saint one week, helping those in need by fighting the enemies of the people; in another week he might be the devil incarnate, breathing fire and smoke as he

plunders all who stand in his way' (8, 2). In a way this is accurate; even in the same story, one can find this ambivalence. However, by restricting himself to the reprint series of 1901 to 1903
(or being restricted to them; the early James stories are very hard
to find), he misses the actual sequence in which the stories were
published; so what appears to be a week to week ambivalence as
older stories are randomly reprinted may actually be a transformation from the early stories of 1881 to 1883 when the James
brothers were presented in a more heroic light to the stories of
1889 and later when they returned to cheap libraries, somewhat
chastened.

Indeed, the outlaws, like the Molly Maguires and the tramps,
eventually found their adversary in the detective; though the
actual James Brothers won public sympathy when Pinkerton
agents attacked their mother's house, killing a child and injuring
their mother, the dime novel James Brothers were displaced by a
heroic Pinkerton detective, Carl Greene, who appeared 'in a
plethora of disguises, always outwitting the outlaws, often
capturing them, but never holding on to them long enough for
the stories to end with him the final victor' (Deutsch 1976, 5).

A similar ambivalence marks the career of Deadwood Dick.
He gives up being a road agent to become a 'regulator', an early
name for a vigilante, fairly early in the series (Beadle & Adams,
though originating the outlaw hero, did not exploit it and would
not publish stories of actual outlaws), working on the boundaries
of the law. By the middle 1880s, however, the outlaw joined the
genealogy of the detective, as Deadwood Dick, Jr. becomes a
detective, in stories often set in Eastern cities, and is fully
distanced from his outlaw past. As in Pinkerton's narrative of the
1877 railroad strike, *Strikers, Communists, Tramps, and Detectives*,
the detective serves to bring the great upheavals under control.

Nevertheless, neither the ambivalence of some portrayals nor
the evolution of the outlaws into detectives or the foils of detective heroes reduces the scandal of their initial impact; the moral
panic itself seems to indicate that the outlaw which emerged in
the late 1870s and early 1880s was a *social bandit*, a figure whose
meaning is not summed up by 'sensationalism.' Unfortunately,
though Daryl Jones' (1978) description of the outlaw character
and persecution-revenge plot is illuminating, his explanation of
the popularity and meaning of the outlaw story in this flowering
between 1877 and 1883 is unsatisfactory: he sees it as 'a projection
of the widespread American preoccupation with the meaning and
value of law' and 'a projection of the average American's

growing alienation in a modern society' (98-99). This is not so much untrue as too general to be explanatory. However, if we look at Eric Hobsbawn's important history and interpretation of social bandits, we can, I think, get a firmer sense of these dime novels.

Social bandits are, in Eric Hobsbawm's (1981) words, 'peasant outlaws whom the lord and state regard as criminals, but who remain within peasant society, and are considered by their people as heroes, as champions, avengers, fighters for justice, perhaps even leaders of liberation, and in any case as men to be admired, helped and supported' (17). Furthermore, they are restricted to peasant societies; 'if the argument of this book is accepted,' Hobsbawm notes, 'they cannot be understood except in the context of the sort of peasant society which, it is safe to guess, is as remote from most readers as ancient Egypt' (130). So, at first glance, it would seem that the category of social bandit is inapplicable to the United States of the Gilded Age. However, there are two qualifications that Hobsbawm makes that are of particular interest to our argument. First, he points out that 'the bandit *myth*' has an appeal that has 'always been far wider than its native environment', surviving through the medium of print into capitalist societies. This is one aspect of the flowering of the outlaw in the 1870s and 1880s; recall that almost half of the stories that Tousey dropped from his Five Cent Wide Awake Library dealt with the exploits of Claude Duval, a 'noble robber' of the seventeenth century. But most of the outlaws were contemporaries — Jesse James was still living when the dime novels were about him were published, and Deadwood Dick, though a fictional character, walked the streets of contemporary Colorado mining towns.

Hobsbawm, in an appendix responding to criticisms of his original argument, takes up this question of 'characters in nineteenth- and twentieth-century America and Australia who seem to fit my pattern of "social banditry" but patently do not seem to belong into a "traditional peasantry" or into pre-capitalist or pre-industrial social environments,' and, in particular, the figure of Jesse James. I will not go into the details of the argument because I am interested here less in the question of actual social banditry — the actions of the James Brothers — than in the representations of those bandits in the dime novels. But his conclusion sheds light on the dime novels as well:

... it was only in an essentially capitalist economy that bank credits, mortgages and the like become central features of what farmers or peasants see as their exploitation, and incidentally features which link the discontent of country people to that of other classes such as artisans and small traders. To this extent the period which turns institutions like banks into quintessential public villains and bank-robbery into the most readily understood form of robbing the rich marks the adaptation of social banditry to capitalism (153).

It was the James brothers' bank robberies and train robberies that gave them their popular support, both in Missouri and with dime novel readers. Indeed train robbery was a new crime: the first one occurred in 1866, and the James Gang turned to robbing trains in 1873 (Broehl 1964, 239-243). The railroad was a popular target; as we have seen, a Pittsburgh crowd burned a railroad yard during the strike of 1877.

The dime novel outlaws also marked this adaptation of social banditry to capitalism, and they are perhaps less sons of Leatherstocking than sons of Molly Maguire, less stories of the Wild West than stories of Labor and Capital. The enemies of the James brothers are Pinkertons not Indians. Read in this light, the mining towns in which Deadwood Dick lives, and his 'concern with social problems', are not anomalous but are central. When Wheeler's trilogy about Deadwood Dick in Leadville was published in the summer of 1879, a Knights of Labor assembly had formed in Leadville, the most productive mining camp in the West; and the following year saw a disastrous strike with the intervention of the National Guard (Lingenfelter 1974, 132, 143; Buchanan 1903, 5-36). The distance between the anthracite mines of Pottsville and Hazelton and the hard-rock mines of Deadwood and Leadville is less than first appears. One finds descriptions of the mines in the Deadwood Dick tales that are not far from those of Daniel Doyle:

> Shafts and tunnels were being pierced into the mountain-side, all the way from the bottom up toward the misty tops, and ore was blasted out and lowered to the gulch-bottom in incline plane cars — or, as in one case, by large buckets from a mighty crane, managed by mule-power. Everywhere were sounds of busy industry in one Babel of noises — the crushing sound of ore-breakers, yells of mule-drivers, the shrieks of steam-whistles, and the ring of axes far up the dizzy mountain, all peculiar to their locality, yet distinct from the sights and sounds of the long street of the magic growing town (WHb, 8).

The climax of *Deadwood Dick on Deck; or, Calamity Jane, the Heroine of Whoop-Up* is a mine explosion plotted by the villain. So it is not surprising that we should find in *Deadwood Dick on Deck* a hero, Sandy, who is 'an enthusiast on the labor question': 'No doubt there are capitalists who would like to step down into the little city of Whoop-Up, and grasp the tyrant's reins in their hands; but they'll be mightily disappointed when they find that very few poor men are so poor but what they can stand firm for their rights' (WHb, 4).

However, once we establish this, we must ask what kinds of stories of labor and capital these are. And here Deadwood Dick remains an ambiguous character. At once a highwayman, bent on revenge for being dispossessed, he is at another time a vigilante regulator enforcing the codes of the mining community, and yet again a mine owner himself. But his mine, described in *Deadwood Dick, the Prince of the Road; Or, The Black Rider of the Black Hills*, is a utopian projection: set in an isolated pocket that he had discovered, it turned 'Paradise ... into a goldmine', a 'scene — not of slumbering beauty, but of active industry and labor'. Nevertheless the flowers are still intact. The miners, who are in 'a prosperous condition', are all Ute Indians; popular racism is employed in order to do away with wage labor for whites. The mine and the valley are entirely secret, and form the base for Deadwood Dick's forays.

Another, less magical, version of the utopian gold mine are the lodes owned and leased by Sandy and Colonel Tubbs in *Deadwood Dick on Deck*; as Colonel Tubbs, the comic rustic figure, explains to the villain, a capitalist from Washington:

> ... we divide up ekal wi' ther boys ... I'd ruther 'a' not fot a cent out o' their hull business, than to have sold et ter men who'd hev hed et all under three or four piratical pairs o' fists, an' w'ile hoarding up their pile, ground ther workin' men down ter Chinamen's wages — 'washee shirtee for fivee cents!' Mebbe ye cum frum out in Pennsylvania, whar they do thet kind o' playin', stranger, but et's orful sure thet ye ken't play sech a trick out hyar among ther horny-fisted galoots o' this delectable Black Hills kentry (WHb, 2).

Here the explicit comparison with the Pennsylvania coal fields is tied to a desire that eastern capitalists and corporations be kept out of the western mines. Though this utopia of dividing it up equal with the boys was never a reality in the hard-rock camps, it was not confined to dime novels either. In Deadwood in 1877, there was an attempt by miners to take over a mine and work it themselves, an attempt that ended with the sheriff calling out the calvary (Lingenfelter 1974, 137).

This by no means exhausts what might be said about the Deadwood Dick tales or the other outlaw dime novels; rather it is an argument that they must be seen in the context of the class conflicts of the Gilded Age, as adaptations of traditional stories of bandits and highwaymen not only to the landscape of the American West but to the social structures of the nation. Indeed, the frontier myths and stories of the nineteenth century have a more direct relation to those class conflicts than is usually thought; as Richard Slotkin (1985, 47) has argued in his persuasive re-interpretation of the myth of the frontier, 'the simple fable of the discovery of new land and the dispossession of the Indians substitutes for the complexities of capital formation, class and interest-group competition, and the subordination of society to the imperatives of capitalist development.' Furthermore, Slotkin argues that 'to the extent that labor spoke as a class "for itself" [in the labor press], it did not adopt the myth-ideological framework of the Myth of the Frontier as an interpretative scheme. Moreover, when it did refer to that Myth, it tended to invert its terms and to choose identification with the forces that the Last Stand myth implicitly condemned' (473-474). This suggests that working-class readers may well have read the dime novel westerns as stories of labor and capital, taking the west as an allegorical republic of outlaws, forming a cooperative commonwealth where 'we divide up ekal wi' ther boys', but threatened by the social structures of the east.

Perhaps what remains most puzzling about this argument is not how Deadwood Dick and Jesse James are related to the railroad strikes of 1877 and why they had such resonance with working class readers; rather it is why the Molly Maguires never developed into these kind of social bandits, why the portrayals of the Mollies remain so ambivalent and contradictory, why the persecution and revenge plot is so infrequently used to tell their story.

It is striking, for instance, that, with the exception of Pinkerton's own account, I have found no dime novels of the Molly Maguires between 1877 and 1883, that is, after the appearance of Deadwood Dick and before the cleanup campaign against the outlaw tales. This may simply be the result of the still inadequate indexes of cheap libraries and story papers. Nevertheless, when Molly Maguire makes the appearance in Tousey's Five Cent Wide Awake Library that I have looked at, it is after the cleanup, and the Mollies are clearly villains.

But if there is no full-fledged Molly Maguire outlaw story,

Irish bandits make their way into the dime novels in this period. So one finds in one of the early James brothers tales, *Frank James on the Trail* (F), an Irish Fenian, Will Brannigan, who 'had a kindly liking for the outlaw brothers, and often helped them out of their difficulties, but would never join their band or share their plunder. "No, Frank," Brannigan would say, "no Brannigan was ever 'wanted' for anything but political offenses."' (F, 2). But Brannigan does join them by the end of the story, after some vigilantes brutally murder the mother of a friend.

And in the Five Cent Wide Awake Library, in the midst of the original James brothers stories, one finds Corporal Morgan Rattler's *The Irish Claude Duval*, a straightforward story of a noble robber who says to one victim: 'you rob and plunder the people of Ireland, while I only take from the tyrant officials of the English government who are gorging themselves with Ireland's blood' (R, 3). He steals the lord's money and wins the heart of his daughter while defending the people of Ireland. This tradition was strong enough to structure much of the discussion of the Molly Maguires. The *New York Weekly* (3 April 1876, 4), for example, once gave a history of the Molly Maguires which defended their incarnation in Ireland as a necessary arm of the tenants against the landlords, while maintaining that such tactics were out of place and criminal in Pennsylvania.

But perhaps the crucial reason for the absence of a Molly Maguire bandit saga can be seen in a comment that Hobsbawm (1981) makes about the James brothers: 'by the time they flourished, Grangerism and Populism were a more coherent response to the problems facing the rural Mid-West than robbery. ... social banditry wanes as modern organized and collective modes of representing class interests become available' (154, 151). The violence of the so-called Molly Maguires did not precede the miners' unions; it came out of the defeat of the union in the Long Strike. But the presence, memory and hope of the miners' union meant that a certain distance was kept between respectable organization and forms of social banditry; thus Daniel Doyle and others made such an effort, not always successful, to separate the union and the Ancient Order of Hibernians from the individual acts of revenge. The acts of Deadwood Dick, Jesse James and the other dime novel outlaws — the Younger brothers, the Dalton Boys, and Joaquin Murieta — were both sufficiently distant from and implicated in the battles of labor and capital to offer a figure of those battles, a figure of vengeance and heroism.

9

Arthurian Knights in Connecticut Factories

Almost all dime novels have a romantic plot; the strikes and murder mysteries are intertwined with seductions, romances and rivalries in love. These cheap stories of labor and capital are also and at the same time stories of sexuality and gender, romances of manhood and womanhood. The disguises and revelations, captures and escapes attempt to resolve not only the ideo-logical antinomies generated by the class conflicts in the republican community but also the contradictions generated when older notions of manhood and womanhood are thrown into question by the new sexual divisions of labor. In the middle class sex/gender system, the solidifying of the 'separate spheres' produced narratives of the self-made man and the domestic woman.[1] The working class sex/gender system, on the other hand, though not entirely separate and isolated from that of the dominant class and its culture, is substantially different: the tales of honest mechanics are not the same as the stories of the self-made man, nor can the narratives of the working-girl's virtue be subsumed under domestic sentimentalism. Even where the words are the same, and that is not often, they are spoken with different accents. The existential dilemmas and ideological contradictions that these producer heroes face are distinct, and their resolutions, though often borrowing from the ideals of middle class respectability, have their own meanings. In the final two chapters I will look at narratives of working class manhood and womanhood in the cheap stories. And in both of the sections that follow, I will use autobiographical accounts as a gauge, clumsy and inexact no doubt, to the way the dime novels of working class manhood and womanhood were read and lived.

Tales of honest young mechanics had appeared regularly, if

not in great abundance, from the 1840s: one of the earliest was *Fleming Field; or, The Young Artisan. A Tale of the Days of the Stamp Act* written in 1845 by one of the most popular novelists of the period, Joseph Ingraham. But the subtitle is revealing; like Lippard's 'legends of the revolution', the tale is set in the past, in a more idyllic work setting before the battle between capitalism and the crafts. In the dime novels with a contemporary setting, the mysteries of the city, the honest mechanic tended to have a cameo role, as in the brief inset tale of John Davis in Lippard's *The Quaker City*. In the late 1840s and 1850s, the first popular working class type developed in the newspaper sketch and the melodramatic theater: Mose, the Bowery B'hoy, a journeyman celebrated as a brawler and fire-fighter in a working-class volunteer fire company. But Mose, a comic figure of the antebellum 'traditionalist' working-class culture, never develops from a stock icon into a formulaic narrative, and by the Civil War, as Peter Buckley (1984, 271) notes, he had sunk into obscurity, 'a strangely static, almost antiquated type'.[2]

However, in the 1870s and 1880s, a new genre of workingman hero tales appeared, stories of skilled mechanics, often in factory settings. These stories of working class manhood, which were published in the nickel and dime libraries, the story papers, and the labor newspapers, and were performed as melodramas, attempted to unite a narrative of an individual's achievement of independence and 'manliness', a romance of chivalric love, and a tale of workers' solidarity. In this chapter I will look at versions of this story of a 'knight of labor' written by two dime novelists, Frederick Whittaker and John E. Barrett.[3]

In 1882, Frederick Whittaker, one of Beadle & Adams' top novel-wrights (in 1886, he claimed to have been paid $3200 for 16 novels a year for Beadle & Adams), whose many cheap stories ranged in subject from pirates to Russian spies, from the Crusades to the Mexican frontier, began writing serials about workingmen for *Beadle's Weekly*.[4] Beginning with *John Armstrong, Mechanic; or, From the Bottom to the Top of the Ladder. A Story of How a Man Can Rise in America* (WTb), he wrote seven stories between November 1882 and December 1884 of young honest skilled mechanics who work their way up from the country, tramping or the orphanage to positions of success and respectability. Their struggle upward entails learning a skill, getting an education, becoming a foreman or even owner of the factory, while at the same time earning the respect of the other workers, fighting together with them in strikes. The strikes in the stories are always won, a marked contrast to middle class novels where, as Fay Blake (1972, 40) has pointed out, strikes are almost invariably lost.

John Armstrong , for example, comes to New York from the country to work in the Excelsior Iron Works. He is arrested for defending a seamstress against the boss's son, is released after her plea, works his way to foreman, having to fight other jealous workers, goes to night school so as to be worthy of the woman he had defended and with whom he has fallen in love (Ella, the seamstress who is now a schoolteacher). Though he learns proper speech and manners, Ella's mother prefers the boss's son (now somewhat reformed). John is caught in the middle of a strike, but his mediation fails and the owners plan to bring in scabs — one thousand Italians who will work at one dollar a day. John joins the workers on strike, and makes a speech at a union meeting. They win the strike, he wins Ella, but marriage, we are told, is not the end of the story. John is now a manager, involved in 'headwork', and, in a series of battles against old enemies at a stockholders meeting, he becomes president of the company. He runs for mayor of New York as the Reform candidate and wins. 'Look up, then, workman of the land, man with the muscle hardened by labor, brain trained in the struggle for life,' the story concludes, 'In America everything is possible for a workingman.'

As the title said: 'from the bottom to the top'. Beadle's advertisement for one of the other stories, *A Knight of Labor; or, Job Manly's Rise in Life. A Story of a Young Man from the Country* (WTe), shows how they were presented:

> Another *speaking* story of work life and struggle — of man and master — of handy hands and sturdy purpose — of country boy fighting his way in the world, with a hammer and will, and out of whose step by step from the village blacksmith shop to the proprietorship of a great carriage manufactory is taught A Splendid Lesson with a Big Moral That, to the young American mechanic, will be a kind of revelation. As a romance of workingman's life it is exceeding full of interest, both personal and associate. In Job, the rough, untutored, hard-headed, almost desperate apprentice, the reader literally has a rough diamond which takes severe cutting to bring out the *facets* of a fine character. That A Woman Does It does not lessen the young blacksmith's heroism, nor detract from the great workman's achievements; and we know the audience interested in

Captain Whittaker's previous creations will give this new work a cordial greeting (*Beadle's Weekly*, 5 April 1884, 4).

This statement to the reader, the 'young American mechanic', tells him not only what to expect in the story but also how to read it. They are pedagogic tales, agents of the 'respectable' rather than the 'rough' tendency in working class culture, inculcating a 'producer's' ethic of work and manhood. Job Manly is himself a rhetorical figure, a personification of a 'manly job'; and David Montgomery (1979, 13) has noted of the word 'manly' that 'the craftsmen's ethical code demanded a "manly" bearing toward the boss. Few words enjoyed more popularity in the nineteenth century than this honorific, with all its connotations of dignity, respectability, defiant egalitarianism, and patriarchal male supremacy.'[5] Whittaker's stories are accounts of how this 'manliness' is won and what it consists of; but, since they are novels and not success handbooks, they are also stories of the contradictions of a craftsman's manly bearing in a society of wage labor.

The workingman hero formula is torn by two different received narrative paradigms, the aristomilitary romance and the bourgeois *Bildungsroman*, the novel of education.[6] The first is built around a typical character — a knight, an outlaw, a rogue — who engages in a series of loosely strung together contests. The second is built around the growth of one individual man, a sentimental education into self-control and the social order. The dime novel's most common terrain is the adventure romance; in the Whittaker novels, one sees this in the series of contests the hero enters — innumerable fistfights, rivalries for women, tests of work skill, courtroom battles, and the climactic strike or election. One particularly interesting version is John Armstrong's contest with the boss's son, Jim Stryker, over speaking ability. Ella's mother likes an orator and thus Stryker who is giving a valedictory speech. John, on the other hand, feels that he can't speak in public and refuses to give a valediction. However, in the middle of the strike, he finds himself addressing the workers, and this is followed by a formal speech at a union meeting. When word of his speeches reaches Ella and her mother, John is clearly the victor.

Set against this somewhat repetitive plot of tests, contests, challenges, and duels, is a story of development and education, of struggling upward. All the heroes must learn self-control (particularly control of the temper that leads them into fistfights), temperance, thrift, and hard work. Often this education is tied to the romantic plot; both John Armstrong and Job Manly fall in love with their teachers. The 'ladder of love' propels the heroes to self-improvement in order to be worthy of the women they love. Both Job Manly and John Armstrong begin speaking dialect (and, we are told, swearing), but they learn to speak 'properly': they develop into 'grammatical' characters. Instead of the magical transformations of workers into noblemen that we saw in the stories of the Molly Maguires, these workers have to learn to be 'gentlemen'. John Armstrong tries to give his father an etiquette lesson concluding that 'the great secret of fine living is to keep clean at all times.' But sometimes the contradictions surface; when John tries to stop his father from drinking his tea from the saucer saying that 'it shows you've no time to wait for it to cool,' his father replies, 'Reckon we hain't, John, when we've got to go to work soon' (WTb,9).

At first glance, these tales of self-improving working men appear to be akin to the Horatio Alger stories of self-made men, particularly if we recall that Alger's stories were less stories of rags to riches than of, in John Cawelti's (1965, 101) phrase, rags to respectability. And the popularity of Alger's stories is often taken as a sign of the power of middle-class ideals of mobility and success, and of the consent given to those ideals by American workers. One may qualify this by disputing Alger's appeal to working-class readers. Warren Susman (1984, 244) argues that Alger aimed at rural and small-town audiences and that 'many city-dwellers found the works foolish and without interest'; moreover, he reminds us that the Alger stories 'may even have been enthusiastically purchased by many who did not believe in their basic value structure or who were not interested in the story as much as in the wealth of realistic detail.' In a similar vein, Daniel Rodgers (1978, 39) has concluded that 'Success writing was many things, but it was not a literature aimed at the industrial wage earner.'

But the Alger case is more complicated than this. For Alger did publish in the dime novel series and story papers that were aimed at industrial workers, like the *New York Weekly*; however, his 'reforming' fiction used the sensational format like a ventriloquist's dummy, trying to capture and reshape its audience. The line between the cheap stories, the sensational fiction that spoke in mechanic accents and resonated within working class cultures, and this reforming fiction is difficult to delineate exactly; it was a boundary that shifted within communities of different sizes, class composition, and ethnic cultures. Nevertheless, one can, I think, draw a line between Alger and Whittaker, for there are important differences between the Alger stories and Whittaker's workingman tales.[7]

Whereas Alger rarely started a boy in a factory, and never showed a boy at work in a factory (Rodgers 1978, 39), Whittaker's tales take boys in the factories as their subject. Moreover, they are also more thoroughly devoted to the *climb* up the ladder than the Alger stories because luck — saving the rich man's daughter, befriending the wealthy young guardian — plays little or no role in them. Job Manly climbs step by step. Far from being accounts of self-made men according to bourgeois standards of success, the Whittaker tales are closer to the ethic embodied in the principles of the Knights of Labor: 'men wholly developed in all the attributes of manhood can not become accumulators. It is only towards those possessing special qualifications of management, of speculation and of foxcraft that the flow of accumulated wealth centres' (McNeill 1886, 484). Speculation and foxcraft, the qualifications of accumulators, are not honorific terms. Job Manly is not a manager, speculator or fox: he wants to '*make things*'.

Thus, the two contradictory narrative formulas — the romance of contests and battles and the story of education and self-improvement — involve a real ideological contradiction which it is the task of the story to resolve. On the other hand there is the ethic of solidarity and mutualism, of the unity of the workers in a strike, of the readiness of the older workers to teach the hero, an ethic that is often tied to manhood based around the sociality of the saloon and the code of the most popular sport (to judge from the *National Police Gazette*), boxing. On the other hand, there is the more individualist ethic of hard work and raising oneself, what David Montgomery (1967, 204) has called 'the ideological syndrome of "free agency", self-improvement, and temperance'. Though the narrative patterns are borrowed from pre-existing generic conventions, they are adapted to work out a genuine ideological antinomy in producer manhood — how to reconcile mutualism with self-advancement. Perhaps the starkest expression of the antinomy is in *John Armstrong, Mechanic*. One sees examples of both ethics: at one point he invokes the mutualist ethic at its most extreme, calling for a general strike: 'If every workman in the United States struck to-morrow on a common plan, they would be masters of the whole country' (WTb,12). But at another moment, he overrides the mutualist ethic of the stint, 'undermining' his fellow workers by enforcing a speedup. Later, when John is caught in the middle of a strike as an assistant superintendent, he decides to join the strikers; he comes and speaks to them, affirming his solidarity. But as he leaves the union meeting, he turns to his father and says that he has decided 'to go to the top of the ladder, and show my fellow workmen how to follow' (WTb,16). This is one attempt to square the circle.

Other attempts to reconcile self-advancement with mutualism produce a variety of plot resolutions, resolutions that often resemble the 'labor panaceas' of the time, the imagination of solutions to what the labor leader George McNeill (1886, 459) called the 'inevitable and irresistible conflict between the wage-system of labor and the republican system of government', solutions which included cooperatives and profit sharing.[8] For John Armstrong, politics becomes the resolution; to be elected mayor is to be a representative, to climb to the top of the ladder while remaining true to his fellows. In *A Knight of Labor*, Job Manly sets up a profit-sharing system where his workers own stock in the company. This device, also used in Martin Foran's labor novel, *The Other Side*, may seem artistically mechanical and politically hopeless but it is narratively perfect, enveloping both Job's 'rise in life' and the image of the cooperative commonwealth. Only in *Larry Locke, The Man of Iron; Or, A Fight for Fortune. A Story of Labor and Capital* (WTd) does the hero, a craneman in a steel works who leads a strike and is the Master Workman of the Knights of Labor, resist the lure of the ladder: when offered a share in the profits of the mill, he turns it down: 'I'd rather be a Master Workman than own a mill, anytime.'[9]

One can get a sense of the power of the Whittaker working-man stories both in their evocation of 'manliness' and in their labored attempts to reconcile self-improvement with mutualism by looking at an autobiography of an iron puddler a couple of years younger than Larry Locke. James J. Davis, whose autobiography, *The Iron Puddler: My Life in the Rolling Mills and What Came of It*, was published in 1922, was born in Wales in 1873 and came to the United States in 1881; he began working in a nail factory at eleven, in the same year that the story of Larry Locke was appearing, and a year later became a helper to an iron puddler. When he came to write his autobiography forty years later, he wrote a book that reads like a workingman hero dime novel.

It is perhaps not surprising. In a discussion of the theory and politics of popular memory, a group of Birmingham cultural historians argue that 'the cultural features of [oral history and autobiographical] accounts are not simply the product of individual authorship; they draw on general cultural repertoires, features of language and codes of expression which help to determine what may be said, how and to what effect. In charting such repertoires, we might start, for example, from the repeated observation of the centrality of storytelling to working class accounts of social reality' (Popular Memory Group 1982, 229). They go on to argue that certain events become 'salient experiences', organizing accounts and highlighting an author's social position. I think one can find in Davis' autobiography a cultural repertoire, a way of telling stories, and a choice of salient experiences that is remarkably similar to the workingman hero dime novels.

There is no evidence that Davis read Whittaker's stories, nor even that he read the nickel libraries or story papers. He does say of himself and his siblings that:

> We were fluent readers, much better readers than our parents, but we had no books. We took the *Youth's Companion*, and it was the biggest thing in our lives. Every week we were at the post-office when the *Companion* was due. We could hardly wait, we were so eager to see what happened next in the 'continued' story. Surely so good a children's paper as the *Youth's Companion* could never be found in any country but America (Davis 1922, 72).

The *Youth's Companion* was one of the most respectable of children's story papers, still suspicious of the absence of parents and the melodramatic heroism of the Horatio Alger stories (Rodgers 1978, 142-144). But the stories Davis tells of his own exploits would lead one to think that he either read the *Youth's Companion* as if it were a Whittaker tale, or, more likely, that the final phrase about 'so good a children's paper' is an adult repression of a wider range of reading in the cheap stories than *Youth's Companion*.

For example: Whittaker's Larry Locke wins his sobriquet of 'boy of iron' in the first installment not from his work in the iron mill but from his victorious fistfight with a bully, 'the terror of all the 'prentices in the mill'. And Davis opens his autobiography with these words:

> A fight in the first chapter made a book interesting to me when I

was a boy. I said to myself, 'The man who writes several chapters before the fighting begins is like the man who sells peanuts in which a lot of the shells haven't any goodies.' I made up my mind then that if I ever wrote a book I would have a fight in the first chapter.

So I will tell right here how I whipped the town bully in Sharon, Pennsylvania (Davis 1922, 17).

The 'fistic duel', as it was called in Tony Pastor's dime novel, *Down in a Coal Mine*, has a place of honor in these stories; it is a 'salient experience', a structuring event in the history of 'manliness'. Another such event is the public speech: recall that one of the climaxes of the John Armstrong story came when he, unaccustomed to public speaking, made his first speech to the striking iron workers, affirming his solidarity and urging caution. And the climax of Davis' autobiography also comes with a speech, as he dissuades his fellow workers from striking: '"Men," I said, "I'm a newcomer here and I never made a speech in my life."' Like John Armstrong his plea for caution wins out over the trouble makers. And Davis adds: 'If this were a novel, it would be fine to record in this chapter that the orator who at the last moment turned the tide and saved the day became the hero of the union and was unanimously elected president. That's the way these things go in fiction. And that is exactly what happened. In due time I found myself at the head of the Local, and nearly every man had voted for me' (Davis 1922, 187-188).

Davis' conception of manhood, of a 'man of iron', is elaborated in metaphors drawn from iron puddling. He writes that

... man's nature is like iron, never born in a pure state but always mixed with elements that weaken it. Envy, greed and malice are mixed with every man's nature when he comes into the world. They are the brimstone that makes him brittle. He is pig-iron until he boils them out of his system ... Lincoln was one who boiled it out in the fires of adversity. He puddled his own soul till the metal was pure, and that's how he got the Iron Will that was strong enough to save a nation ... The stubborn earth is iron, but man is iron too. (103, 109, 87).

This rhetoric leads him to scorn reformers and uplifters who see life in the mills as terrible: '"Men are ground down to scrap and are thrown out as wreckage." This may be so, but my life was spent in the mills and I failed to discover it ... I lusted for labor, I worked and I liked it' (97-98). It is a line that Job Manly might have spoken. But the rhetoric is also used to reinforce the racism

176

that was so central to nineteenth-century white popular culture; Davis says that 'Some races are pig-iron; Hottentots and Bushmen are pig-iron. They break at a blow. They have been smelted out of wild animalism, but they went no further; they are of no use in this modern world because they are brittle. Only the wrought iron races can do the work' (72). Davis also shared in the cultural form that best testifies to the contradictions of nineteenth-century racism; his greatest delight was performing in blackface in local minstrel shows.

Despite the confidence of the rhetoric of iron men and the narratives of fistfights, the autobiography is as split by the contrary ethics of mutualism and self-advancement as are the dime novels of Frederick Whittaker. In his chapter, 'The Puddler Has a Vision', he clearly speaks in the accents of mutualism: 'Love of comrades had always been a ruling passion with me. I joined my union as soon as I had learned my trade, the Amalgamated Association of Iron, Steel and Tin Workers of North America [it is also Larry Locke's union] ... Sympathy is the iron fiber in men that welds him to his fellows' (134). But in other places he defends the wage system and affirms its mobility; he moves 'from tin worker to small capitalist' saying that 'the laborer who does not turn capitalist and have a house and garden for his old age is lacking in foresight.' As much as one has sympathy for the underdog, 'the upper-dog must be the better dog or he couldn't have put the other dog down' (137). His story is filled with contempt for communists and anarchists who are slackers and sick men, not unlike those in John Barrett's stories, to which I will turn later. Davis' solution lies in a school for orphans sponsored by the Loyal Order of Moose, a solution not unlike Job Manly's profit-sharing carriage factory, and in his rhetorical figures, which, like Whittaker's, have their power: 'I have been a puddler of iron and I would be a puddler of men. Out the best part of the iron I helped build a stronger world. Out of the best part of man's metal let us build a better society' (275).

Whittaker also finds his most successful resolution of the antinomy of mutualism and self-advancement in a rhetorical figure, one with particular significance: the phrase 'knight of labor'. Here the two plots and two ethics are violently juxtaposed, and, since this metaphor is the name of the leading working class organization of the 1880s, it is worth looking at in some detail.

The strangeness of the term, 'knights of labor', struck German socialists of the time as one of the pecularities of the Americans.

Friedrich Engels (1887, 494) spoke of the Knights, 'the first national organization created by the American working class as a whole', as 'a truly American paradox, clothing the most modern tendencies in the most medieval mummeries'. One of the sources of Engels' knowledge of American workers was his correspondent, Friedrich Sorge, and Sorge too, in his articles about the American labor movement for *Die Neue Zeit* (1891-1895, 247-248), noted the paradox of the Knights: 'At first sight it appears strange that in this great republican community secret organizations, not by any means only the Knights, are able to achieve such importance. Undoubtedly the affected secretiveness, the stuff of ceremonies, and the obsession with titles of the Anglo-Saxon natives (other people's also) places the American folk character in an unfavorable light.' But, after citing Marx's comments in the *Eighteenth Brumaire* about the ruses of class representation, he concludes that there is no contradiction between secret organizations and republican institutions: 'the rubbish of secret orders and ceremony in the United States points simply to a certain youthfulness, an immaturity in the movement, as in the life of the people, and is deliberately cultivated by clever intriguers, petty-bourgeois reformers, quacks and politicians.' In a way Sorge was correct, not so much in the deliberate cultivation of secrecy by intriguers, but in the relation of secrecy to a relatively undeveloped working class movement. The secret Knights were a descendent of organizations like Lippard's Brotherhood of the Union; indeed a short history of the Knights of Labor by its founders opens with the invocation, 'Philadelphia, the City of Brotherly Love, the home of Lippard and of the Brotherhood of the Union, has the honor of being the birth-place of the Noble Order of the Knights of Labor' (McNeill 1886, 397). And the early, secret Knights were often accused of being connected to the Molly Maguires. This secrecy added to the power of their image in popular fiction and the popular culture at large. Nevertheless, the Knights abandoned their oaths and complete secrecy as they grew more powerful, and Frederick Whittaker's Job Manly gives a sense of their image in the 1880s: 'He found no terrible secrets in the initiation, but only a set of signs and grips by which the members recognized each other at times when a strike was on foot' (WTe,19). But if the secrecy began to fade as the organization grew, the 'medieval mummeries' did not.

There were those at the time who thought the name not well chosen. S.M. Jelley (1887, 196), in a description of the Knights of

Labor, noted in 1887 that 'many of the Knights have expressed themselves to the effect that the term is too much like those of orders with which the Knights are distinctly at war.' And this was true: the knight is accented in a variety of ways in the late nineteenth century. There was a revival of interest in chivalry throughout American society in the 1880s, and it usually was the basis of a conservative ethos; Henry Seidel Canby noted that in the 1890s, historical romances, books like Charles Major's bestselling *When Knighthood Was in Flower* (1898), became 'a landslide, millions of copies circulating among all classes except the proletariat'.[10] It was against this revival of chivalry, largely anti-republican and anti-egalitarian, that Mark Twain set his contradictory novel of the Connecticut Yankee, the mechanic Hank Morgan, in King Arthur's Court.

Despite this occasional sense that the rhetoric of chivalry belonged to anti-republican and anti-producer discourse, the term, 'knight of labor', is usually used as a popular honorific in working class culture; in his autobiography, Joseph Buchanan (1903, 172), a labor agitator and editor, will unself-consciously refer to someone as 'a true knight and my trusting friend'.

The 'knight of labor' makes one of its earliest appearances in the dime novel in the stories of Frederick Whittaker, beginning with *Larry Locke, the Man of Iron*.[11] Larry Locke, a craneman in a steel mill, becomes an organizer of the 'Amalgamated Union of iron-workers' and a Master Workman of the Knights of Labor. Larry Locke's story has the subtitle, 'a story of labor and capital'; and, unlike the others, with their subtitles of his 'rise in life', making 'his way in the world', and 'from the bottom to the top of the ladder', it has little of the self-advancement plot and much of the mutualist plot. Larry marries another orphan, Red Moll, and though they have a respectable household, he does not go through the night school education and the reform of manners and speech the other Whittaker heroes do. His respectable marriage and home are threatened when he is robbed of his mortgage money and unjustly arrested; however, at the end, after all is won and he is made a manager, he turns down a chance to share in the profits:

> ... a workman I am, and always shall be. The Knights of Labor made me what I am ... Till there are no more bosses and slaves, and till the time when work won't be looked on as a favor to be asked, I'm going to stick to the Knights. I'd rather be a Master Workman than own a mill, anytime. When the time comes that every honest workman in

America belongs to the Order, and all stick together, as we should do, every workingman shall see more happiness, than he ever saw before. Heaven send the time, and God speed the just aims of the KNIGHTS OF LABOR! (WTd, 40).

Larry Locke is the hero of mutualism and solidarity, Whittaker's one Master Workman.

The story is in part a straightforward exposition of the principles of the Knights, first as the organizer arrives and explains the Order to the iron-workers, and second, in the trial of Larry Locke for assault. The trial establishes that the Knights do not require false testimony and absolute secrecy, the old accusations against the Molly Maguires. When a newly initiated Knight is nervous about revealing the aims of the Order on the witness stand, he is told that there is no secrecy: 'the objects of the Knights ... are to raise the condition of the workingmen of this country in the scale of civilization, and to enable them to live in greater comfort.' And when Larry himself takes the stand, he gives an eloquent account of the Knights. However, perhaps because there is some overlap in the story between the Knights and the Amalgamated Union, there is little exploration of the figure of the 'knight of labor' itself.

This elaboration of the 'knight of labor' comes in a more problematic story of early 1884, Whittaker's *A Knight of Labor; or, Job Manly's Rise in Life. A Story of a Young Man from the Country*. In this story Job Manly arrives from the country to work in a carriage factory, and finds a union shop. Far from echoing Larry Locke, Job refuses to join the pernicious 'lords of labor', and is persecuted by his fellow workers. Later, another worker says that he is 'beginning to sour on the Order ... I don't see where the good comes in. The Order never yet made a strike succeed.' To which Job replies: 'Is it beginning to make you feel that you are the slaves and the men who control the Order are masters? ... I defy any society or Order, whatever it may be, that tries to stop me from going to work' (WTe,17). However, as the greenhorn becomes more experienced in the shop he learns the values of solidarity and joins the Union and the Order: 'He began to appreciate how they must have hated him before ... they were not by any means the men he had pictured them [that is, villains]; but, on the contrary, simple, unlettered workmen, who were afraid they might lose the means of making a living by reasons of the selfishness of their employers, and so had combined together to make the employer do as they wished'

(WTe,19). By the end, when Job owns and runs a carriage factory, we see 'Dignity Lodge K. of L.': 'The order that Job once thought to be his persecutor had turned out, in his prosperity, to be the best friend he had, and he had given the building for the use of the new Lodge thereof' (WTe,36).

This story ends up extolling the Knights of Labor all the more effectively partly because of Job's initial hostility toward them, but also because of its use of the figure of the 'knight of labor' itself. In disentangling a popular metaphor, it is useful to consider its contraries, the terms that are counterposed to it; often the power of the figure lies in its condensation of several semantic oppositions. There are at least four such oppositions working in the figure of the 'knight of labor', and one sees these in Whittaker's tale. The first sets knights against monarchs and aristocrats. In an analogical construction, the contemporary social order is viewed through the lens of an earlier social cleavage. So as accumulators and non-producers are stigmatized as an aristocracy, as lords of labor and as monarchists subverting the republic, the workers are seen as knights, as vassals: George McNeill (1886, 463) writes that 'the cotton oligarchy (lords of the loom) ... [are] amassing princely fortunes, and creating in our midst a vassal or permanent wage-labor class.' Whittaker does not use the opposition in exactly this way, but his narrative does move from a vision of the evil 'lords of labor' to the good 'knights of labor'.

The second opposition is a diachronic rather than a synchronic construction; it sets the pre-capitalist values associated with knights against the new capitalist order. David Montgomery (1980, 204) notes this, writing that 'the workers' mutualistic ethic had pre-capitalist sources ... The very name "Knights of Labor", and the Order's incessant appeal to "chivalry" against gluttonous commercialism underscore this romantic use of popular memories and traditions, just as did the medieval pageantry of anarchist parades, the ornate regalia of craft unions, and the invocation of crafts' patron saints.' This use of chivalry against the present is clearly found in Whittaker's story, particularly in the character of Axel Petersen, the 'Norse' nobleman and master craftsman who represents a time and place where there is no division of labor: 'we are taught our trade from the bottom to the top' (WTe,5). Axel teaches Job 'what he himself knew, not only of manly exercises, but of the work of his trade, and of the learning that is necessary if a man wants to get on in the world' (WTe,7). In a reverse of Twain's Hank Morgan, Axel is a combination of a medieval knight and artisan who comes into Job's present.

However, this temporal opposition is also often inverted in the popular rhetoric, as the knights of *labor*, the aristocracy of *toil*, are posed against the knights of old. At a later point in Whittaker's often contradictory story, Axel, who is no longer a figure of the ideal artisan but has become Count Smedburg, asks Job: 'A knight of labor? What do you mean by that? Labor is a thing to be avoided; and no gentleman labors if he can help himself.' But, disinherited for his love of a commoner, Axel comes to learn the nobility of labor: 'I will go to *work*, as you say. I will take care of my wife.' Job can then say that Axel too is a 'true Knight of Labor, and that is a title I value more than you can value all your proud titles of nobility' (WTe,26).

The final meaning of the knight lies in its relation to the lady, its place in the rhetoric of working class manhood. During a long romantic interlude, Job Manly tells Cora: 'I am no knight of the old times, to go about robbing peasants and calling on the name of my lady. I am a knight of the new time, Miss Cora — a knight of labor ... a true Knight of Labor would always work hard to deserve his lady. I told you that I knew I was your inferior [she is a schoolteacher], and I was only good enough to lean on in time of trial, but anything further I knew was out of my power. Well, now I have resolved to end this and know my fate, be it bad or good. I am able to support a wife and I ask you to be mine' (WTe,24,26). Of course she accepts; as the advertisement had promised, she brings out the facets of this rough diamond, reflecting to herself that 'He had grown to a man. What a change!'

Thus the ideals of chivalry come together with the notion of manliness, of a 'manly job'. In the midst of a challenge to the present order these stories drape themselves in the costumes of a past order; the knight reconciles the story of education, undergoing trials of self-improvement to be worthy of a lady, with the story of 'fistic duels' and secret brotherhoods, the ideology of self-advancement with the ideology of mutualism.

However Whittaker was not the only dime novelist to tell stories of knights of labor. Six months after the conclusion of Whittaker's *A Knight of Labor; or, Job Manly's Rise in Life. A Story of a Young Man from the Country* in the *Beadle's Weekly* issue of 28 June 1884, the *New York Weekly* began serializing John E. Barrett's *A Knight of Labor; or, The Master Workman's Vow* (Bb). Barrett was less of a novel-wright than Whittaker; he may have written as few as four story paper serials. And he had a significant role in the labor movement; an associate of Terence Powderly, the Grand Master Workman of the Knights of Labor, in Scranton, Pennsylvania, he was born in Ireland, arrived in the United States in 1871, and was the editor of the Scranton *Truth* after 1884 (Powderly 1940, 237).

Barrett had written a serial for the *New York Weekly* in 1877 about the railroad strike, *Love and Labor; or, The Perils of the Poor. A Tale of the Present Great Strike* (Ba), and both *Love and Labor* and the 1884 *A Knight of Labor* have a similar plot. Neither are stories of the education of a young mechanic; rather they are tales of workingmen unjustly arrested and imprisoned. In both stories, an opposition is set up between the great city, New York, and the milltown in Pennsylvania. In both stories, when a young man or young woman secretly leaves for New York, a working-man is accused of his or her murder; after a series of adventures, the young runaway sees a newspaper account of the trial of the accused, and, in a variation of the old fantasy of attending one's own funeral, they return and reveal themselves, clearing the workingman. The first story is set against the 1877 strike, and a locomotive fireman, Harry Hinton, a moderate but respected leader of the striking railroad men, is accused, in the midst of a battle between the vigilance committee and the crowd, of murdering his sweetheart. Harry's individual plight is paralleled to that of the strikers, and it is not until Annie, who had fled to New York because of a misunderstanding, returns that both Harry and the strikers are victorious; Harry becomes a mine superintendent and marries Annie.

A Knight of Labor is slightly more complex. Here Ruth Watkins, the daughter of Reese Watkins, a steel worker and the master workman of the Knights of Labor, runs off to New York with Basil Brandon, the son of the president of the steel works. The master workman had vowed to kill Basil if he dishonored his daughter, so when a corpse is found in the river, he is arrested for murder. The Knights rally behind him, but it is a losing struggle until Basil returns from his misadventures in New York, clears Watkins, and shows his honorable nature. The story ends with the cross-class marriage of the son of the steel magnate and the daughter of the master workman.

This story uses the Knights of Labor in two quite different ways. First, like the Whittaker stories, it simply depicts the Knights, show-ing their solidarity, reciting statements of their principles, and generally serving the educative and informative function that has always characterized popular fiction. One sees the Knights rally behind Reese Watkins when he is beaten and called a tramp by the people at the millionaire's home, and hears their class-inflected, masculinist rhetoric: 'let us teach those ruffianly aristocrats, who are not content with squeezing out our life-blood on low wages, but who also want to invade the sanctity of our homes, and sacrifice the purity of our daughters, that there is a God in Israel, and that they are not yet beyond the reach of law' (Bb,30). The reader also learns that the Knights are neither 'nihilists' nor 'communists'. One of the evil characters is Facility Jack Dabble, a lazy, alcoholic and extremist follower of the anarchist Most; though he begins as a member of the Knights assembly, his attempt to burn their hall and kill a newsboy lead to his expulsion, after which he goes to work for the capitalists in their attempt to frame Reese. This strenuous anti-radicalism (when the story was reprinted in the Log Cabin Library, the scene depicted on the cover had the caption: 'The powerful young blacksmith seized the communist and shook him vigorously') seems to be common to dime novels, both in the workingmen tales and in the range of stories which set detectives after anarchists and communists (see, for example, Anthony P. Morris's *Old Cincinnati on his Mettle; or, On the Trail of the Anarchists* [M]).

However, the Knights have another function in this story which is integral to the plot, and not merely an informative illustration. When Basil, the son of the steel works president, returns from the great city, he comes in disguise as Dick Russell, looking for work in the steel mill. He is told by a Knight that there is a strike brewing, that, though the Order opposes strikes, in this case there is no other solution. Russell's first reaction is to insist on his 'right' to work and take someone else's place: 'Is not this a free country? Can I not sell my labor for what I please?' 'Yes, I suppose you can,' he is told, 'but if you be much of a man, and I think you are, it will make you feel mighty mean when you see the streets of Throckton filled with idle men, to think that you are eating the bread that belongs to some little family ... Join us. Stand with us, and assist us in resisting what is an injustice to yourself as well as to us. You will find that the honorable, manly course to pursue' (Bb,27). Russell is convinced of the 'honorable, manly course' and becomes a Knight of Labor. After he reveals himself as the missing Basil and clears the master workman, he intercedes for the men with his father, the president of the steel works, and becomes the superintendent, rescinding the wage cut. But it is only after he has taken the guise of a workingman, and been accepted as a Knight of Labor, that Basil is worthy to marry Ruth, the daughter of the master workman. The cross-class marriage required an imaginary crossing of class by the young steel baron; rather than the workman revealed to be a gentleman, the gentleman becomes a knight of labor.

But Barrett's novel is not only one of manly knights of labor in the steel town of Throckton; a large portion of it takes place in New York, and its protagonist is not a knight of labor, but Ruth Watkins, a working girl. It is as if Barrett had fused in one story Frederick Whittaker's tales of working class manhood and Laura Jean Libbey's stories of working class womanhood, which first appeared in 1882, and to which I will now turn.

10

Only a Mechanic's Daughter

Three months after the conclusion of Frederick Whittaker's serial, *Larry Locke, the Man of Iron*, in the *Beadle's Weekly* of 12 January 1884, Larry's 'sister' appeared in the pages of the *Fireside Companion* in the first working-girl novel written by Laura Jean Libbey: *Leonie Locke; or, The Romance of a Beautiful New York Working-Girl* (LBa). Over the next twenty years, Leonie would be followed by many working-girls in the pages of the *Fireside Companion* and the *Family Story Paper* in serials by Libbey, Emma Garrison Jones, Lillian Drayton, Charlotte M. Stanley, and Mrs. Alex McVeigh Miller, among others. Though little collected and little studied, the working-girl novel is one of the major genres of the cheap stories, dominating a number of the major story papers and a host of cheap libraries.[1] It is also a central narrative of working class womanhood, resolving in a variety of imaginary ways the contradictions between wage work and the gender ideologies of the dominant culture. In what follows I want to look at the genesis of the working-girl story out of the crisis of the ideology of domesticity, at the ways that Libbey's narratives work, and, with the help of the autobiographical account of Dorothy Richardson, at the ways the stories of Leonie Locke were read and lived.

Like the stories of honest mechanics, stories of working women first appeared in the 1840s. Joseph Ingraham, whose *Fleming Field, the Young Artisan* was an early example of the mechanic genre, also wrote an early example of a working-girl story: his *The Beautiful Cigar Girl; or, The Mysteries of Broadway*, published in 1844, was a fictionalization of the Mary Rogers murder case, the same case that was basis of Poe's tale, 'The Mystery of Marie Roget'. However, as we saw with the tale of the mechanic, the story of the working woman was usually a set piece within the mystery of the city; and the tale of Nora, the handloom weaver's daughter in Lippard's *The Nazarene*, is the characteristic form of the working-girl tale in the 1840s.

The first full-fledged working girl heroine appeared in the wake of the public outcry about the plight of needlewomen in outwork and sweatshops in the 1860s. The penny press and the story papers declared themselves the champions of the 'poor seamstress'; indeed the editor of the *New York Weekly*, Francis S. Smith, a supporter of the Working Women's Protective Union (an association of middle class reformers which gave legal and employment assistance to working women), wrote a popular serial, *Bertha, the Sewing Machine Girl; or, Death at the Wheel*, in 1871, and, as Mary Noel (1954, 277-278) notes, 'practically every story paper had a crop of Berthas or factory girls in the seventies.' Smith's serial was quickly adapted for the melodramatic stage, and was produced at New York's Bowery Theater in August, 1871. According to Dorothy Pam (1980), who has written the major study of working-girl melodramas, *Bertha, the Sewing Machine Girl* was the first in a genre that was to last into the first decade of the twentieth century; they were part of a popular theater which had a working class audience and a repertoire clearly distinguished from that of the middle class theater.[2]

In the same year that Bertha, the sewing machine girl, made her appearance in the story papers and on the stage, Elizabeth Stuart Phelps published her novel of a mill town, *The Silent Partner*. The juxtaposition is telling, for Phelps' novel is one of the last in the extraordinary series of domestic novels of mid-century, and in its exploration of the alliance between Perley Kelso, the daughter of a 'gentleman manufacturer', and Sip, the factory girl, it marks the limits of the domestic ideology, and in some ways completes and transcends the domestic novel.

It is striking that none of the recent, ground-breaking interpretations of the domestic novel, neither those that celebrate it as a genuine women's fiction, 'a monumental effort to reorganize culture from the woman's point of view, ... remarkable for its intellectual complexity, ambition, and resourcefulness' (Tompkins 1980, 81), nor those that criticize it for its 'anti-intellectual sentimentalism' which 'provided the inevitable rationalization of the economic order' (Douglas 1977, 12-13), fully explains the reasons for the breakup of the domestic ideology and the demise of the domestic novel in the late 1860s, a collapse not only of a genre but also of a middle class hegemony over women's culture and the ideologies of womanhood.[3] I would suggest that the work of

Elizabeth Stuart Phelps, whose mother was a domestic novelist and who thus marked a second generation of the domestic novel, can be seen as a symptom of this crisis of sentimentalism in at least three ways. First, the most common suggestion about the decline of sentimentalism has centred on the traumatic cultural effects of the Civil War, which shattered the well-regulated kinship networks, domestic routines, and Protestant certainties of the white middle class household. That Phelps' first, extraordinarily popular novel, *The Gates Ajar* (1868), is explicitly an attempt to reconstruct the vision of a benign God and a domestic heaven in the face of the war dead, is testimony to the war's contribution to the erosion of the domestic ideology. A second form that the crisis of sentimentalism took was the 'discovery' of the productive marginality of middle class women, the naming of the idle, 'parasitic' woman. This took fictional form in the novels and stories of sick and invalid women, which Phelps began to write in the late 1870s and 1880s, a genre which gave stark testimony to the paralysis of sentimental ideology.[4]

However, the third force that broke up sentimentalism seems to me the most important: it was the new visibility of class, of working women in the culture. The domestic novel was largely blind to working class women; it was a genre based around the kin networks and households of the families of white merchants and manufacturers. The few domestic novels that treated factory life tended to use already anachronistic pictures of the early mill girls at Lowell as their examples of working women (Siegel 1981, 86-99); the boarding house system with its paternalistic attention to the moral education and supervision of the mill girls was the organizational equivalent of sentimental ideology. An anecdote that epitomizes the place of working women in sentimental culture is related in Anthony Wallace's (1978, 52) study of Rockdale, Pennsylvania. Wallace reconstructs the culture of a network of cultivated women of the 'managerial class' of Rockdale (manufacturers, mill owners, merchants, and gentlemen farmers, and their wives and children) through the correspondence of Clementina Smith and Sophie DuPont. At one point, Wallace notes, 'Clementina and Sophie read, and approved, a novel about a factory girl by the well known English authoress, Charlotte Elizabeth.' The plot of this novel, *Helen Fleetwood*, is a useful gauge against which to measure the works of Laura Jean Libbey: the heroine 'takes employment in the carding room of a great factory, perseveres in Christian virtue despite the coarseness of her companions and the hostility of the irreligious, and then returns to her village to die, still a maiden, of overwork, an unjust beating by a supervisor armed with an iron bar, and consumption.' Libbey's heroines, we will see, are quite different: they are identified with, not against, the other working girls, are too resourceful to be beaten by supervisors (though they are threatened), and they never die.

It was Elizabeth Stuart Phelps who first seriously treated working women in the domestic novel. Her 'silent partner' is the deaf-mute, Catty, who dies a redemptive death in a flood to cement a Christian sisterhood between the cultivated woman and the factory woman, both of whom decide not to marry. But the 'silent partner' is also all of the working women who demonstrate the ineffectiveness of Perley's sentimental philanthropy, the partner that comes to speak in her own accents (even though the content remains a version of sentimental Christianity) at the end of novel. 1871, thus, can stand as the end of the sentimental hegemony, marked by Phelps's post-sentimental novel of the 'labor question', and the appearance of a working class heroine of stage and story paper, Bertha, the sewing machine girl.

So Laura Jean Libbey, the young college-educated daughter of a Brooklyn surgeon, came to a genre and a public that had already formed in the theaters and the story papers; but she also inherited the conventions of 'highly-wrought fiction', the story paper serials and dime novels of writers like Ann Stephens (the author of Beadle's first dime novel), Metta Victor (who wrote for Beadle and the *New York Weekly*), E.D.E.N. Southworth (who wrote mainly for the *New York Ledger*), Mary Agnes Fleming (who wrote mainly for the *New York Weekly*), and 'Bertha M. Clay' (Street & Smith's house pseudonym). These novels are too often subsumed under the category of domestic fiction, though, as Nina Baym (1984, 208) has shown, contemporary reviewers — when they noticed them at all — saw them as 'the domestic novel's antithesis: a feverish, florid, improbable, melodramatic, exciting genre'.

Baym suggests that 'what might have united the readers and writers of domestic and high-wrought fiction was their deployment of an essentially similar plot, the story of female trials and triumph' (209). However, this plot that unites 'women's fiction' at an fairly abstract level (indeed it can be seen in Libbey's working-girl novels as well) takes on quite different accents in its genteel and sensational versions, as Alfred Habegger's (1981, 209) fine reading of Southworth's *The Hidden Hand* demonstrates:

'If there is no reconciling [Southworth's heroine] Capitola with our sense of Victorian femininity, neither is there any reconciling her with the supergood, hard-working, self-disciplined heroines of so many 1850s women's novels.' As Sarah Josepha Hale, the editor of *Godey's Lady's Book*, wrote, Southworth's work was 'beyond the limits prescribed by correct taste or good judgement' (Freibert and White 1985, 70). These sensational serials attracted their wide audience among young working-class women and continued to flourish alongside the working-girl novels of the 1880s and 1890s.

Libbey's combination of the working-girl heroine and the sensational women's serial made her a star of the fiction industry and, by 1910, the *Bookman* was able to note that in the trade any book of the genre was known as a 'Laura Jean Libbey' (Peterson 1983, 20). Though there are stories of her teenage writings being accepted by Robert Bonner's *New York Ledger*, she began writing regularly for the *Fireside Companion* in 1882 at the age of twenty; in the next twenty years she wrote at least 52 different serials for two major story papers.[5] About seven of them are 'classic' working-girl stories; a number of others have closely related heroines despite their settings in Newport and other vacation spots of the rich.

Her intention, she wrote Robert Bonner, was to write '*young love stories* — pure, bright — with a vein of deep romance and pathos running through them — a story for the masses' (Walcutt 1971, 2:402). And a quick plot summary of *Leonie Locke; or The Romance of a Beautiful New York Working-Girl* yields the basic Libbey formula. Leonie, new to the great city, is forced to go to work because of a sick father who soon dies. She attracts the unwanted attentions of the villain, Charlie Hart, who is the foreman at the shop where she works as a fur sewer. She is rescued by the junior member of the firm, the wealthy young Gordon Carlisle, and they fall in love. The plot, which is a series of abductions and escapes, pivots around two issues: the problem of the cross-class marriage with its contraries of love and money, and the dilemma of a forced and false marriage. The first of these is relatively straightforward. The wealthy young man must choose between being disinherited and giving up love. Gordon chooses Leonie, rightly according to Libbey's meta-physic of love. Unfortunately, his mother deceives both Gordon and Leonie, telling Leonie that Gordon would never choose her over money, and telling Gordon that Leonie chose some quick cash over a disinherited son. The roles are then reversed; by a stroke of fortune, Leonie becomes an heiress, and Gordon, disinherited and disguised, becomes her impoverished tutor. At the end, there is a much delayed recognition and explanation; they realize that each has chosen love over money, and they marry, getting both love and money.

The second dilemma is somewhat stranger, but no less characteristic. The villain, after several abductions and affronts, deceives the heroine into marriage (in *Leonie Locke* Leonie signs a paper she thinks is a charity but is really a declaration of marriage in invisible ink), thus putting her into his power and separating her absolutely from the hero. Eventually, the falseness of the marriage, never consummated, is exposed, and she is free to marry the hero. The significance of this plot can be seen in a variety of striking titles: 'Kidnapped at the altar', 'did she elope with him?', 'was she sweetheart or wife?', 'married by mistake'. This 'wife in name only' plot, to use the title of an often reprinted Bertha Clay novel, allows Libbey and other novelists to combine in the same story a romance leading to the happy ending of marriage *and* a displaced marriage story, often implicitly criticizing the metaphysics of romantic love, where the heroine is subject to a villainous husband who 'loves' her. Thus the novel is both a romance and a masked divorce story.[6]

There are three principal aspects of the Libbey novels that I want to look at: the return of the seduction plot and its meaning for working class womanhood; the significance of the transformation of working-girl into lady; and the way these stories were read. One of the striking characteristics of the working-girl story is the return of the seduction plot to the novel of womanhood. Earlier, I cited Nina Baym's argument about the importance of the eclipse of the seduction plot in the domestic novel of mid-century; its return is equally significant. The seduction/rape plot is, I have argued, more a story about class than gender, and it is in these novels of class that it once again becomes central. The seducers are all of a higher class than the working girl; some are only foremen using their power in the shop, but more often they are sons of the factory owner with no respect for a working girl. These are also seduction tales from the women's point of view, unlike those of Lippard; here we find working women successfully defending themselves against the villains. Nevertheless, there are similarities: Leonie is held captive in a red-brick building that houses a young gentlemen's club, not unlike Monk Hall. But these are all stories of Pamela, not of Clarissa. None of

Libbey's heroines is seduced or raped; they always escape in the nick of time. In a sense these are tales of heroic working class resistance to the unwanted advances of the wealthy and powerful.

It has been suggested that this concern for the working woman's 'virtue', and the centrality of this resistance to seduction and rape, is a conservative aspect of Libbey's novels, an acquiescence to the dominant genteel sexual codes. Cathy Davidson (1981, 3-4) writes of 'Libbey's socially conservative fables' that 'all of the novels preached the same simple and not very original message: A young girl who remains virtuous (i.e., virginal) can ultimately expect to secure not only a husband and happiness, but a fortune too.' However the concern for 'virtue' is more complicated. Just as the rhetoric of self-improvement found in the Alger tales changes when it is narrated in tales of working class manhood, so the meaning of 'virtue' shifts in tales of working class womanhood. For in the rhetoric of the late nineteenth century bourgeois culture, a working woman could not be virtuous, regardless of her virginity; in the memorable phrase from an 1874 working woman's letter to the *Workingman's Advocate* (that Alice Kessler-Harris [1982, 75] has called our attention to), 'why is it can a woman not be virtuous if she does mingle with the toilers?' Middle class popular novels of mid-century often 'revolved around the question of whether mill employment was compatible with virginity' and usually concluded that it was not (Siegel 1981, 87).

An indication of how widespread the sense of the immorality of factory women was can be seen in as relatively sober a work as Carroll Wright's *The Working Girls of Boston*. This 1884 report of the Massachusetts Bureau of Statistics of Labor concludes with a section on 'the moral condition of working girls': 'it has often been said that the shop girls are an immoral class, that it is largely from their ranks that prostitution is recruited, and the vile charge has often been made that in great stores where many girls are employed, an engagement often depends upon the willingness of the saleswoman or shop girl to become the intimate friend of either the proprietor or head of department. ... In addition to our desire to ascertain the general moral condition which surrounds the working girls of Boston, we have had a very strong desire to ascertain the truth or falsity of these damaging assertions and charges' (Wright 1884, 118). His conclusion is that 'the working girls are as respectable, as moral, and as virtuous as any class of women in our community' (118). Nevertheless the energy and prominence that Wright gives the matter indicates the public perception.

One solution to this collective reputation was the organization of working girls' clubs in the 1880s and 1890s by an alliance of working women and middle class reformers. Priscilla Murolo, in a study of the working girls' clubs of New York (1981, 10-11), has argued that 'for working women, individual sexual decorum was not only an end in itself but also a means to a collective end. . . . To working women in the clubs, "being right" was not a private matter between the individual and god. It was a matter of public concern and one which helped define an individual's relationship to other women of her class. She could practice group solidarity and represent them well. Or she could adopt an ethic of individualism and risk lowering an already-low public opinion about the character of the "working girl"'[7] The working girls' clubs were, one might say, the organizational equivalent of the working girl novel, as the boarding house system had been to the sentimental novel. Thus one might see Laura Jean Libbey's working-girl narratives as lying between Wright's investigations and conclusions and the articles published in *Far and Near*, the journal of the Working Girls' Clubs, under titles like 'Why Do People Look Down On Working Girls?'. Neither the reformer's scientific discourse nor the actual writing of the working girls, they nevertheless must be seen as attempts not to mimic genteel codes of womanhood but to establish a working class virtue that was excluded from those genteel codes. That it shared certain key terms — particularly the association of virtue with virginity — does not make it an identical discourse. In the defiant speech of Leonie Locke — 'You are no gentleman, sir . . . to insult an honest unprotected girl in this manner! . . . I am only a poor unprotected working-girl, but let me tell you this, sir: I would rather die — yes, die — than become your wife' (LBa, 1,3) — and in the hero's genuine respect — 'My sympathies always have been and ever will be, with those noble young girls who earn their bread by their own honest labor, . . . and every true gentleman will voice my sentiments. . . . And whenever I hear any one speak illy of a working-girl, I lose my respect for that person, for I know that they are shallow of heart and silly of head' (LBa, 7) — lie the burden of Libbey's novels. Unlike the seduction novels that occasionally occur in middle class fiction, which focus on the fallen woman,[8] the Libbey stories are tales of the woman who does not fall, despite drugs, false marriage, physical violence, and disguise. Against middle class sympathy for the fallen is set working class virtue.

There are three aspects of this 'virtue', this working class womanhood, that stand in striking contrast to the middle class womanhood of the late nineteenth century. One is the attitude toward manual work itself. Though one will not find in these stories the same kind of pride in craft and ethic of workmanship that one finds in the honest mechanic tales, there is a strong sense of the dignity of work. Second, there is an almost complete absence of the Christian piety and evangelism that characterize the domestic novel. Though these are often allegorical and typological novels, they are not based on Christian types. One is more likely to find tags from Shakespeare than from the Bible. The Christian metaphysic of redemptive love is replaced by a metaphysic of romantic love, one that Libbey herself promulgated in short columns of advice that accompanied her serials in the story papers. The full significance of romantic ideologies of love for ethnic working class women who grew up in households dominated by various forms of patriarchy and with equally various forms of women's power is an issue too complex to attempt to deal with here.[9] Suffice it to note that the Libbey novels presented love, sexuality, and marriage in individual terms that were in marked contrast to most working class families. Unlike the majority of Libbey's working women readers, who lived at home with their parents, Libbey's working-girls are usually orphans without siblings, unprotected but independent. The barriers to love and marriage are the machinations of the villains, not the objections of parents.

The third distinctive characteristic of the working class womanhood in these novels is the stress on physical action and violence. Sally Mitchell (1981, 151), discussing the British penny weeklies of the same era, notes that 'the chief difference between this fiction and the reading of the middle class ... is the overwhelmingly physical nature of the action.' The fistfights of the honest mechanic stories are replaced by a series of assaults, abductions and imprisonments. Throughout all of this the heroine not only maintains her virginity, but also proves to be an able and resourceful escape artist. Her abilities to fight back remind us that the working-girl heroine has a sister in the cheap stories who is even less bound by gentility, the western heroine, from Frederick Whittaker's 'Amazons' in the West to Edward Wheeler's Calamity Jane.[10] Since the western dime novels were less tied to the everyday reality of workers, they made fewer concessions to respectability. Thus, just as the outlaw flourished more in the mining camps of Leadville than in those of Pottsville, so a physically active, non-genteel woman flourished more in the streets of Deadwood than in those of New York. Nevertheless, from Capitola, the cross-dressing 'tomboy' who fights a duel in Southworth's 1859 *The Hidden Hand*, to Old Sleuth's 1885 *The Lady Detective*, 'a story of a woman placed in an essentially unfeminine position ... and more than holding her own with desperate law-breakers without any sacrifice of her womanly attributes', the heroines of the cheap stories skirt the boundaries of genteel codes.[11] Indeed, the predominance of representations of physical action and violence in the dime novels may also indicate a different accenting of 'virtue' in working class culture. Both Christine Stansell's study of working women of the Bowery in antebellum New York and Kathy Peiss's study of New York working women at the turn of the century suggest that young working women developed an etiquette and sexual style that was markedly different from middle class 'respectability', and that this can be seen in dress, dance styles, and public behavior at commercial amusements and in the street. And it is striking that the Libbey novels rarely take place in the home; the working-girl finds both villain and hero in public places: in the streets, on the trains and streetcars, in the parks, and in the workshop.

This reading of the Libbey novels as tales of working women's resistance and manifestos of a working class womanhood and 'virtue' is, however, thrown into question by two transformations that occur in the stories: the rapid move out of the world of work and shop, and the revelation that the working girl is an heiress, that she is really a 'lady'. As Joyce Shaw Peterson (1983, 26) argues: 'Libbey openly decries the popular tendency to equate working girl with easy morality and disreputability and replaces this stereotype with an equation of working girl with innocence and misfortune worthy of respect and sympathy. But Libbey's equation is proved false at the end of the book when it is revealed that the working girl is really a born lady and only taking her rightful status at last.' Indeed, often, the revelation occurs long before the end of the book; Leonie Locke becomes an heiress about a third of the way into the story, and her life as a garment worker comes to an end. However, as my earlier argument about similar transformations in stories of working-men/nobles might indicate, I do not think that this magical transformation should be interpreted as 'proving false' the earlier vindication of the working woman's virtue or as 'eroding' Libbey's 'assertions of democratic values'. Indeed there are good reasons for interpreting this transformation in exactly the opposite way, as the culminating assertion of the working woman's virtue and heroism.

First, if one looks at the narratives of factory women to which these stories respond, the reasons for their wish-fulfilling fantasy become clearer. In the stories of fallen women or of factory women beaten down to death (as in the story the Rockdale bourgeois women read), there is no magical transformation, no working woman revealed as a disinherited lady; the 'realism' of bourgeois fiction represented workers as victims, sometimes sympathetically, but always keeping them in their place. The working woman was neither a lady nor a cheated heiress. The working-girl novels, on the other hand, not only made her an active agent in her world, without minimizing the threats and hardships she faced, but also asserted that she had been cheated, that the babies had been switched in the cradles, that the evil stepsister was an usurper.

Libbey's central imaginary resolution — 'that the rich should wed with the poor ... just as the Lord intended it' (LBa,10) — stands as both a simple wish-fulfillment for her readers and as a utopian vision of reorganized society. But the marriage of the rich and the poor does not yield two rich people; all of Libbey's heroines are still 'working-girls' at the end. As the narrator says at the end of *Leonie Locke*:

> The great sensational story found its way into the daily papers, as sensational stories always do; and many a working-girl read the story of Leonie Locke, and their honest hearts thrilled as they read the story of her struggle against adverse fate. She had been a working-girl like themselves; she had known all their privations, the early rising, hurried toilet, and hurrying steps to the work-shop. She had known what it was to toil late and early for the sweet bread of life, and had known all their sorrows and the pitiful desolation and fear of being discharged from work.

Cinderella does not forget her origins.

For these are Cinderella stories; Libbey's novels that do not focus on working girls usually surround the heroine with evil and envious step-mothers and step-sisters that force her into a position not unlike that of a working girl or servant. And it is worth recalling that in non-capitalist tribute and kinship societies, the fairy tale was the story of peasants and slaves; the genealogical myths and legends were the legitimating narratives of the warrior and priestly classes. The importance of the Cinderella story in the working-girl narratives is, I think, a sign of the powerlessness of working women. Consider the differences between the stories of knights of labor and Libbey's ladies of labor. The magical transformation from working-girl to heiress is much more radical in Libbey; there is a more violent juxtaposition of the upper ten and the lower million, a juxtaposition emphasized by the shift of scene from the mill town to the great city of New York. (This geographical shift between a Pennsylvania mill town and New York is well illustrated in Barrett's *A Knight of Labor* which, as I noted, has a working-girl tale inset within the main story.) The mediations that make up the story in the workingman tales, the variety of virtues that make an honest mechanic — the acquisition of a craft, the solidarities of the union, the public life of local politics and courtroom scenes — are not present in the working-girl stories. These mediations structure and inflect class conflicts in the stories as in the small towns themselves. The working-girl stories tell of a class confrontation that is at once more direct, for theirs is a violent world of male predators and jealous rivals, and less social. The persecution of the working girl takes place in a private world of sexual harassment; the class conflict is condensed into the personal confrontation of a villainous boss and a virtuous working woman. The isolation of the heroine foregrounds the relative absence of friendships between women in the Libbey novels. Though active jealousy and the refusal to have 'girl friends' is a characteristic of Libbey's female villains, none of her heroines is able to establish more than fleeting friendships with other working girls. Dorothy Pam, whose study of the working-girl melodrama takes her into the first decade of the twentieth century, argues that it is not until after 1900 that the melodrama features scenes of solidarity between working girls.

There are several other fairy tale aspects to the stories that tell us to read the transformation as a metaphor: the working-girl is a working-girl *and* a lady. First, there is the inversion of the plot when the good wealthy lover is literally disinherited and returns to the working-girl-turned-heiress as a 'poor and obscure' tutor. The cross-class love affair is repeated in reverse, and he, to be worthy of the working-girl, must not only respect her but must also become a poor man. Second, the transformation of working-girl into lady almost always follows her closest encounter with death: in one story she is rescued from suicide in the East River; in another she has been tied to a railroad track and passes out; in a third she is about to be buried, pronounced dead by doctors, when a lover detects signs of life in the casket. The transformation is a rebirth, a second chance. Finally, in Libbey's novels, as in Whittaker's *Nemo*, there is a distinction within the upper ten between good and evil. The evil figures of wealth — the snobbish parents who disinherit the young man that loves the poor working-girl — are millionaires and capitalists. The good figures of wealth — the working-girl's real father — are judges, senators, generals and colonels: figures of the republic who have been led astray in some way and come to regret the actions that disinherit the working girls. A characteristic case in a quasi-working girl story, *Viola, the Beauty of Long Branch; or, Only a Mechanic's Daughter. A Charming Story of Love and Life at the Sea Shore* (LBd), sets Viola as her cousin's maid because her uncle, General Wallingford, disapproved of his sister's marriage to Richard Sterling, 'a handsome young mechanic'. By the end, Viola is rich, as a result of her father's invention, and the General's mistake in rejecting the mechanic is put to right.

These allegories are still under the sign of the patriarch; one could not argue that Libbey's novels are a part of a nineteenth century feminist culture any more than one could argue that Whittaker's and Barrett's stories of knights of labor are a 'proletarian fiction' in the sense of a revolutionary socialist culture. However, it is equally wrong to see Libbey's stories as simply 'socially conservative fables', agents of the dominant culture in colonizing working class imagination.

One avenue into the place of Libbey's novels in working women's reading and imaginations is the autobiographical narrative by Dorothy Richardson, *The Long Day: The Story of a New York Working Girl*, which was published in 1905, and which includes a discussion between women workers in a box factory of the novels of Laura Jean Libbey. It is not the most unequivocal source: little is known of Dorothy Richardson, of when the experiences related took place, or when the account was actually written. It seems clear that she was of a middle class background and did not share the culture of her fellow workers in the box factory. We hear those workers' voices through her prose and in the situations that she sets up. Nevertheless, the very contrast between her culture and theirs gives us some sense of working women's culture and the place of cheap stories in it. I want to look at two aspects of Richardson's account: the telling of the story of Libbey's *Little Rosebud's Lovers* to her by Mrs. Smith and Phoebe; and Richardson's own contradictory assessment of the popular novels.

When Mrs. Smith asks Dorothy Richardson, 'Don't you never

read no story-books?', Richardson enthusiastically replies that she does. But when asked whether she has read *Little Rosebud's Lovers*, she not only reveals that she has not, but that she has not read any novels by its author, 'a well-known writer of trashy fiction'. Indeed *Little Rosebud's Lovers; or, The Cruel Revenge* (LBc) was written by Laura Jean Libbey in 1886, and was reprinted many times after. It is not a working girl novel; rather it is a Cinderella tale. Little Rosebud, the daughter of a judge, is mistreated by her step-mother and step-sister, and, later, becomes a maid to her cousin. Though 'only a servant', she attracts two virtuous lovers and two villainous lovers, and is married twice leading to a variety of assaults, abductions and escapes. At the end, her marriage to one of the villains proves to be a false one — the magistrate's term of office had run out — and she is free and legally married to the hero who had rescued her from being buried alive.

Mrs. Smith proceeds to tell Dorothy Richardson the story of *Little Rosebud's Lovers*, and in that account there are several interesting emphases and discrepancies from which we might draw some suggestions about working women's readings of Libbey. First, Mrs. Smith puts a major emphasis on Rosebud's fall in fortunes, when she becomes homeless, without money, and abandoned by her 'husband'. In effect, she reads the story as if Rosebud were one of Libbey's working-girl heroines. Second, when confronted by a discrepancy in her account by Phoebe — how could Rosebud take the train to New York if she had no money (in fact, Libbey carefully allots Rosebud 'a hundred dollars or more' for her trip) — Mrs. Smith first says that rich men's daughters can travel anywhere on a pass, and then resorts to 'it's only a story and not true anyway.' (78) The investment that Mrs. Smith has in the story does not depend on its absolute fidelity to daily life, rather on the fact that it is 'more int'resting, besides being better wrote' than other novels. Furthermore, her reading of Rosebud as a helpless, penniless orphan in New York would be disrupted by a too close attention to her hundred dollars in gold coins or her privileges as a rich man's daughter on the trains.

What realism Mrs. Smith finds in Libbey is in her characterizations of typical men and women. She exaggerates the villainy of Libbey's female villains, and dwells on the men who are villains. Paul Howard, who is not one of Libbey's more developed characters, is elaborated by Mrs. Smith: 'he was a terrible man; he wouldn't stop at nothing, but he was a very elegant-looking gentleman that you'd take anywheres for a banker or 'Piscopalian preacher ... he just fascinated women, the way a snake does a bird, and he was hot stuff as long as he lasted, but the minute he got tired of you he was a demon of cruelty.' So the characters are re-interpreted through types known and imagined in the culture, types which are themselves modified by the popular stories.

Finally, and most unexpectedly, Mrs. Smith tells only the first half of the story, leaving her hearers to believe that Rosebud died of her sufferings. The miraculous rescue from being buried alive and the subsequent second marriage and happy ending are entirely left out of Mrs. Smith's account. This may be due to Richardson's editing, to the nature of serialization which must have left many stories half read and abandoned, or to a seemingly uncharacteristic preference for a tragic rather than happy ending. Louis Gold (1931, 48), who served as Libbey's secretary at one time, recalled that the happy ending of a wedding was invariable: 'only once did she write a story with an unhappy ending; the storm of protesting letters she received discouraged her from making another such blunder.'

What can we conclude from Richardson's story of Mrs. Smith's story of Libbey's story? Not much, perhaps. Clearly, the appeal of the basic wish-fulfillment had its power. Richardson tells of the women in the box factory choosing imaginary names for themselves out of the story books and Sadie Frowne, a New York garment worker, said of the romances of Charlotte Brame (a writer often linked to Libbey) that 'she's a grand writer and makes things just like real to you. You feel as if you were the poor girl yourself going to get married to a rich duke' (Katzman and Tuttle 1982, 56).

And there may be, indeed, a peculiar and unintended realism at work. In her discussion of aristocratic costume romances of the British penny weeklies, Sally Mitchell (1981, 158) argues that 'the absurd conventions of the aristocratic romance provided a set of characters and situations that were actually less foreign to working women than were those found in the domestic novels written for the middle class. Money and social position gave the Duke's daughter [like Rosebud] — at least in the novelist's imagination — a freedom of action unknown to the genteel governess or the cloistered daughter of the family.' Like the knights of labor, the ladies of labor borrowed older costumes to figure contemporary lives.

Dorothy Richardson's conclusions about the reading of her

fellow workers have a curious contradiction. At the end of her account, she writes that:

> It is a curious fact that these girls will not read stories laid in the past, however full of excitement they may be. They like romance of the present day, stories which have to do with scenes and circumstances not too far removed from the real and the actual. All their trashy favorites have to do with the present, with heroes and heroines who live in New York City or Boston or Philadelphia; who go on excursions to Coney Island, to Long Branch, or to Delaware Water Gap; and who, when they die, are buried in Greenwood over in Brooklyn, or in Woodlawn up in Westchester County. In other words, any story, to absorb their interest, must cater to the very primitive feminine liking for identity (Richardson 1905, 301).

This conclusion, which, as far as setting is concerned, is substantiated by a reading of Libbey, stands uneasily next to one of Richardson's earlier conclusions. When she described the plot of Alcott's *Little Women* to the other workers, she tells us, Phoebe's reaction was, 'that's no story at all — that's just everyday happenings. I don't see what's the use putting things like that in books ... They sound just like real, live people; and when you was telling about them I could just see them as plain as plain could be. ... But I suppose farmer folks likes them kind of stories ... they ain't used to the same styles of anything that us city folks are' (86). So a story, to be a story, had to be set in a contemporary time and knowable landscape, but its plot had to be out of the ordinary; 'everyday happenings', according to this working woman's aesthetic, did not make a story. The story was an interruption in the present, a magical, fairy tale transformation of familiar landscapes and characters, a death and rebirth that turned the social world upside down, making proud ladies villains, and working-girls ladies.

Conclusion: Happy Endings?

In 1900, the *Bookman* announced 'The Extinction of the Dime Novel' (Dred 1900). Though somewhat misleading — cheap sensational fiction continued to flourish into the twentieth century — it epitomizes a widespread and not inaccurate sense that the dime novel passes into history at the turn of the century. A number of publishers went out of business in the 1890s including Beadle and Adams, whose demise seemed to mark the end of an era. Both the dime novel and story paper formats were dying out in the face of the Sunday newspaper and the pulp magazines. Cheap libraries continued but were now entirely the provenance of children; as often happens, out-of-date popular fiction became children's fiction. By 1907, the *Atlantic Monthly* had published a eulogy of the dime novel, Charles M. Harvey's 'The Dime Novel in American Life'. Though Harvey's opening parallels that of W.H. Bishop, writing in the *Atlantic* 28 years earlier — 'Are not more crimes perpetrated these days in the name of the dime novels than Madame Roland ever imagined were committed in the name of liberty? It looks that way. Nearly every sort of misdemeanor into which the fantastic element enters, from train robbery to houseburning, is laid to them' — this is no longer a serious question for the *Atlantic*'s readers, and Harvey moves quickly to elaborate a newer and quite different view of dime novels. They now have become a token of nostalgia: 'What boy of the sixties can ever forget Beadle's novels!' He sketches the outlines of a history in which cheap fiction is no longer seen as the reading of working people but as the reading of all American boys. The central question has shifted from the paternalistic and humanistic one of Bishop: is this reading better than no reading? to the more general historical issue: 'what did the dime novel stand for? What

influence did it have on the minds of its readers? What forces did
it represent in the evolution of American society?' The answer
Harvey gives would have surprised any middle class critic of a
generation earlier: 'The aim of the original dime novel was to
give, in cheap and wholesome form, a picture of American wild
life.' And their influence is equally wholesome: they 'incited a
love of reading among the youth of the country. ... It can be
truthfully said that the taste and tone of the life of the generation
which grew up with these tales were improved by them.' Finally,
they are incorporated into the main current of American culture:
'From Beadle's day onward most of the dime novels have been
American. ... In reading them the American boy's soul soared
and sang.' It is a remarkable re-writing of the dime novel: no
longer is the archetypal reader the factory girl; no longer are they
the reading of the other, the 'lower classes' and the 'foreigners';
no longer need they be replaced with 'better literature' and more
uplifting reading. They are now 'our' collective American boyhood. Though Harvey's essay was an occasional one, it was
symptomatic; for this image of the dime novel has dominated
almost all subsequent histories and criticism.

Why this change in the image of the dime novel? Having
attempted to restore to the dime novel its mechanic accents, and
to replace it in the working class culture where nineteenth-
century observers originally found it, I will conclude by
suggesting that this cultural revaluation of the dime novel was
the result both of an ideological rewriting of the lineaments of
the dime novel, a rewriting prompted by the failure of leisure
reform in the face of the culture industry, and of a genuine
change in sensational fiction at the turn of the century, a change
that can be seen in other aspects of working class culture as well.

The rewriting of the meaning and character of the dime novel
is best seen in the celebration of the dime novel western and in
the myth of Horatio Alger. By the turn of the century, the dime
novel western had taken on a new cast, as the genteel tradition
came under attack from a new middle-class culture. As a result,
the nineteenth-century split between the genteel and dime-novel
western heroes was effaced, and, as Richard Slotkin (1985, 558-
559) notes, ironically 'the new "realistic" writers (Garland,
London, Norris, Wister) drew on the themes and interests of the
"red-blooded" dime-novel tradition, and asserted its authenticity
as a vision of western history; while the genteel, feminized,
historically pretentious tradition was dismissed as the product of
an effeminate sentimentality.' However, in this revaluation of the

dime-novel western, its mechanic accents were often obscured. The genre that had used the frontier setting not only for escapist adventure but to stage social conflicts through figures of bank and train robbers, striking cowboys and range wars, and to imagine the utopian social relations of a cooperative common-wealth, was incorporated, after the closing of the frontier and the defeat of populism, into a new elegiac myth of the West embodied in Owen Wister's *The Virginian* (1902), and coming to dominate much of twentieth-century American culture.[1]

If the appropriation of the dime-novel western involved a univocal reading of those stories, the canonization of Horatio Alger involved a strategic misreading not only of Alger but of his place in the history of the dime novel. I have already argued that Alger was not a typical dime novelist, but a ventriloquist using the dime format in order to reform working-class reading and culture. Though Alger's initial successes, the Ragged Dick series published in the respectable juvenile magazine *Student and Schoolmate*, were fairly well-received by reviewers who saw them as an alternative to dime novel fiction, his subsequent stories, published in Street and Smith's *New York Weekly*, were not particularly successful, suspected both by the genteel culture he represented and the sensational public he addressed. 'At the behest of his new publishers,' his most recent biographer (Scharnhorst 1985, 94) notes, 'Alger began at once to write more sensational and violent fiction.' This lost him the support of the librarians and reviewers of genteel culture without gaining him the support of a mass public: the several attempts to establish juvenile story papers based on Alger's moral fables were failures, and Scharnhorst (1985, 121) concludes that 'no one, it seems, was getting rich off Alger, least of all his publishers.' Indeed, Alger's greatest success comes after his death in 1899; not only did he find his largest readership between 1900 and 1915, but beginning in the 1920s his formulaic stories were interpreted as the archetypal narrative of capitalism. By the mid-twentieth century, Alger had become a part of the mythology of American capitalism, and stood as the quintessential dime novelist.[2]

Together, the revaluation of the dime novel western and the promotion of Alger as the typical dime novelist allowed an ideo-logical appropriation of the dime novel as the wholesome reading of American boys, telling tales of western expansion and inculcating the values of self-made success. But the need to thus appropriate the dime novel derived from the success of the culture industry and the failure of leisure reform. As Francis

Couvares (1984, 120) concludes in his cultural history of Pittsburgh, 'at the dawn of the twentieth century in Pittsburgh, commerce overmatched reform and contributed to the remaking of working-class culture. Militant leisure reform only accelerated the rush of working people (and many of their betters) into the arms of merchants of leisure who were fashioning a new mass culture.' The expansion of the culture industry led the cultural arbiters of the middle classes not only to abandon the hostility of their immediate predecessors toward the dime novel but to celebrate its 'Americanness'; as a fading cultural form, the dime novel was commonly invoked as a nostalgic sign of the past glories of popular culture and a measure of present degradation.

But the change in the image of the dime novel was not only a product of these ideological reevaluations and selective appropriations. For there were genuine changes in both sensational fiction and working class culture that left the dime novel behind, a vestige of the plebian, producer culture of the nineteenth century. These changes can be seen most dramatically in the fate of the dime novel detective and in the appearance of Frank Merriwell in the 1890s. Though I have not devoted a chapter to the dime novel detective, largely in order to avoid the twentieth-century reification of the detective story genre, I have repeatedly told the story of the increasing domination of the formulas of the dime novel by the detective. The process by which narratives of the city, of the Molly Maguires, of tramps, and of outlaws all became narratives of detectives had a contradictory political meaning. At times, detectives substituted for outlaw heroes, much as G-men were to replace gangsters in the movies of the depression, and tales of class conflict were turned into crime stories; at other times, the detective became a mechanic hero, as in the tales of populist detectives. Much of this ambivalence derived, I have argued, from the multiplicity of disguise; the early detective heroes were anonymous sleuths who could assume any disguise, any accent. This changes in the 1890s, particularly with the figure of Nick Carter. As J. Randolph Cox (1981, 12) has written, 'Nick Carter ... signalled a break with the established tradition ... [he] is truly the pupil of the old detectives who came before him, for he represents a new American hero.' Indeed Nick Carter outlives the dime novel, flourishing in pulp magazines and radio serials. Disguise is still central; the covers of the Nick Carter Library showed 'Nick Carter in Various Disguises': a Chinese boy, a dandy, a woman, a farmer, an Irish political boss, and a black boy. But the central picture made it clear that he is really a young, muscular, white Anglo-Saxon man. The disguises and accents of the earlier detectives had not been resolved in such an unequivocal and stable signifier.

Nick Carter was joined in 1896 by a similar dime novel hero, Frank Merriwell. For the next two decades, Merriwell (and his brother Dick and his son Frank Jr.) appeared in stories of prep school and college life and sports. Like Nick Carter, Frank Merriwell outlived the dime novel; and like Carter, Merriwell was a figure of the Anglo-Saxon chauvinism of the turn of the century. Though sensational fiction remains a contested realm — indeed there is another moral panic about Jesse James stories in 1903 — the popularity of Nick Carter, Frank Merriwell and the imperialist heroes of Douglas Wells is a sign of the breakdown of the producer heroes who dominated the nineteenth-century dime novel; Larry Locke's education in the iron mill gives way to Frank Merriwell's education at Yale. Indeed, even Laura Jean Libbey began to turn away from the working-girl story toward the subjects that dominated the Merriwell dime novels — sports, schools and empire — setting love stories amidst baseball, golf, and West Point, and telling the tale of the 'heroine of Manila ... for whom gallant Commodore Dewey risked his life.'

The reasons for and meaning of this change in sensational fiction cannot be fully answered without a study of the pulp fiction of the early twentieth century and of its relation to the emerging film industry and the new working class of immigrant laborers from eastern and southern Europe and the Black share-cropping South. It is conceivable that such a study would question the representativeness of Nick Carter and Frank Merriwell just as this book has questioned the representativeness of Horatio Alger and the dime novel western. However, without that study, I would suggest that the eclipse of the plebian, producer narratives of the dime novel, and the ascendency of stories of upper-class schoolboys and heroic all-American detectives, is the result of a fragmentation of working-class culture at the turn of the century. 'It has been common of late,' David Montgomery (1980, 201) notes, 'for historians to detect in the rhetoric of American workers a deep and abiding faith in the republican institutions created in the eighteenth century, which guided the [workers'] movement through its many forms until the depression of the 1890s, and then was somehow lost or trans-formed.' Montgomery goes on to argue that a number of structural and political changes — the merger movement and the development of a more collectivist capitalism, the recomposition

of the working class, the global and imperial role of the United
States, and the counter-attack against the labor movement —
disrupted the 'sense of moral universality among "the
producers", which directly challenged both the ethic of acquisi-
tive individualism and "monopoly corruption" of the republic'
(215). Though working class militancy was not destroyed, 'no
single set of values, no commonly accepted vision of the
republic, any longer guided the many streams of working-class
struggle into a single-minded flood of protest' (211). One can see
the loss of this 'moral universality' in the sensational fiction of
the turn of the century; as the master allegory of the producer's
republic fades, its mechanic heroes — from Arthur Dermoyne to
Leonie Locke — begin to disappear, no longer able to represent
the nation. A new national allegory based on a resurgent racism
and imperial ventures in the Carribean and the Pacific comes to
form the master plot for the cheap stories of Nick Carter and
Frank Merriwell.

* * *

> The critic has actually imposed upon the world the superstition
> that a painting by Raphael is more valuable to the civilizations of
> the earth than is a chromo; and the august opera than the
> hurdy-gurdy and the villagers' singing society; and Homer than
> the little everybody's-poet whose rhymes are in all mouths today
> and will be in nobody's mouth next generation . . . the
> superstition, in a word, that the vast and awful comet that trails
> its cold luster through the remote abysses of space once a century
> and interests and instructs a cultivated handful of astronomers is
> worth more to the world than the sun which warms and cheers all
> the nations every day and makes the crops to grow.
>
> Mark Twain, 1889

How do we judge dime novels? Throughout this book, I have
steadfastly opposed the tendency of the historian or sociologist
of mass culture and leisure to focus on the production and
consumption of escapist entertainment and ignore its forms and
contents. Nevertheless, I have skirted the issue of cultural evaluation, resisting the literary impulse either to denigrate or celebrate the aesthetic qualities of these stories by comparing them
to the 'classic', 'canonic' works of narrative fiction of their time.
Moreover, though I have argued that certain novels and writers
are more representative of the unmanageable mass of sensational
fiction than others, I have tried to avoid the temptation of

creating a counter-canon of the 'best' dime novelists or dime novels. It seems unlikely that we need to recover any particular dime novel or dime novelist in a new paperback edition; as in the case of newspapers, it is more important that their cultural significance be recognized by the maintenance of library collections, the development of more adequate bibliographies, and the publication of microform editions. For the most part, therefore, I have taken the route of the cultural historian, examining and interpreting common if often despised texts to illuminate the cultures that produced and consumed them, arguing that they can be seen as the dream work of the social, the slips and jokes of a political unconsious.

Nevertheless, there is a kind of evaluation that cultural history ignores at its peril: the historical evaluation of a cultural form or genre, of its successes and failures, its limits and possibilities. It is a judgement not on any individual text, author, or reader, but on the cultural formation itself, the kind of evaluation that establishes 'renaissances', 'reformations', and 'cultural revolutions', moments when new forms flower and moments of 'decadence' and 'academicism'. Such evaluations are and ought to be controversial, for they are not disinterested; they represent the engagement of the present with the past, the construction and appropriation of a period with its generic and aesthetic systems. How, in this light, do we judge the moment of the dime novel?

The cultural formation of the dime novel derives its energy and crudity from the conjuncture of the birth of a culture industry with the emergence of an American working class. Its narrative formulas gain their resonance largely from their closeness to working class ideologies, from the mechanic accents of the producer culture to which its readers, writers, and earliest publishers belonged. As the first cheap, mass-produced, and national cultural medium, the dime novel had a particular importance in popular life: before the emergence of mass literacy (which the dime novel stimulated and depended upon) written narrative had never challenged the centrality of oral narratives; after the development of film and broadcasting, written narratives returned to a subsidiary role in popular narrative. Nevertheless, precisely because the dime novel depended upon the ability to read — the acquisition of a complex notational system by its consumers — its prose remained rudimentary. So whereas the stories of the fiction factory were as powerful as any told by the crafted novel, its discourse never reached the rhetorical range or complexity of that tradition. It was not until film and broad-casting allowed highly skilled craftworkers to produce cheap stories that did not rely on the audience's ability to decode a notational system that popular narratives can match their discourse to their stories.[3]

One may gauge the success and failure of the dime novel, its limits, possibilities and achievements, by considering it against the work of Mark Twain, the classic American writer closest to the dime novel in practice, influence, and audience. Twain began his career with one foot in the fiction factory, but was able to step into the literary world of the gilded age; this personal history left a contradictory scarring. On the one hand, he wrote, in a letter of 1867, that he was not going to write for the story paper the *New York Weekly* (which had reprinted his Sandwich Island letters first published in the Sacramento *Union*): 'Like all other papers that pay one splendidly, it circulates among stupid people and the *canaille*' (Neider 1982, 55). On the other hand, by 1890, he claims to have been misjudged by the critics of the culti-vated class: 'I have never tried in even one single instance to help cultivate the cultivated classes ... I never had any ambition in that direction, but always hunted for bigger game — the masses. ... My audience is dumb, it has no voice in print, and so I cannot know whether I have won its approbation or only got its censure. ... I have always catered for the Belly and the Members ... I never cared what became of the cultured classes' (Neider 1982, 202). Indeed almost uniquely, Twain bridged the gap between the audiences of the cultivated novel and the dime novel; as an emblem we might take the dual publication of *Adventures of Huckleberry Finn*: serialized in the *Century*, a leading magazine of the cultivated middle classes; and sold as a subscription book, a form of publishing only a step removed from the dime pamphlets and story weeklies (as Howells noted, 'no book of literary quality was made to go by subscription except Mr. Clemens' books, and I think these went because the subscription public never knew what good literature they were' [Kaplan 1966, 62]).

Twain's contradictory stance allows us to set his successes and failures alongside those of the dime novel. First, in Twain's failure lies the dime novels' success. Whatever may be said of the complexities of *A Connecticut Yankee in King Arthur's Court*, Twain's novel fails to embody the class realities of his master mechanic, Hank Morgan, both by its historical displacement and by its technological focus. A dime novel fistfight in the opening scene takes Morgan out of the Connecticut present and allows Twain to construct a figure for the modern world by conflating — in a move paralleled throughout nineteenth-century middle class culture — the master mechanic with the salesman, the man who could make anything, who praises manual labor, and speaks in defense of trade unions, with the man who will sacrifice much for an effect, who can sell stove polish to people without stoves. Any conflict between capital and labor is suppressed for the sake of an imagined conflict between past and present. I do not mean to dismiss the interest of Twain's juxta-position of social systems, indeed modes of production, in *Connecticut Yankee*; Twain's profound ambivalence toward the world of the Yankee results from the way that Arthurian Britain figures *both* the slave South (whose defeat by the Yankee is celebrated as a liberation) *and* the societies of the American Indians (whose defeat by the Yankee is seen as a massacre). Nevertheless, the reduction of the world of Yankee capitalism to the figure of Morgan signals Twain's inability to narrate that contemporary world, a world the dime novel mapped. Thus, against Twain's story of Hank Morgan, one may place Daniel Doyle's dime novel of Harry Morgan; and against the conceit of a Connecticut Yankee cast into King Arthur's court, one might place the tales of 'knights of labor' with their elaborate play on the ambiguities of knighthood and chivalry in a capitalist culture.

But Twain's successes mark the limits of the dime novel: what the dime novel fails to achieve is *Huckleberry Finn*. In part, this is merely to recognize once again the discursive impoverishment of the dime novel. For Twain's accomplishment in *Huckleberry Finn* lies perhaps more in his discourse than in his story, in his trans-formation of dialect, both white and Black, into a vernacular, a linguistic transformation that no dime novelist (indeed no other contemporary novelist) was able to accomplish.

But the comparison also highlights the dime novel's funda-mental evasion of race. One could argue that all significant American popular cultural forms are inflected and inscribed by race, that American popular culture is a mulatto culture. This does not mean that it is an 'integrated' culture, and it certainly does not mean that it is not a racist culture. But from the minstrel show to rock n' roll, from the melodramas of *Uncle Tom's Cabin* to the film of *The Color Purple*, popular culture has been not only a dialogic confrontation of Black and white performers but a syncretic fusion of forms and a map of racial fears, fantasies, and utopias.

From this perspective, the dime novel was a failure. The dime novel industry was largely isolated from Black audiences and Black writers; moreover, no narrative formulas were developed that could tell a racial story, as the few accounts of race in the dime novels show. J.B. Dobkin (1986, 50) searched through 8000 nickel library serials of 1879-1910, and found 'no black hero figure', about fifty Black characters important to the story line, and the virtual disappearance of Black characters after 1906-1907. For the most part, what he and other scholars find are conventional, static, and negative stereotypes.[4] An apparent exception, the emergence of a Black detective in several stories like Old Cap Collier's *Black Tom, The Negro Detective; Or, Solving a Thompson Street Mystery* (OL9) and Prentiss Ingraham's *Darkie Dan, the Colored Detective; or, The Mississippi Mystery* (I), is instructive. *Black Tom* sets a detective story in the midst of New York's Black community: 'Black Tom the detective was a mysterious individual who came and went into and out of the negro quarters of the city, like a phantom.' But after this Black detective solves the mystery of a white woman's corpse found in the Black part of town, and enables an impoverished white woman garment worker to reclaim her rightful inheritance, we discover that he is a white detective in disguise. Though a reader *might* have read this as a metaphorical disguise — the detective is both Black and white — the text does not encourage this. Unlike the working-girl stories where the lady reaffirms at the end that she is still a working-girl, and unlike the story where the nobleman ends by calling his record as a miner the proudest and best of his career, the white detective is clearly an impersonator: as the story ends, 'Nick Miller received much praise for his wonderful work, and his clever impersonations of the mysterious individual known as Black Tom, the negro detective.' Prentiss Ingraham's Darky Dan, on the other hand, is a Black detective hero; but the narrative price of this figure is the reconstruction of slavery. Set in the South, Dan stays with his master after emancipation, and his 'detective work' is in service to his white master and the master's family.

The dime novel did occasionally employ the narrative formula which is at the heart of *Huckleberry Finn*, and which Leslie Fiedler (1982, 15) has discussed at length: the 'myth of an idyllic anti-marriage: a lifelong love, passionate though chaste, and consummated in the wilderness, on a whaling ship or a raft, anywhere but "home", between a white refugee from "civilization" and a dark-skinned "savage", both of them male.' This romance is consummated in the coal mines of Pennsylvania in two of the Molly Maguire dime novels discussed earlier: in Tony Pastor's story, the hero's ever faithful friend is Injun Joe; and in Albert Aiken's story, the hero is aided by a 'deformed black', Banty Bob, the 'black angel' who saved him on a Civil War battlefield. These figures are, to use the vocabulary of Propp's study of folk tales, donors; and as Fredric Jameson (1972, 67-68) has argued, 'what Propp's discovery implies is that every How (the magical agent) always conceals a Who (the donor). ... The basic interpersonal and dramatic relationship of the narrative tale is therefore neither the head-on direct one of love nor that of hatred and conflict, but rather this lateral relationship of the hero to the excentric figure of the donor.' The success of *Huckleberry Finn* and the reason it continues to be contested in American culture lies in part in its elaboration of this relationship between white hero and Black donor, even though the narrative of Huck and Jim degenerates into the dime novel imagination of Tom Sawyer. The dime novel instances of this story, however, always remain secondary to the main narratives, occasions for racist humor at the expense of the 'sidekick'. The dime novel remains firmly within the racist parameters of the nineteenth-century producer culture, lacking even the minstrel show's carnivalesque staging of the boundaries of race. If the dime novels' accents are those of the mechanic, its color is white.

* * *

'And they lived happily ever after', says the fairy tale. ... The fairy tale tells us of the earliest arrangements that mankind made to shake off the nightmare which the myth had placed upon its chest. ... The wisest thing — so the fairy tale taught mankind in olden times, and teaches children to this day — is to meet the forces of the mythical world with cunning and with high spirits. ... The liberating magic which the fairy tale has at its disposal does not bring nature into play in a mythical way, but points to its complicity with liberated man.

Walter Benjamin, 'The Storyteller'

Fairytales and colportage are castle in the air par excellence, but one in good air and, as far as it can be true at all of mere wishing-work: the castle in the air is right.

Ernst Bloch, 'Happy End, Seen Through and Yet Still Defended'

Perhaps nothing is held against popular stories more than

their dependence on happy endings, on, in Henry James's (1888, 590) words, 'a distribution at the last of prizes, pensions, husbands, wives, babies, millions, appended paragraphs, and cheerful remarks'. There are good reasons for this prejudice, this suspicion. In many of the novels of 'realism' and 'sentimentalism', the happy ending was a sign that all was right in the world, that everything worked out in the end. All could be confidently encompassed in the everyday happenings of middle class life. In the twentieth century, the most powerful articulation of this suspicion of the happy ending has been in the critique of the culture industry by Max Horkheimer and Theodor Adorno; they saw mass culture as ruled by illusory promises of fulfillment and facile reconciliations.

But the suspicion of happy endings is often taken too far; as Horkheimer and Adorno themselves noted, the aesthetics of tragedy can too easily become mystifying ideologies of the 'tragic sense of life'. The unhappy endings of a certain bourgeois 'realism' are often simply the conventions of an aesthetic of slumming, static depictions of degradation. The literary history of the strike story might lead us to reconsider the ideological implications of the happy ending in dime novels: as I noted above, in nineteenth-century genteel fiction, strikes were always lost; in the dime novel, strikes are always won. A similar contrast was noted in the novels of working women: in the genteel novel the Rockdale women read, the working woman dies tragically; in the Libbey dime novels, the heroine triumphs magically. These unhappy endings are surely not simply realistic depictions of a harsh world, but myths of a supposed necessity; and if the happy endings are escapes, they are escapes from the nightmares of bourgeois myths.

Though the happy endings of dime novels are often nothing more than the fiction factories' path of least resistance, they also, like those of fairy tales, enact utopian longings. Ernst Bloch (1986, 367-368), who, along with Walter Benjamin, has defended the politics of the fairy tale, drew the comparison between the fairy tale and the dime novel, which he called by its German name, colportage:

> But colportage consistently manifests features of fairy tale; because its hero does not wait, as in the magazine story, for happiness to fall into his lap, he does not bend down to pick it up either like a bag thrown to him. Rather its hero remains related to the poor thickskin of the folk-tale, the bold boy who sets corpses on fire, who

takes the devil for a ride. ... The romanticism of the robber thus shows a different face, one which has appealed to poor folk for centuries, and colportage knows all about it. ... Here there is immature, but honest substitute for revolution, and where else did it express itself but in colportage. ... Consequently the need for re-evaluation of this genre, by virtue of the highly legitimate wishful image in its mirror, is especially evident.

I have tried to begin this re-evaluation, stressing the utopian moment of the dime novels, revealing their magical and meta phoric transformations as figures of desire, allegories of recon-ciliation. I have argued that this is how their disguises were read, and their accents understood. Though they were not 'accurate pictures' of working class life, not 'just everyday happenings', the pressure of the real persisted, as the labored, willful and some-times absurd happy endings — Job Manly's profit-sharing scheme or Little Rosebud's resurrection from the casket — attest. And the 'distribution at the last of prizes, pensions, husbands, wives, babies, millions, appended paragraphs, and cheerful remarks' that James objected to is usually, in dime novels, a *redistribution*, an expropriation of the expropriators.

Notes

Chapter 1

1. For an account of the business history and circulation of the early story papers, see Barnes 1974, 1-29. The *Ledger* claimed a circulation of 377,000 by 1869, and the *New York Weekly* boasted 350,000 in 1877 (Noel 1954, 130,138). Later in the century, the competition was keen; in 1892, the *Weekly* had a circulation of 250,000, the *Fireside Companion* 200,000, the *Family Story Paper* 150,000, *Saturday Night* 100,000, and the *Ledger* 100,000 (*N.W. Ayer & Sons American Newspaper Annual*, 1892).
2. For examples of this sort of commentary, see Pearson, 1929; Matthews, 1923; Robinson, 1928, 1929.
3. This emphasis is continued in the most substantial recent work, Daryl Jones' *The Dime Novel Western*, 1978, as well as in the first major microform collection of dime fiction, University Microfilms International's *Dime Novels: Popular American Escape Fiction of the Nineteenth Century*.
4. Durham 1966, vi. As a comparison, Lyle Wright's bibliographies of American fiction for 1850-1900, which omit all dime novels and serialized fiction, have a total of 9,003 entries.
5. See W. Wright, 1975, for a fine discussion of the western in twentieth-century culture. Hoppenstand 1982 is a recent reprinting and reassessment of dime novel detectives.

Chapter 2

1. Francis Scott Street (born 1831) and Robert DeWitt (born 1827) began as clerks in publishing houses. A few of the early writer/entrepreneurs had college educations: Maturin Murray Ballou, Gleason's collaborator, had dropped out of Harvard, Park Benjamin had attended Harvard and Washington College, and Orville J. Victor, Beadle's editor, had graduated from the Seminary and Theological Institute of Norwalk, Ohio. Saxton, 1984, 221 notes that eight of the ten publishers of the first-wave penny dailies began as artisans.
2. Wilentz, 1984, 131. My account of the printing industry and trades draws heavily on Wilentz.
3. The Panic of 1893, however, contributed to the demise of dime novels, cheap

libraries, and story papers for three principal reasons: first, the United States Book Company, the huge trust formed by John Lovell to consolidate cheap story production in 1890, proved a victim of the Panic; second, the establishment of an international copyright in 1891 had reduced the profits coming from pirated editions of British books; and third, dime novels succumbed to the competition of the new forms of cheap publishing fostered by the depression years, the 'magazine revolution' of 1893 (Frank Munsey cut the price of his monthly magazine from a quarter to a dime in October 1893; by April 1895, circulation had risen from 40,000 to 500,000 [Peterson, 1956, 6-11]) and the 'yellow' press.

4. See Adimari, 1935, 1956; Beadle Dime Novel, 1900; Boyle, 1939; Brown, 1932; Burgess, 1902; Cook, 1912; Coryell, 1929; Jenks, 1904; Johannsen, 1950, vol. 2; Lewis, 1941; Monaghan, 1952; Pachon, 1957; Patten, 1964; Reynolds, 1982.

5. Noel, 1954, 167. Noel has the best account to date of the controversy. See also the long quotation from the trial testimony in Pearson, 1929, 191-194, and a related case discussed in Pachon, 1986.

6. One gets this sense from the biographical dictionary of the Beadle authors in Johannsen, 1950, 2:3-314. See, for example, the careers of Charles Dunning Clark, Welden Cobb, Anthony Morris, James Alexander Patten, and Nathan Urner.

7. Michael Schudson's (1978, 89) use of Walter Benjamin's distinction between story and information in his analysis of late nineteenth-century newspapers may illuminate dime novels as well; he distinguishes the 'sensational' new journalism of Hearst and Pulitzer from the journalism of the Ochs *New York Times* by distinguishing the ideal of the 'story' from the ideal of 'information'. 'When telling stories is taken to be the role of the newspaper,' he writes, 'the news serves primarily to create, for readers, satisfying aesthetic experiences which help them to interpret their own lives and to relate them to the nation, town or class to which they belong.' He goes on to identify these newspapers of the 'story' with a working class readership. It is arguable that the 'sensational' dime novels and story papers played this role before the rise of the 'sensational' yellow press in the 1890s. The story papers emerged out of a split between the story and information functions of the newspaper; and the 'yellow press' and Sunday newspapers of the 1890s attempted to recuperate the story aspect of journalism. Indeed, many accounts of the dime novel's decline place the blame on the competition of the sensational press, which, under the guise of reporting the 'news', was able to venture further from genteel codes into the world of vice and immorality. See, for example, Bellows, 1899, 99: 'People who would not for a moment tolerate vicious fiction read with avidity the scandals of the papers because they are set forth as facts. ... That portion of the daily press which is known as Yellow Journalism threatens the dime novel's very existence.'

8. Bishop, 1879, 390-391. Noel, 1954, 123 also writes of the *Fireside Companion* being based on narrativized melodramas. This process is particularly evident in the case of the factory-girl stories discussed in chapter ten, and in the dime novelists who also wrote for the melodramatic stage: Albert Aiken wrote his story of the Molly Maguires (discussed in chapter seven) for the story paper, the *Fireside Companion*, and for theatrical production. (Johannsen, 1950, 2:3-314. See also the career of Bartley Campbell). See McConachie 1985 for a discussion of the relation between melodrama and its working-class audience in antebellum New York.

9. For the connection between the dime novel and another part of the culture industry, spectator sports, see Messenger, 1981, 100-107.

Chapter 3

1. Since concepts of class are widely debated and have different meanings in different theoretical vocabularies, let me outline my use of the concepts drawn from the Marxist tradition. First, I follow Erik Olin Wright's (1985) discussion of class analysis, where he distinguishes between the analysis of *class structure*, 'the structure of social relations into which individuals (or, in some cases, families) enter which determine their class interests', and of *class formation*, 'the formation of organized collectivities within that class structure on the basis of interests shaped by that class structure' (9-10). 'Classes,' he argues, 'have a structural existence which is irreducible to the kinds of collective organizations which develop historically (class formations), the class ideologies held by individuals and organizations (class consciousness) or the forms of conflict engaged in by individuals as class members or by class organizations (class struggle), and that such class structures impose basic constraints on these other elements in the concept of class' (28).

    Second, one must also distinguish between at least two levels of abstraction in class analysis: the analysis of modes of production where classes are seen as 'pure types of social relations of production, each embodying a distinctive mechanism of exploitation' (10), and the analysis of specific social formations, where one rarely finds pure classes but rather fractions of classes, and alliances between classes as the result of specific historical combinations of distinct modes of production, uneven economic development, and the legacy of earlier class struggles. (On levels of abstraction in class analysis, see also Katznelson, 1981, chapter 8.) At the first, 'higher' level of abstraction, my study assumes that the United States between the 1840s and 1890s (particularly the north and mid west, the centers of dime novel production and reception) was fundamentally organized by the capitalist mode of production; its 'basic' or 'fundamental' classes were capitalists and workers; other classes were, in Wright's term, 'contradictory class locations', or, in Wolff and Resnick's (1982; 1986) term, 'subsumed classes'. However, most of my study is pitched at the second, 'lower' level of abstraction. Here I draw particularly on the analysis of the transformation of American class structures in Gordon, Edwards, and Reich, 1982; on the histories of the working classes by the 'new' labor historians — Gutman, Montgomery, Couvares, Ewen, Fink, Kessler-Harris, Laurie, Levine, Peiss, Rosenzweig, Ross, and Wilentz, among others — which focus on the class fractions and class alliances among the popular or subaltern classes; and, for the history of the dominant classes, on the work of Batzell, Bledstein, Halttunen, Pessen, Wallace, Warner. On middle-class formation, see the excellent essay by Blumin, 1985. In general, by the working classes, I include craftworkers, factory operatives, common laborers, domestic servants, and their families; by the capitalist classes, I mean manufacturers, large merchants, bankers and financiers, the patrician elite and their families. The contradictory class locations include small shopkeepers, small professionals, master artisans and clerks: I will examine later their relation to the rhetoric of the 'producing classes' and the 'middle classes'. David Montgomery's (1967, 29-30) interpretation of the 1870 census concludes that:

> Of the 12.9 million people in all occupations, only 1.1 million (8.6 per cent) can be listed as nonagricultural employers, corporate officials, and self-employed producers or professionals. Thus the business and professional elites, old and new, totaled less than one tenth of the nation's economically active population. ... 67 per cent of the productively engaged Americans were dependent for a livelihood upon employment by others. Industrial manual workers, or what would now be called 'blue collar labor'... numbered just over 3.5 million souls, or 27.4 per cent of the gainfully employed.

Agriculture accounted for 52.9 per cent of the gainfully employed: 24.2 per cent were farmers, planters and independent operators; 28.7 per cent were agricultural wage earners. Domestic servants made up 8 per cent of the gainfully employed; white collar workers — clerks and salespeople — 3 per cent.

My work is *not* a contribution to the history of 'class structure' in the United States, but rather to the history of 'class formation' in the United States. As Katznelson (1981, 207) writes, 'Class society exists even where it is not signified; but how and why it is signified in particular ways in particular places and times is the study of class formation.' In particular, my study is meant as a contribution to the history of 'class consciousness', or what I would prefer to call the *rhetoric of class*, the words, metaphors, and narratives by which people figure social cleavages. The ideological struggles to define social cleavages are determined by the existing class structure but they also play a part in the formation of class organizations and in class struggles. (Przeworski, 1985 and Therborn, 1980 are perhaps the best theoretical discussions of the ideological constitution of classes.)

2. The evidence of collectors and enthusiasts is even vaguer; they tend to stress the 'respectable' people who read dime novels and Albert Johannsen's list is characteristic: 'bankers and bootblacks ... lawyers and lawbreakers ... working girls and girls of leisure, President Lincoln and President Wilson' (Johannsen, 1950, 1:9). Edward Pearson, in his early book on dime novels, has a chapter devoted to readers' reminiscences; but the correspondents to whom he sent his questionnaire are largely established professionals: editors, librarians, professors. In the middle class homes of their childhood, dime novels were often prohibited and usually read by children on the sly; indeed this image has become part of the commonsense knowledge about dime novels.

3. Quoted in Shove, 1937, 19. This assessment raises the question of the readership of the *New York Ledger*, an issue worth considering. For anyone who wishes to argue for an overlapping rather than discontinuous reading public in nineteenth century America, the *Ledger* is a key journal. It attained the highest circulation of any magazine or story paper by reaching a cross-class, 'popular' audience with stories, poems, and articles by leading writers and intellectuals including Edward Everett, Henry Ward Beecher, George Bancroft, Henry Wadsworth Longfellow, Harriet Beecher Stowe, and Fanny Fern. Thus, Mary Noel, focusing primarily on the *Ledger*, concludes that the story papers had a largely middle class audience. And, in her study of ante-bellum responses to fiction, Nina Baym (1984, 18) includes the *Ledger* in the same discursive universe as the major middle-class magazines, from *Godey's*

to *Harper's, Graham's* to the *Atlantic.*

This, I would argue, is misleading. Far from being a representative journal, the *Ledger* achieved its wide circulation by uniquely straddling the boundary between the two worlds of genteel and sensational culture. It was the most respectable story paper, the least respectable magazine. Indeed, when appealing to advertisers, it claimed to be the 'leading high-class illustrated family weekly paper in America' (*N.W. Ayer & Sons American Newspaper Annual,* 1892, 1403.) Its genteel contributors came to it not because they felt it was part of their culture but because Bonner paid so well. When Bonner convinced Edward Everett, the former president of Harvard, to write fifty-two weekly columns in 1858 and 1859 in return for a substantial contribution to the Mt. Vernon fund, which was preserving Washington's home (and with which Everett was involved), E.L. Godkin, then a correspondent for the London *Daily News,* summed up the response of the genteel culture, and marked the gap between it and the *Ledger*:

> The great topic of the quidnuncs for the last few days has been Edward Everett's extraordinary undertaking to write for the New York *Ledger,* a two-penny weekly magazine, circulating nearly three hundred thousand copies. ... It is filled with tales of the 'Demon Cabman', the 'Maiden's Revenge', the 'Tyrant's Vault', and a great variety of 'mysteries' and 'revelations'; and, in short, barring its general decency of language, belongs to as low and coarse an order of literature as any publication in the world. The proprietor [Robert Bonner] was four or five years ago a journeyman printer, but by lavish use of puffery in aid of this periodical has amassed a large fortune, *a la* Barnum. ... To the astonishment of the whole Union the ex-ambassador, ex-secretary of state, ex-president of Harvard University, ex-editor of the 'Greek Reader', the scholar, the exquisite, the one aristocrat of the 'universal Yankee nation', has accepted the proposal. ... If you knew the sensation which this incident has caused here amongst genteel people, you would hardly expect me to add a line to my letter after reciting it (Ogden, 1907, 1:179-180).

On the other hand, though Everett (1860) himself accepted Bonner's proposal with 'great misgivings', he concludes his series of articles with a peroration of the *Ledger,* beginning with an awed account of visiting the story paper's production plant, remarking on its circulation of four hundred thousand, and concluding with an invocation of its readers:

> It has simply aimed to be an entertaining and instructive Family newspaper, designed, in the first instance, to meet the wants of what is called, in a very sensible and striking paper in Dickens' Household Words, ... the 'Unknown Public'. The New York 'Ledger' is the first attempt in this country, on a large scale, to address *that* public; and the brilliant success, which has attended it thus far, is a strong confirmation of the truth ... that the time is coming when 'the readers, who rank by millions, will be the readers who give the widest reputations, who return the richest rewards, and who will therefore command the services of the best writers of the time' (488).

4. As noted above, William Wells Brown's *Clotelle* was published in dime novel format during the Civil War, part of Redpath's abolitionist attempt to reach Union soldiers. There is some evidence that one of Beadle's authors was Black (see entry for Philip S. Warne in Johannsen, 1950, 2:289), and Victoria

Earle Matthews may have written for the story papers (see Penn, 1891, 375-6). However, most fiction by black writers was published in Black newspapers and journals; the Black Periodical Fiction Project, headed by Henry-Louis Gates, has not found a Black equivalent of dime novels. For a discussion of the relation between dime novel conventions and early Afro-American fiction, and of the Afro-American fiction reading public in the late nineteenth century, see Carby, 1987.

5.   The history of readers and the reading public is very undeveloped for the United States; the unsatisfactory typology of the 'brows' dominates most literary and cultural history, and as Henry Nash Smith pointed out, this has not been adequately articulated with social class. Kaser, 1984 is one of the few studies of nineteenth century American reading, and it confirms the importance of dime novel reading by soldiers in the Civil War. However, accounts of the British, French, German, and Russian reading publics offer suggestive parallels. In England, one finds a similar explosion of cheap stories — the 'penny dreadfuls' and weekly newspapers — in the 1830s and 1840s. Richard Altick (1957, 83) argues that 'it was principally from among skilled workers, small shopkeepers, clerks, and the better grade of domestic servants that the new mass audience for printed matter was recruited during the first half of the century.' The staple of this cheap printed matter was sensational fiction, but it is important to note that this was a shift in reading matter. The first cheap reading matter for artisans was radical political journalism, and the desire to read was often connected to working class political activity and self-improvement. The fiction industry picked up a reading public after the failure and abandonment of political aspirations, particularly of Chartism (L. James, 1963, 25). By the end of the century, reading had spread throughout the working class. A recent examination of a U.S. Department of Labor study of British workers in 1889 and 1890 finds:

> almost all [families] had family members who were literate. At least 80 percent of those interviewed in every industry bought books and newspapers. These proportions apply to both laborers and the highly skilled in textiles, although in heavy industry the unskilled were less likely to read and spent smaller sums on books. ... This extensive, but limited taste for reading is confirmed by Lady Bell's interviews of Middlesborough workers around 1900. Of 200 families she interviewed, only 15 percent did not care to read or had no reading member. Yet most chose just newspapers and light novels. ... The literary world of most workers therefore mixed sports, crime, and general news with romantic or sensationalist fiction (Lees, 1979, 183).

On the British reading public, see Altick, 1957; L. James, 1963; Leavis, 1932; Mitchell, 1981; Neuberg, 1977; Webb, 1955. On the French popular reading public in the early nineteenth century, see Allen 1981; 1983.

German workers had similar reading tastes. The equivalent of the dime novel in Germany was the 'colporteur novel' of the 1870s and 1880s which was sold in installments and combined cheap prices with sensational fiction (Fullerton, 1977; 1979). See also Steinberg, 1976.

Brooks, 1985 offers an excellent history of both the Russian reading public and sensational fiction, the 'literature of the *lubok*', in the late nineteenth and early twentieth century, with suggestive cross-national comparisons.

In the United States, the research that is closest to a history of the reading public is the sociological studies of reading in the library science of the 1920s to 1940s, work exemplified by that of Douglas Waples. (For a history and overview of this work see Karetzky, 1982; Steinberg, 1972; see also Waples and Tyler, 1931; Waples, Berelson and Bradshaw, 1940.) A small part of this work focused on factory workers (see Gray and Munroe, 1930, 81-91; Ormsbee, 1927, 75-95; Rasche, 1937) and, though the period studied is the 1920s, it is suggestive for our purposes. A number of conclusions were drawn from the surveys carried out. First of all, newspapers were by far the most common reading matter of young workers (all of the surveys were primarily focused on young adult workers), followed by fiction magazines, the 'pulps'. Newspapers were read largely for sports, crime news and fashion, and the fiction magazines carried 'sensational' and 'salacious' stories. There was clear gender division in the reading of pulps, with the striking exception of *True Story*, Macfadden's innovative pulp of the 1920s which carried stories said to be true and written by readers; it was read by men and women alike. The gap between middle class reading and working class reading in the 1920s can be gauged by Hazel Grant Ormsbee's comment on finding that *True Story* was far and away the most read magazine by young working class women: 'Even though it may be found on all the street corner news stands, and indeed at almost every stand where magazines are sold, its name is probably not even known to the many persons who are familiar with most of the magazines in the second class [i.e., the middlebrow magazines like *Saturday Evening Post* and *Ladies' Home Journal*]' (Ormsbee, 1927, 80). There was also a close connection between reading and the movies: movie magazines and the novels that movies were based on were both common reading. The conclusions of these studies are summed up by Gray and Munroe: 'the quality of some of the material read is very good. On the other hand, there is a surprisingly large amount of reading of cheap, sensational material. ... In fact, the need of elevating the reading interests and tastes of young workers presents a very grave problem' (Gray and Munroe, 1930, 89). This desire to 'reform' workers' reading has roots in the era of the dime novel.

A second general conclusion developed out of Douglas Waples' comparisons of people's expressed subject interest with their actual reading. He found that there was 'almost no correlation between the workers' expressed reading interests and what they read in the newspapers and similarly little relation between these interests and their magazine reading.' Waples concluded that the most important determinant of what is read is accessibility, particularly in the case of workers who read mainly newspapers (Karetzky, 1982, 99). This reading research of the 1920s and 1930s does offer some important insights and data, though it is marred by the condescension and moralism of the researchers and by the complete distrust of fiction in general and sensational fiction in particular. Another product of the 1920s sociological imagination, Helen and Robert Lynd's *Middletown*, is particularly interesting because, while confirming the general observations of the reading researchers for the 1920s, finding important cleavages in reading material by class and gender in Middletown, it compares workers' reading of the 1920s with that of the 1890s. The Lynds find three major changes: the general decline of the workers' self-improving reading culture that was manifested in the independent Workingmen's Library, which has disappeared by the 1920s; the increase in public library circulation which has replaced 'buying of cheap paper-covered books in the nineties and the reading of books from the meager Sunday School libraries'; and the slackening of attentiveness to reading: 'more things are skimmed today but there is less of the satisfaction of "a good evening of reading". There appears to be considerably less reading aloud by the entire family' (Lynd and Lynd, 1929, 229-242).

6. Larcom, 1889, 244, 105-106, 190. See for details, 99-106, 226-247. 'Libraries' here refers to the various series of cheap novels that appeared after the *Lakeside Library* of 1875.

7. Neither Beadle & Adams nor Street & Smith seem to have ever used the word 'railroad' or 'railway' in a series or story paper title, and the only instance mentioned in the histories of publishing, Shove, 1937 and Stern, 1980, is the American reprints of the English Routledge *Railway Library*.

8. Indeed there is a struggle over a similar sort of reading at the workplace by Cuban tobacco workers in the 1860s. As Ambrosio Fornet (1975) writes, 'the proletariat found in Reading — in "the enthusiasm to hear things read", as an editorial writer in *El Siglo* put it — the era's most democratic and effective form of cultural diffusion.' It began in 1865 in the large tobacco factory of El Figaro, with each worker contributing time to make up for the working time lost by the reader. 'From there,' Fornet goes on, 'readings sprang up in other workshops in Havana. ... Wherever sedentary group work was carried out, the idea found supporters.' Readings included newspapers, histories and novels. The first struggles over reading had to do with owners wanting to select and approve the material to be read, but the campaign against reading escalated and by May, 1866 the political governor issued a decree that prohibited 'the distraction of workers in tobacco factories, workshops or any other establishment by the reading of books or periodicals, or by discussions unrelated to the work being carried out by these same workers'.

9. For an account of a similar reaction to commercial fiction by the German Social Democrats, see Trommler, 1983, 64-67.

10. Little is known of Weldon Cobb's life. I suspect that his serials written for the *Workingman's Advocate* preceded his success in the commerical story papers and cheap libraries; perhaps they brought him to the attention of the fiction entrepreneurs. For the biographical data that exists, see Johannsen, 1950, 2:56; and Johannsen, 1959, 43. Unfortunately, Johannsen has no record of Cobb's connection to the *Workingman's Advocate*.

11. I am indebted to Joseph DePlasco for calling my attention to Foster and to the fiction in the *Labor Leader*.

12. Another example of this kind of labor fiction is the novel of Knights of Labor organizer T. Fulton Gantt, *Breaking the Chains*, which was found and has been edited and republished by Mary Grimes, 1986.

Chapter 4

1. Herbert Gutman's (1976) pioneering essay on working class culture has been developed and qualified by a number of local community studies in the last decade. The major works on the conflicts within and about working class culture and leisure include those of Paul Boyer, 1978, Francis Couvares, 1984, Elizabeth Ewen, 1985, Kathy Peiss, 1986, Roy Rosenzweig, 1983, and Stephen Ross, 1985.

2. For an account of a library controversy over workers' reading as early as

222

1828, see Wilentz, 1984, 149. For an account of the Workingman's Library in Muncie, Indiana, see Lynd and Lynd, 1929, 232.

3. Bremner 1967, xx. I am indebted to this introduction to the republication of Comstock's *Traps for the Young* for the details of Comstock's career.

4. The *North American Review* greeted Beadle's early dime novels with a remarkably favorable review in 1864. Individual novels are assessed, a procedure that will not be repeated in later discussions of cheap stories, and they are found to be 'unobjectionable morally, whatever fault be found with their literary style and composition'. The review ends on an optimistic note, envisioning dime novels as a possible public benefactor, and wishing them success in raising the character of cheap literature (W. Everett, 1864).

5. Kent Steckmesser, 1965, and Richard Slotkin, 1985, have shown that the story of Kit Carson was narrated in dramatically different fashions by genteel and sensational fiction and biography: I will discuss this in chapter 8. On the other hand, Nina Baym (1984, 208-209) maintains that a similar plot unites the genteel domestic novel and its 'antithesis', the 'high-wrought fiction' of the story papers: I will take issue with this interpretation in chapter 10.

Chapter 5

1. Indeed, the major microfilm edition of dime novels is entitled *Dime Novels: Popular American Escape Fiction of the Nineteenth Century*.

2. The principal attempts to theorize popular culture in this way are Jameson, 1979 and Hall, 1981. For historians of working class leisure that avoid Stedman Jones' just criticisms, see Rosenzweig, 1983; Couvares, 1984; Ewen, 1985; and Peiss, 1986.

3. Gramsci, 1973, 80, 145. Gramsci's writings on serial fiction have been translated in Gramsci 1929-1935; I have drawn on the excellent editorial notes for the situation of Gramsci's writing.

4. My argument has parallels with Jane Tompkins' (1980) soteriological reading of Stowe's *Uncle Tom's Cabin*, a novel that moves from domestic realism to national allegory. It is also indebted to Sacvan Bercovitch's (1978) discussions of the persistence of Puritan typology in American culture. My notion of a master plot of republican figures and types parallels Bercovitch's claims for the jeremiad: 'the jeremiad became the official ritual form of continuing revolution. Mediating between religion and ideology, the jeremiad gave contract the sanctity of covenant, free enterprise the halo of grace, progress the assurance of chiliad, and nationalism the grandeur of typology ... a major reason for the triumph of the republic was that the need for a social ideal was filled by the typology of America's mission ... it provided what we might call the figural correlative to the theory of democratic capitalism. It gave the nation a past and future in sacred history, rendered its political and legal outlook a fulfillment of prophecy, elevated its "true inhabitants", the enterprising European Protestants who had immigrated within the past century or so, to the status of God's chosen, and declared the vast territories around them to be their chosen country' (1978, 140-141). However, I would disagree with two major aspects of Bercovitch's argument. First, he sees American culture as characterized by 'an *ideological* consensus'. The Puritans 'established the central tenets of what was to become (in Raymond Williams's phrase) our "dominant culture". And

because there was no competing order — no alternative set of values except the outmoded Old World order they rapidly discarded — the ideological hegemony that resulted reached virtually all levels of thought and behaviour' (xii-xiv). Though there has been no successful counter-hegemonic challenge to capitalism in the United States, the hegemony of the dominant classes, in the sense of genuine cultural — as well as economic and political — leadership based upon popular consent, has not only been contested but has evaporated at various times in American history. Bercovitch tends to reduce the concepts of 'hegemony' and 'dominant culture' — which connote in Gramsci and Williams unstable and historically conditioned balances of forces between classes and social groups — to the timeless 'consensus' of American exceptionalism. Second, Bercovitch falls into a rhetorical determinism, a 'formalism' in the strict sense, when he sees any use of the form of the jeremiad or the typology of America as 'a mode of cultural cohesion and continuity ... a fundamental force against social change' (204-205). This seems to deduce social meaning from formal analysis; I suggest that the same form or convention may take on quite different meanings and have significantly different effects in different historical and social circumstances. Thus, the typology of America is used by nineteenth-century workers as the figural correlative of the 'cooperative commonwealth' against 'democratic capitalism'.

5. Janice Radway's (1984, 199) ethnographic study of contemporary popular fiction readers makes a similar argument about the way romances are read as myth and as novels: 'The romance-rading experience, in short, appears to provide both the psychological benefits of oral myth-telling and those associated with the reading of a novel.'

6. Habegger's remarks come in the context of a provocative discussion of nineteenth-century American realism; he calls realism 'the literature of writers with some democratic freedom': 'While realism pays close attention to the facts of the contemporary social scene, corrects some of the current stereotypes, and tries to represent the causal flow of events, allegory offers a timeless scene, a universe of static types and symbols rather than causal change, a view of behaviour that sees the actor or hero as the matrix for competing absolutes or abstract types, and facts that require interpretation rather than recognition followed by action. Allegory is the product of mind living under absolutism and hence projects an implacable world of abstract types — precisely the type of world projected by the violated will ... in allegory, unlike realism, the individual is in chains' (1982, 111-112). While agreeing with Habegger's general interpretation, I would qualify his account of nineteenth-century American realism; its emergence, which depends upon the ability to conceive significant individual agency, was a product not only of democratic freedoms but of the class power of the writers and readers of that fiction.

7. The centrality of the study of genre and convention for marxist cultural history and criticism has been argued most powerfully by Fredric Jameson, 1975; 1981; 1982, and Franco Moretti, 1983. (See also Williams, 1977, 173-186). Jameson, 1981, 106; 1975, 157, writes that:

> genres are essentially literary *institutions,* or social contracts between a writer and a specific public, whose function is to specify the proper use of a particular cultural artifact. ... Generic criticism may thus be seen as a process which involves the use of three variable terms: the individual

work itself, the intertextual sequence into which it is inserted through the ideal construction of a progression of forms (and of the systems that obtain between those forms), and finally that series of concrete historical situations within which the individual works were realized. ... So generic affiliations, and the systematic deviation from them, provide clues which lead us back to the concrete historical situation of the individual text itself, and allow us to read its structure as ideology, as a socially symbolic act, as a protopolitical response to a historical dilemma.

He argues that there is a privileged relation between historical materialism and genre study: 'the first extended exercise in Marxist literary criticism — the letters of Marx and Engels to LaSalle about the latter's verse tragedy, *Franz von Sickingen* [and, we shall see, Marx's discussion of Eugène Sue] — was indeed essentially generic; while the most developed corpus of Marxist literary analysis in our own time, the work of Georg Lukács, spanning some sixty years, is dominated by concepts of genre' (Jameson, 1981, 105). Franco Moretti makes a similar argument in his recent *Signs Taken for Wonders* (1983, 9,12-16,19.). Like Jameson, he sees 'the best results of historical-sociological criticism ... in works aimed at defining the internal laws and historical range of a specific genre: from the novel in Lukács to the baroque drama in Benjamin, from French classical tragedy in Goldmann to the twelve-note system in Adorno.' His project is to bring to literary history a sense of what the *Annales* school called *longue durée*, an idea of 'normal literature'. Rather than a focus on 'events', great works and great authors, the concept of genre requires 'emphasis on what a set of works have in *common*. It presupposes that literary production takes place in obedience to a prevailing system of laws and that the task of criticism is precisely to show the extent of their coercive, regulating power.' 'Is the task of the historian of culture,' he asks, 'always and only to ask what, in the past or the present, makes possible the "separation" of an elite from the mass of the public? Is it not rather to deal with the mass conventions, the great ideological agreements by which each age is distinguished from others? But — it might be objected — the average production of a given genre is unreadable and boring now. I do not doubt it. But it is precisely this unbearable "uncontemporaneity" that the historian must seek out.' In this way a history of literature could 'rewrite itself as a sociology of symbolic forms, a history of cultural conventions'.

8.   Cawelti sees a popular fiction formula as a combination or synthesis of a number of specific cultural conventions with a more universal story form or archetype. A genre, Cawelti argues, is when a formula or set of formulas comes to be looked at by its creators and audiences as a distinctive literary class with certain artistic potentials and limitations. A genre, he says, is a formula looked at aesthetically. I would amend this slightly to say that a genre is a class of narratives whose producers and audience recognize it self-consciously as such, whether that recognition is aesthetic or commercial. See Cawelti, 1976, 6. I treat this issue at more length in my own 'genre study' of the spy thriller: Denning, 1987.

9.   Recent histories of the 'language of labor' by William Sewell and Gareth Stedman Jones offer a particularly interesting counterpoint to this work. Sewell's account (1980, 11) of the language of nineteenth-century French artisans is an effort in 'reconstructing the meanings of the words, metaphors, and rhetorical conventions that they used to talk about and think about their experience'; though he does not turn to popular story-

telling and commercially produced popular fiction, the impulse to dwell on the rhetorical forms that artisans used is based on an accurate sense that political ideologies are not coherent, fully elaborated systems of ideas articulated by exceptional authors but are embedded in a variety of symbolic forms. Similarly, Gareth Stedman Jones (1983, 94) has argued that categories of historical analysis like 'experience' and 'consciousness' conceal the material and historical effects of language. In a provocative revision of the classic dictum of *The German Ideology* — 'we do not set out from what men say, imagine, conceive, nor from men as narrated, thought of, imagined, conceived, in order to arrive at men in the flesh. We set out from real, active men, and on the basis of their real life-process we demonstrate the development of the ideological reflexes and echoes of this life-process' — Stedman Jones writes: 'In contrast to the prevalent social-historical approach to Chartism, whose starting point is some conception of class or occupational consciousness, it [his essay] argues that the ideology of Chartism cannot be constructed in abstraction from its linguistic form. An analysis of Chartist ideology must start from what Chartists actually said or wrote, the terms in which they addressed each other or their opponents.' This is not intended as a return to an idealist historiography nor as a denial of the material conditions of existence of this ideology. Rather it is an attempt to free 'class' from a position as a fixed point, to stress that 'the term "class" is a word embedded in language and should thus be analyzed in its linguistic context' (7-8). Again Stedman Jones' argument has the virtue of calling attention to the discourse of workers and the vocabulary, symbolic forms and figures of class through which they saw and experienced the world.

Neither Sewell nor Stedman Jones pay much attention to narratives; their central concern is reconstructing the terms of working class political discourse from writings and speeches in the radical and workers press, from what Stedman Jones calls 'the public political language of the movement'.

10. This conception of ideology has been most developed in the work of Fredric Jameson (1977b; 1981) who has attempted to link methods of narrative analysis to those of ideological analysis. A characteristic formulation argues: 'the ideological representation must ... be seen as that indispensable mapping fantasy or narrative by which the individual subject invents a "lived" relationship with collective systems which otherwise by definition exclude him insofar as he or she is born into a pre-existent social form and its pre-existent language' (Jameson, 1978, 394). His notion of the ideologeme offers a way of mediating between this narrative conception of ideology and traditional notions of ideology:

> the ideologeme [the minimal unit of larger class discourse] is an amphibious formation, whose essential structural characteristic may be described as its possibility to manifest itself either as a pseudoidea — a conceptual or belief system, an abstract value, an opinion or prejudice — or as a protonarrative, a kind of ultimate class fantasy about the 'collective characters' which are the classes in opposition. (Jameson, 1981, 87.)

11. Recent surveys of nineteenth-century American fiction have charted an increase in representations of workers and workers' lives during the century. While working-class life was virtually ignored as a subject between 1820 and 1840, there were no fewer than 65 novels 'which took as their main theme the condition of the urban labor force' between 1840 and 1870 (Siegel 1981, 77). But even these were a small fraction of what was to come. Fay

Blake (1972, 3), using a somewhat different index, the representation of strikes in fiction, says that 'before the Civil War it is hard to find any novels at all that deal with working class life. . . . Beginning about 1870 a number of novels include strikes as part of the plot.' Her list of novels that portray strikes provides a relative measure: 13 between 1840 and 1870, and 54 between 1871 and 1900. However, these surveys of workers and strikes in novels worked primarily from the Lyle Wright bibliography of American fiction, which exludes dime novels, story paper serials, and the cheap libraries, and thus is not an accurate picture of popular fiction after 1840. If one were to catalog the novels of working-class life, the stories of labor and capital, that appeared in these forms (a bibliographic task that has scarcely begun), one would find not only a similar increase between mid-century and the later decades, but a far greater number and proportion of these stories.

12. Again, Gramsci's notes on serial fiction (1929-1935) offer suggestive examples of the analysis of figures of social cleavage. See in particular his comments about the class significance of narratives of revenge ('one could say that the day-dreams of the people are dependent on a (social) "inferiority complex". This is why they day-dream at length about revenge and about punishing those responsible for the evils they have endured. . . . What man of the people does not believe he has been treated unjustly by the powerful and does not dream about the "punishment" to inflict upon them?' [349,348]); the origins of the character of the 'superman' ('perhaps the popular "superman" of Dumas should really be considered as a "democratic" reaction to the concept of racism with its feudal origin and should be put alongside the glorification of "Gallicism" in the novels of Eugène Sue' [358]); and the way fictional characters, rather than celebrated writers, are central to the popular imagination ('the heroes of popular literature are separated from their "literary" origin and acquire the validity of historical figures. Their entire lives, from birth to death, are sources of interest and this explains the success of "sequels" even if they are spurious. . . . The term "historical figure" should not be taken in a literal sense . . . but figuratively in the sense that the fantasy world acquires a particular fabulous concreteness in popular intellectual life' [350]).

13. The best overall account of the struggle between 'union' and 'incorporation' in the culture of the late nineteenth century is Trachtenberg, 1982.

14. I borrow this term from Stuart Hall (1981, 233), who writes that the language of the tabloid press 'is neither a pure construction of Fleet Street "newspeak" nor is it the language which its working class readers actually speak. It is a highly complex species of linguistic *ventriloquism* in which the debased brutalism of popular journalism is skilfully combined and intricated with some elements of the directness and vivid particularity of working-class language. It cannot get by without preserving some elements of its roots in a real vernacular — in the "popular". It wouldn't get very far unless it were capable of reshaping popular elements into a species of canned and neutralized demotic populism.'

Chapter 6

1. Unfortunately, there is no detailed comparative study of the 'mysteries of the city', which is perhaps the first international popular genre. My discussion draws on several essays on particular writers: Umberto Eco,

1979, and Peter Brooks, 1984, on Eugène Sue; Peter Buckley, 1984, on Ned Buntline; Anne Humphreys, 1985, on G.M.W. Reynolds; and Werner Sollors, 1986, and Patricia Herminghouse, 1985, on the German-American writers. See also Siegel, 1981.

2. The other major innovation in the publishing world of Jacksonian Philadelphia was the 'movement to make magazines for ladies and ladies for magazines', in the words of Philadelphia's main literary historian (Oberholtzer, 1906, 228), the creation of monthly magazines for the genteel and cultivated women of the class of merchants, financiers, and manufacturers. There were a number of these magazines, usually costing three dollars a year, with titles like *The Ladies' Literary Portfolio* and *The Ladies' Garland*: the major ones were *Godey's Lady's Book*, founded by Louis Godey in 1830 but emerging into the height of its popularity and influence in the 1840s after Sarah Josepha Hale came to Philadelphia to edit it in 1841, and *Graham's Magazine*, founded in 1840 and edited for a short time by Edgar Allan Poe. These magazines published verse, sketches, and domestic stories, as well as full color fashion plates and steel engravings. They catered to and reflected the marked improvement in the consumption patterns, the 'lifestyle', of the families of merchants and manufacturers. As Warner, 1968, 66, summarizes it:

> In the years between 1827 and 1860 the new middle class enjoyed a number of important advances in everyday consumption. The bare floors, whitewashed walls, and scant furniture of middle-income eighteeth-century homes gave way to wool carpeting, wallpaper, and all manner of furnishings. The houses themselves became relatively cheaper and grew in size from three rooms to four-to-six rooms in row houses or flats in row houses. The children slept one to a bed, and indoor toilets became common in their homes. In contrast to the eighteenth century when the middle-income house generally included the shop, the husband now commonly worked in an office, store or shop outside his home, and the first-floor front room became a parlor instead of a work room. Mid-nineteenth-century families of the new middle class did not need to put their children to work in the family trade or shop; they could take full advantage of the new public grammar school education. Finally, they had grown prosperous enough to attend the increasing variety of offering of commercial downtown entertainment.

    Commercial entertainment included the new magazines. It is also important to note, as Warner does, that 'almost every item on this list of middle-class consumption gains lay beyond the reach of Philadelphia's artisan population.'

3. For details about Peterson, see Korey, 1980, 229-235 and Shove, 1937, 53-56. Actually Peterson's books were relatively expensive; the shilling 'extras' had been put out of business by increased postal rates and Peterson's cheapest line cost 25 cents. Nevertheless, until the appearance of Beadle's in 1860, T.B. Peterson was synonymous with cheap stories.

4. The biographical details on Lippard are taken from the excellent unpublished critical biography by Emilio De Grazia, 1969.

5. The other two types were his 'legends' of the American Revolution, stories of Revolutionary battles and heroics, published in the story papers and then collected in volumes like *Washington and His Generals; or, Legends of the Revolution* and the popular *Blanche of Brandywine; or, September the Eleventh,*

1777. A Romance Combining the Poetry, Legend, and History of the Battle of Brandywine; and his revolutionary allegory, *The Entranced; or, The Wanderer of Eighteen Centuries,* a tale that ranges from Nero's Rome to the European revolutions of 1848, from medieval Florence to the contemporary United States, as two giant allegorical characters, the wanderer Adonai and the Arisen Washington, witness class struggle and oppression through the ages, and ends with a vision of the deliverance of workers by the sword of Washington.

6. See Umberto Eco's, 1979, 132, discussion of the 'sinusoidal structure' of the serial novel, where, instead of the constant and accumulating curve of the self-contained narrative, one finds an episodic structure of 'tension, resolution, renewed tension, further resolution, and so on'.

7. Siegel, 1981, 61-75, notes that:

> Between 1820 and 1870 enterprising authors [in the U.S.] produced no fewer than seventy-five books which promised the public an inside look at the plutocracy. Paradoxically, these productions delighted in detailing the material abundance enjoyed by the city's upper class and, at the same time, courted the common man by ridiculing the excesses of a new moneyed elite.

And Humpherys, 1985, 13, sees in G.M.W. Reynolds

> a straightforward, perhaps unconscious expression of two elements in the popular mind: the desire for a better life defined predominantly by what the populace perceives as better in the lives of those 'above' them and a contradictory tendency to want to destroy that very desired life because those that had it were seen as exploiting those that didn't.

8. Taylor, 1977, 307. In a similar vein, Blumin, 1984, 17, notes that the mysteries 'did very little to illuminate life in the metropolis.' On the genre represented by Foster, as well as by Junius Henry Browne and James Dabney McCabe, see Blumin, 1984 and Taylor, 1977. The close relation between these works and the 'mysteries of the city' is indicated by Foster's attempt to write a 'mystery of the city': *Celio, or New York Above-Ground and Under-Ground,* 1850, of which Taylor notes, 'this disappointing story seems to owe more to the influence of the popular Philadelphia writer, George Lippard, than to Foster's first-hand contact with the raw material of life in New York City' (307-308).

9. The key discussion of the prostitute in nineteenth-century fiction, particularly that of Sue, is Brooks, 1984. Buckley, 1984, 442ff draws on Brooks in his discussion of the prostitute in Buntline.

10. There are a number of excellent recent studies of the domestic novel, a genre and literary practice that shares a fluctuating and not always clear border with cheap, sensational fiction and the fiction factories: see Baym, 1978; Douglas, 1977; Kelley, 1984; and Tompkins, 1980.

11. On the view of the Revolution in dime novels, see Curti, 1937.

12. Here I follow the loose periodization suggested by the historian of women, Mary Ryan, 1979, xvii, who has argued that there have been three distinct patterns in the sex/gender system of the United States: 'first, the integral position of women in the patriarchal household economy of the seventeenth century; second, the segregated woman's sphere under industrial capitalism; and finally, the integration of females into once-male spheres during the twentieth century.'

13. The concept of a vanishing mediator is developed for narrative analysis in Jameson, 1974; the classic formulation of the notion of a mediator that vanishes is Marx, 1867, 187.
14. Ziff, 1981, 100. However, I prefer the nuances of Terry Eagleton's, 1982, 88, comment about the seduction narrative: 'Sexuality, far from being some displacement of class conflict, is the very medium in which it is conducted.'
15. These same voyeuristic passages are the basis for Leslie Fiedler's, 1970, xiii-xiv, explanation of the eclipse of the seduction narrative and his argument that Lippard's work was aimed at an exclusively male audience:

> It should be clear that the literature of the 1840s is a specific sub-genre of popular literature — not merely produced by men only but intended for an exclusively male audience. It was, therefore, doomed, to a temporary eclipse at least, not only by the more ambitious literature contemporary with it, the work of, say, Balzac and Dickens — but also by the pop literature which immediately succeeded it: those genteel best-sellers of the 1870s [the 1850s and 1860s is more accurate] ... which represented an attempt to come to terms with the re-emergence of a bourgeois female audience — first appealed to by Richardson — as the controllers of the literary market place. In any case, it is the temporary dissolution of a politically minded male audience with a taste for sub-pornography, in favor of the domestically oriented female audience with a taste for pure sentimentality which explains the loss of approval suffered by Lippard's kind of fiction.

Fiedler's evidence as to Lippard's male audience is entirely stylistic; he compares descriptions of the female form in passages from Lippard and from the London story paper, the *Family Herald*. The male novel of the 1840s, says Fiedler, has a style which 'tends toward the breathless, the ecstatic, the rhapsodic'; 'conventional marks of punctuation give way to dashes or dots to indicate the replacement of logic by passion' (xiv-xv). This is convincing as far as it goes; nevertheless, one would like other sorts of evidence. The idea of separate gendered reading publics is possible; that one should replace the other in controlling the literary marketplace is unlikely. Lippard himself addresses his readers as 'the young man and young woman' in *The Quaker City* and as 'every honest man and woman' in *The Nazarene*. The popularity of his works would indicate that they crossed the boundaries of a gendered audience; indeed, the development of specifically gendered audiences for fiction is more likely a part of the larger creation of separate spheres that is occurring at this time.

16. De Grazia, 1969, 139. Unfortunately, no source for this statement is given, so it is difficult to evaluate this 'denunciation'.
17. An advertisement bound with Foster, 1850.
18. The place of republicanism in American ideology has been the subject of much recent historiography; see Appleby, 1985, Hanson, 1985, Ross, 1979. The delineation of a specifically artisan republicanism is particularly convincing in the work of Bruce Laurie, 1980, Sean Wilentz, 1984, and Eric Foner, 1980, 58, who writes:

> Workingmen responded to these developments [the emergence of the factory system, the dilution of craft skill, the imposition of a new labor discipline in traditional craft production, the growing gap between masters and journeymen, and the increasing stratification of the social order, especially in the large eastern cities] within the context of an

ideology dating back to the Paineite republicanism of the American Revolution. The central ingredients in this ideology were a passionate attachment to equality (defined not as a leveling of all distinctions, but as the absence of large inequalities of wealth and influence), belief that independence — the ability to resist personal or economic coercion — was an essential attribute of the republican citizenry, and a commitment to the labor theory of value, along with its corollary, that labor should receive the full value of its product.

Dan Schiller, 1981, convincingly interprets the penny press in the light of artisan republicanism: his argument about the audience of the penny press complements my assessment of the dime novel audience. Schiller writes: 'that craftsmen — the artisans and mechanics of the burgeoning Eastern cities, with a much smaller number of "large merchants" and "wealthy people" — formed the primary public for the cheap press is, I think, indisputable' (9-10). Refuting earlier studies of the penny press, he shows that the merchants and mechanics of the 1830s and 1840s were not a single 'middle class' or 'common man', but were antagonistic classes in conflict: 'It is entirely correct to call the antipathy between the sixpennies and the cheap commercial papers a form of "class conflict", but it was not a battle between old aristocrats and a new middle class; rather, it was a battle between contemporary privilege and monopoly, typified perhaps best of all by the banks, and artisan-backed equal-rights' (53). Recent studies of artisan ideology in Britain (Stedman Jones, 1983) and France (Sewell, 1980) would indicate that the European 'mysteries of the city' emerged in a not dissimilar ideological context.

19. Marx was critical of both. On Reynolds' politics, see Humphreys, 1985; on the entanglement of rhetoric and ideology in Sue, see Eco, 1979.

20. On Lippard's Brotherhood of the Union, see Butterfield, 1955; on its place within the labor movement, see Wilentz, 1984, 367-368.

21. 'Szeliga' was the pseudonym of Franz Zychlin von Zychlinsky. A particularly helpful discussion of Marx's treatment of Sue can be found in Prawer, 1976, 86-102.

22. Indeed, Lippard's hero worship passed from narrative to politics when he celebrated Zachary Taylor, the Mexican War general, in his *Legends of Mexico* and then campaigned for him in the election of 1848. By the middle of 1849, however, he had reconsidered his enthusiasm for the Mexican War and lost faith in the revolutionary qualities of Taylor. For an excellent discussion of Lippard's dime novels of the Mexican War, see Slotkin, 1985, 192-198.

23. This is, in a way, Marx's verdict on Sue's fiction, though that assessment is entangled in Marx's parallel critiques of Sue's political proposals and of the German critic Szeliga's interpretation of Sue.

24. Howard Erlich, 1972, 62, has called attention to the graphic aspects of *The Quaker City*, arguing that 'the work fails ... because it tries to adapt the visual organization of the diorama or panorama to the Gothic novel.' See also the suggestions of Ridgely, 1974, 86.

25. See Sollors's (1986, 144-148) discussion of Klauprecht, and Herminghouse's (1985) discussion of Börnstein. On the dime novel western, see Smith, 1950, and Jones, 1978.

26. For a history of the Philadelphia riots, see Feldberg, 1975, 1980, and Montgomery, 1972.

27. For a rejection of Lippard's explanation and a discussion of the class and ethnic dynamics behind the riots, see Montgomery, 1972, 58.

28. On Duganne, see Curti, 1937, 772; and Zahler, 1941, 45. Zahler notes that the *Iron Man*, edited by Duganne, and Lippard's *Quaker City* were two of three radical papers published in Philadelphia. Duganne's poetry was also published in a variety of labor papers. On Duganne and the Know-Nothings, see Johannsen, 1950, 2:86 and Scisco, 1901, 240.

29. For the history of the Killers and the election night riot, see Laurie, 1980, 151-159.

30. On 'white egalitarianism', see Saxton, 1984; on abolitionism and the labor movement, see Foner, 1980, 57-76.

Chapter 7

1. I have relied on Broehl, 1964, Aurand and Gudelunas, 1982, and, to a lesser extent, Bimba, 1932 for overall accounts.

2. George Munro not only used Pastor's name as the author of a number of serials, but published ten-cent songbooks like *Tony Pastor's 'Down in the Coal Mine' Songster*. On Pastor, see Noel, 1954, 123-124.

3. For details of newspaper coverage and specific quotations, see Bimba, 1932, 13,14,86 and Broehl, 1964, 307. Broehl points out that 'the Yost case was a matter of personal grudge. . . . Nothing in the trial had tied the Yost murder to labor-union activity.'

4. Broehl, 1964, for example, sometimes uses the terms interchangeably, as in his characterization of John P. Jones, a murder victim.

5. The first installment of *The Slate-Picker* is accompanied by a sentimental poem about a slate-picker by the editor, Francis S. Smith.

6. A biographical sketch of Aiken can be found in Johannsen, 1950, 2:8-9.

7. See Montgomery, 1976, 115. Herbert Gutman, 1963, 47, argued that 'the small businessmen and shopkeepers, the lawyers and professional people, and the other nonindustrial members of the middle class were a small but vital element in these industrial towns. Unlike the urban middle class they had direct and everyday contact with the new industrialism and with the problems and outlook of workers and employers.'

8. Though I have not found circulation figures for the story papers in the spring of 1876, *Ayer & Son's Manual Manual for Advertisers* (3rd Edition, June 1877) shows Street & Smith's *New York Weekly* at 150,000, far surpassing the *Fireside Companion*'s 35,000 and the *Saturday Journal*'s 30,000.

9. For useful discussions of these narratives, see Hartsfield, 1985, 39-73, and Reilly, 1976. On the origins of the detective in popular fiction, see Cox, 1981, Hartsfield, 1985, 105-118, Hoppenstand, 1982, and Stewart, 1980.

10. A similar attitude toward the detective may be found in George McWatter's (1871, 647-653) semi-fictional detective narrative which sees the detective as a 'representative man', and offers a striking example of the popular rhetoric of class:

> There are but two great classes in civilization, — the oppressed and the oppressors, the trampled upon and the tramplers. To the latter class belongs the detective. . . . He is the outgrowth of a diseased and corrupted state of things, and is, consequently, morally diseased himself. His very existence is a satire upon society. . . . He makes friends in order to reap the profit of betraying them . . . aside from the fact that the detective, in his calling, is often degraded to a sort of watchman or ordinary policeman, to help the big thieves, the merchants, etc., protect them-

selves from the small thieves, who are not able to keep places of business ... his calling is a very noble one, and a singularly blessed one,
inasmuch as it is the only one which I call to mind, by which hypocrisy
is elevated into a really useful and beneficent art. ... In all he is a representative man; for throughout all the departments of trade and business,
from the greatest to the least, all are swindlers, to more or less extent.
Nobody better than the detective knows how absurd and ridiculous it is
to talk of 'honesty in trade', for he is quite as likely to be called upon to
ferret out and arrest a forger or a cheat in the respectable ranks of business as he is to entrap a common pickpocket.

11. See Stern, 1980, 81-88 for a sketch of Carleton; she quotes Ralph Gardner as
noting that 'since a number of Carleton's books were reprints of stories
originally published in *New York Weekly*, it is safe to assume that there was a
close business connection, and possibly a partial ownership of the Carleton
organization by Street & Smith.'

12. The Pinkerton story had an even firmer hold on middle class fiction than on
the dime novel. Several novels retold the tale of Molly Maguire terror in the
forty years after the hangings. Patrick Justin McMahon's *Philip; or, The
Mollie's Secret. A Tale of the Coal Regions*, 1891, makes James MaParland the
hero of the novel. Rev. R.F. Bishop's *Camerton Slope*, 1893, explicitly states
that his facts are drawn from 'Allan Pinkerton's narrative of the part taken
by his organization in hunting down this "midnight, dark-lantern,
murderous-minded fraternity."' But despite his claim to have 'at an early
age entered the mines as a driver', his genteel Protestantism takes over. His
town, Camerton, is more 'American' than the other mining towns, and it 'in
general represented a higher order of social life; the homes were cleaner and
better kept.' The Camerton miners will not join the strike, and the book
ends with a heroic vigilance committee exiling five Mollies from the area.
And as late as 1915, Arthur Conan Doyle turned to the Pinkerton account
for a Sherlock Holmes novel, *The Valley of Fear*, which drew much of its
American section from Pinkerton. See Blake, 1972, 37-39, 211, 215, 218-220,
for a discussion of these and three other middle class novels that deal with
the Molly Maguire case.

Chapter 8

1. This is what Seelye, 1963 argues in an otherwise useful essay. For a brief but
interesting discussion see Rodgers, 1978, 226-228.

2. For a discussion of Harris' novel, see Ringenbach, 1973, 13-14. Ringenbach,
1973 treats the 'discovery' of the tramp by various legal, scientific and
reforming discourses; Monkkonen, 1984 offers an excellent collection of
essays on tramps in America.

3. Quoted in Seelye, 1963, 541. On the way the tramp served as a 'mediating
symbol' tying strikers to savages, see Slotkin, 1985, 481.

4. See Enslin, 1971, 102 for the early publication history, and Slotkin, 1985,
307-308, for a brief discussion of Alger and tramps.

5. Indeed the idea of the riots produced on stage was not so strange: Francis
Couvares, 1984, 42-43, noted the 1878 production at Pittsburgh's Fifth
Avenue Lyceum of Bartley Campbell's *The Lower Million*, which depicted
events of the railroad strike of 1877 and employed 'veteran rioters' as extras.
Unlike Whittaker's story of tramps, however, Campbell's play resembled

the workingman hero tales that I will discuss in the next chapter.

6. Johannsen, 1950, 1:256, usually the most reliable bibliographic authority, dates the first story 15 October 1877; however, Durham, 1966, xii dates it 25 July 1877 which has the poetic truth of placing it right in the midst of the two weeks of national railroad strikes.

7. This is a phrase from Smith, 1950, but it also structures the work of Jones, 1978 and the Durham, 1966 reprinting of *Seth Jones* and *Deadwood Dick on Deck*.

8. On the Carson narratives, see Henry Nash Smith himself, 1950, 81-89, Kent Steckmesser, 1965, 13-53, and Richard Slotkin, 1985, 200-207. Slotkin offers the most persuasive interpretation of the two myths of Carson.

9. The full story of the crackdown or 'cleanup' of the outlaw stories has not been told. The main secondary sources are Smith, 1944; Settle, 1966, 190 (who cites a letter that apparently deals with the 1903 suspension); and Deutsch, 1976. Jones, 1978, 79, says that 'the Postmaster General threatened Frank Tousey with the loss of second-class postal privileges' and cites Smith, 1944 as a source; however, though Smith implies this possibility, he does not establish it. It is also possible that it was the result of Anthony Comstock's campaign; Bremner, 1967, xx, writes that 'in the mid-1880s [Comstock] successfully prosecuted book dealers for selling "criminal story papers" and "stories of bloodshed and crime".' Puffer, 1980, 300, supports this when he writes 'it was the publication in 1884 of stories of London court life that led to [Tousey's] arrest and interrogation by Anthony Comstock, postal inspector and secretary of the Society for the Suppression of Vice. To get the prosecution dropped, Tousey promised to destroy the offending plates. Comstock and his group regularly attacked publishers, authors, booksellers, and newsdealers in an attempt to stop what they thought unwholesome literature. Tousey yielded to this pressure in 1883 by abruptly stopping all stories about outlaws.'

Chapter 9

1. There is a wide and growing literature on the relation between the sex/gender system of the nineteenth-century American middle class and the novel; see for example Cawelti, 1965; Douglas, 1977; Habegger, 1982; and Halttunen, 1982.

2. For a brief but illuminating discussion of the mechanic in mid-century popular fiction, see Siegel, 1981, 83-86; on the figure of Mose, see Buckley, 1984, 271-342, and Blumin, 1984, 20-28.

3. I will concentrate on the commercial fiction of the cheap libraries and the story papers. For a discussion of a sensational story published in a labor newspaper, see Susan Levine's (1984, 143-147) discussion of the Boston *Labor Leader's* story *Ella Inness: A Romance of the Big Lock-Out; or, How a Knight Won the Prize*. And for a discussion of 'melodrama and comedy ... based on local and working-class themes' in Pittsburgh, see Couvares, 1984, 41-43.

4. *Beadle's Weekly* was a continuation of the Beadle & Adams story paper, the *Saturday Journal*, under a new name. For Whittaker's biography and Beadle publications, see Johannsen, 1950, 2:300-302. On his earnings, see Noel, 1954, 131. See also Slotkin's (1985, 500-510) excellent discussion of his popular 1876 biography of Custer. I am indebted to Virginia Moskowitz, the Mount Vernon, NY, City Historian, for her help in tracking down the career of Frederick Whittaker.

5. On the cult of manliness, see also Couvares, 1984, 56.
6. The term 'aristomilitary romance' comes from Martin Green's (1979) important study of the relation between adventure fiction and imperialist ideologies.
7. The distance of Whittaker's tales from middle class codes is further highlighted by the fact that the Alger stories themselves, far from being completely respectable, were attacked throughout the 1880s for their sensationalism. See Daniel Rodgers's (1978, 140-143) brief but excellent discussion of Alger.
8. For a discussion of various 'solutions' to the wage system see Rodgers, 1978, 40-64.
9. Slotkin's (1985) discussion of Whittaker's 1876 biography of Custer offers an interesting counterpoint to the interpretation of these tales, though he stresses Whittaker's similarities to Alger rather than his differences. The Custer biography also unites the aristomilitary romance and the narrative of education: Slotkin calls Whittaker's Custer 'an amalgamation of a Cooper Frontiersman-aristocrat and an upwardly mobile Horatio Alger boy hero. . . . He combines in his character and career aspects of the chivalric knight and of the new man of "that great industrial class from whom so many of our original men are springing"' (503, 505). And Whittaker struggles with the antinomies of self-advancement and mutualism, findig a synthesis in the Civil War army (507-510).
10. Quoted in Fraser, 1982, 9. For the middlebrow 'best-sellers', see Hart, 1950, 180-200 and Mott, 1947.
11. This story underwent several small changes in the New York Dime Library edition of December 1903 which I used; in comparing this edition with the two (of eleven) installments of the original serialization in Beadle's Weekly that I located, the principal change was the deletion of all references to the 'Amalgamated Union of the iron-workers in the United States' in the later edition. Whether this was done in the first reprinting in 1886 or in the second reprinting in 1903, I don't know. It is interesting that the novel represents a victorious strike in a period when the Amalgamated Association of Iron and Steel-Workers had lost the 'great' strike in Pittsburgh in 1882, and 'in the latter part of 1882 and the first seven months of 1883 [Larry Locke was first serialized in October 1883], twenty strikes and one lockout occurred, nearly all of which were precipitated by the workmen, and ended disastrously' (McNeill, 1886, 307). I am indebted to David Montgomery for calling my attention to the possible changes in the story. See also my Bibliographic Note.

Chapter 10

1. Peterson, 1983 is the first significant discussion of Libbey and the working-girl novel, but see also Utter and Needham, 1936, 328-367. For a list of representative titles, see Godfrey, 1983, 69-71. Leonie Locke was Libbey's fourth serial for the Fireside Companion but her first working girl story.
2. Stansell, 1986, has an excellent discussion of the early figures of working women in antebellum labor, reform, and journalistic discourses, including the figure of the 'starving seamstress' (72-74, 110), the figure of the factory girl (125-128, 139), and the figure of Lize, the Bowery Gal, the companion of Mose (91-100).

3. This characterization oversimplifies an important area of research and critical debate. Besides Douglas, 1977 and Tompkins, 1980, see Baym, 1978 and 1984; Kelley, 1979 and 1984; and Tompkins, 1985.

4. For a fine discussion of Phelps' late writings, see Stansell, 1972.

5. There may be more. Libbey wrote for the *Fireside Companion* between October 1882 and January 1886, and between January 1890 and late 1897, and for the *Family Story Paper* between February 1886 and late 1889, and between January 1898 and 1901. She also wrote some stories for the *New York Ledger*. Her novels were reprinted in many cheap libraries, including the Library of American Authors, the Hart Series, and Munro's Library of Popular Novels. I am indebted to the excellent bibliographies of Edward LeBlanc (see Bibliographic Note) for the publishing details of the two principal story papers. Most of the treatments of Libbey contrast her to either Dreiser or Alger. Davidson and Davidson 1977 and Godfrey 1983 both develop the connection between the working-girl stories and Dreiser, revealing more about Dreiser than about the working-girl stories in the process. Peterson, 1983 and Davidson, 1981 see Libbey as a female equivalent of Alger. This seems to me based on a popular misreading of Alger; she seems closer to the young mechanic tales discussed in the last chapter.

6. I borrow the term 'masked divorce story' from Sally Mitchell, 1981, 156.

7. I am indebted to Priscilla Murolo for sharing her work on working girls' clubs, and her suggestions about their relevance to Libbey's novels.

8. See the excellent discussion by Mitchell, 1981.

9. See Sarah Eisenstein's (1983, 126-128) discussion of the romanticism of young women workers, and Elizabeth Ewen's (1985, 228) account of 'new ideals of romantic love ... taking precedence over customary values' among Jewish and Italian women in New York's Lower East Side. Ewen's book, with its attention to the interplay of economy and culture, offers much towards an understanding of a significant part of Libbey's audience.

10. For a discussion of the dime novel western heroine, see Smith, 1950, 112-120.

11. The interpretation of Capitola as a 'tomboy' is persuasively made by Alfred Habegger, 1981 and 1982; the description of *The Lady Detective* comes from a March 29, 1890 advertisement for the Old Sleuth Library.

Conclusion

1. On the development of the Western, see Cawelti 1971, and Wright, 1975. I do not mean to imply that the twentieth-century Western is an entirely uncontested genre; an attention to the pulp and paperback Western would probably reveal not merely a variety of formulas but the ways those formulas have been inflected by contemporary social conflicts. An example is Jane Tompkins's excellent paper on Louis L'Amour delivered at the 1985 American Studies Association Convention .

2. The best discussion of Alger is Scharnhorst, 1985; see in particular his discussion of the controversy over sensationalism (117-123), and his history of Alger's reception and reputation (149-156). He shows that despite the nineteenth-century attacks on Alger, Alger was usually distinguished from dime novels proper; Alger himself wrote that 'sensational stories, such as are found in the dime and half-dime libraries, do much harm, and are very

objectionable. Many a boy has been tempted to crime by them. Such stories as "The Boy Highwayman", "The Boy Pirate", and books of that class, do incalculable mischief' (Scharnhorst, 1985, 120). On the suspicion of Alger among figures of genteel culture, see Heins's (1974, 120-121) discussion of the nineteenth-century reviews of Alger, which includes the comment in *St. Nicholas*, a genteel children's magazine, that Alger's *Brave and Bold* 'is of the "sensational" order, while the characters are such as we do not meet in real life — and we are very glad that we don't meet them.' On the failure of the Street and Smith story paper, *Boys of the World*, see Reynolds, 1955, 37, 51-52; on the failure of Munsey's *Golden Argosy*, see Scharnhorst, 1985, 132. The assessment of Alger's greater posthumous readership comes from Mott, (1947, 158-159). On Alger's place in the myth of the self-made man, see Cawelti, 1965.

3. I borrow the distinction between story and discourse from structuralist narrative theory. Chatman, 1978, 19, gives a useful summary: 'Structuralist theory argues that each narrative has two parts: a story (*histoire*), the content or chain of events (actions, happenings), plus what may be called the existents (characters, items of setting); and a discourse (*discours*), that is, the expression, the means by which the content is communicated.'

4. Despite the scholarly emphasis on the dime novel western, Roger Nichols 1982, 49, notes, few scholars have given attention to the depiction of Indians in dime novels; moreover, 'surprisingly few westerns paid much attention to the Indians, and those which did rarely offered new ways to depict them.' See also Simmons, 1981, on nativism and racism in the dime novel and Smith, 1980, on stereotypes of Mexicans.

Bibliographic Note

The bibliography of dime novels, story papers, and cheap libraries is still very undeveloped; many of the series and serials lie in uncharted reams of decaying rag and pulp. It remains difficult to find particular novels, to establish the works of particular writers, and to track the various reprintings of stories. Johannsen 1950 is still the most exhaustive bibliography, providing a valuable map of the publications of Beadle and Adams. Butterfield 1955 has a good bibliography of Lippard's work. The series of bibliographic listings published by Edward T. LeBlanc as supplements to *Dime Novel Round-Up* are invaluable; I used the following ones:

Cox, J. Randolph. 1974. *The Nick Carter Library*. Fall River, Mass.: Edward T. LeBlanc.
—— 1975. *New Nick Carter Weekly*. Fall River, Mass.: Edward T. LeBlanc.
—— 1977, 1980. *Nick Carter Stories*. Two Parts. Fall River, Mass.: Edward T. LeBlanc.
—— 1985. *Magnet Detective Library*. Fall River, Mass.: Edward T. LeBlanc.
Craufurd, Ross. 1976. *The New Sensation and The Sporting New Yorker*. Fall River, Mass.: Edward T. LeBlanc.
—— 1979. *Our Boys and New York Boys Weekly: The Great Tousey-Munro Rivalry*. Fall River, Mass.: Edward T. LeBlanc.
Mayo, Chester G. 1960. *Good News*. Fall River, Mass.: Edward T. LeBlanc.
Rogers, Denis R. 1958. *Munro's Ten Cent Novels*. Fall River, Mass.: Edward T. LeBlanc.
Steinhauer, Donald L. No Date. *Golden Days*. Fall River, Mass.: Edward T. LeBlanc.

I am also greatly indebted to Edward LeBlanc for the use of the following unpublished bibliographic listings:

LeBlanc, Edward T. *Family Story Paper*.
—— *Fireside Companion*.
—— *New York Weekly*.

237

LeBlanc's Bibliographic Listings of The New York Detective Library, Old Cap. Collier Library, Old Sleuth Library, Old Sleuth Weekly, Young Sleuth Library, Bob Brooks Library, and Secret Service are published in an abbreviated form in Hoppenstand 1982.

Cheap Stories

As I noted in the discussion of Whittaker's *Larry Locke*, there were changes between one printing and another in dime novels, so later editions must be used cautiously; nevertheless, one is often forced to use later editions. The bibliography of cheap stories below lists the abbreviations of the stories cited in the text, the details of the probable first edition, and the details of the edition I quote from. Since the stories often change formats, I have cited the *chapter* number, *not* the page number, in the text, except in the cases of Brown, Lippard, Pinkerton, and Whitman.

Al Aiken, Albert. *The Molly Maguires; or, The Black Diamond of Hazelton. A Story of the Great Strike in the Coal Region. Fireside Companion* #436-#449 (6 March 1876 — 5 June 1876).

AL Alger, Horatio Jr. *Tony, the Tramp. New York Weekly* 31:#32-#42 (26 June 1876 — 4 September 1876).

Ba Barrett, John E. *Love and Labor: or, The Perils of the Poor. A Tale of the Present Great Strike. New York Weekly* 32:#41-33:#3 (24 September 1877 — 3 December 1877). Reprinted as *The Hillsburg Tragedy; or, Murdered for Gold.* Log Cabin Library #114 (21 May 1891).

Bb——— *A Knight of Labor; or, The Master Workman's Vow. New York Weekly* 40:#4-#15 (1 December 1884 — 16 February 1885). Reprinted in Log Cabin Library #85 (30 October 1890).

BE Bellamy, Charles. *The Breton Mills; A Romance of New England Life. Labor Leader* 20 October 1888 — 1 March 1889.

BR Brown, William Wells. *Clotel; or, The President's Daughter. A Narrative of Slave Life in the United States.* London: Partridge & Oakey, 1853. Reprinted by New York: Collier Books, 1970. Revised for first United States edition as *Clotelle: A Tale of the Southern States.* Redpath's Books for the Camp Fires #2 (1864).

C Cobb, Weldon. *Reuben Dalton's Career; or, A Struggle for the Right. A Story for Workingmen. Workingman's Advocate* 5 April 1873 — 19 April 1873.

Da Doyle, Daniel. *Molly Maguire, The Terror of the Coal Fields. New York Weekly* 31:#17-#33 (13 March 1876 — 3 July 1876).

Db——— *The Slate-Picker; or, The Slave of the Coal Shaft. New York Weekly* 31:#33-#44 (3 July 1876 — 18 September 1876).

F *Frank James on the Trail.* Morrison's Sensational Series #46 (1 July 1882). Reprinted in *Eight Dime Novels,* edited by E.F. Bleiler. New York: Dover Publications, 1974.

I Ingraham, Prentiss. *Darkie Dan, the Colored Detective; or, The Mississippi Mystery.* Beadle's Dime Library #134 (18 May 1881).

LBa Libbey, Laura Jean. *Leonie Locke; or, The Romance of a Beautiful New York Working-Girl. Fireside Companion* #858-#873 (7 April 1884 — 21 July 1884). Reprinted in Munro's Library of Popular Novels #264 (23 November 1897).

LBb——— *Little Leafy, the Cloakmaker's Beautiful Daughter. A Romantic Story of a Lovely Working Girl in the City of New York. Family Story Paper* #661-#673 (5 June 1886 — 26 August 1886). Reprinted by New York: J.S. Ogilvie Publishing Company, No Date.

LBc——— *Little Rosebud's Lovers; or, A Cruel Revenge.* The Library of American Authors #16 (1886). Reprinted by New York: J.S. Ogilvie Publishing Company, No Date.

LBd——— *Viola, the Beauty of Long Branch; or, Only a Mechanic's Daughter. A Charming Story of Love and Life at the Sea Shore. Family Story Paper* #773-#786 (28 July 1888 — 27 October 1888). Reprinted as *Only a Mechanic's Daughter. A Charming Story of Love and Passion.* New York: Norman L. Munro, 1892.

LPa Lippard, George. *The Quaker City; or, The Monks of Monk Hall. A Romance of Philadelphia Life, Mystery and Crime.* Philadelphia: G.B. Zieber & Co., 1844. Published in installments. Reprinted as *The Monks of Monk Hall.* New York: Odyssey Press, 1970.

LPb——— *The Nazarene; Or, The Last of the Washingtons. A Revelation of Philadelphia, New York, and Washington, in the Year 1844.* Philadelphia: G. Lippard and Co., 1846. Published in installments. Reprinted by Philadelphia: T.B. Peterson, 1854.

LPc——— [A Member of the Philadelphia Bar, pseud.] *The Killers. A Narrative of Real Life in Philadelphia, in which the deeds of the Killers, and the great Riot of election night, October 10, 1849, are minutely described.* Serialized in *Quaker City Weekly,* beginning 1 December 1849. Reprinted by Philadelphia: Hankinson and Bartholomew, 1850.

LPd——— *The Empire City; or, New York by Night and Day.* New York: String & Townsend, 1850. Published in installments. Reprinted by Freeport, N.Y.: Books for Libraries Press, 1969.

LPe——— *New York: Its Upper Ten and Lower Million.* Cincinnati: H.M. Rulison, Queen City Publishing House, 1853. Published in installments. Reprinted by Upper Saddle River, N.J.: The Gregg Press, 1970.

M Morris, Anthony P. *Old Cincinnati on His Mettle; or, On the Trail of the Anarchists.* Old Cap. Collier Library #517 (18 November 1893).

OD O'Donnell, Sergeant. *Coal-Mine Tom; or, Fighting the Molly Maguires.* The Five Cent Wide Awake Library #620 (23 July 1884).

OLa Old Cap. Collier. *Black Tom, the Negro Detective; or, Solving a Thompson Street Mystery.* Old Cap. Collier Library #486 (22 April 1893).

OLb——— *On to Washington; or, Old Cap. Collier with the Coxey Army.* Old Cap. Collier Library #545 (30 May 1894).

PA Pastor, Tony. *Down in a Coal Mine; or, The Mystery of the Fire Damp. Fireside Companion* #302-? (11 August 1873 — ?). Reprinted under same title with author, Old Sleuth, in Old Sleuth Library #48 (29 March 1890). Reprinted under title *Foiled by Love; or, The Molly Maguire's Last Stand* in Old Sleuth Weekly #44 (1909).

PI Pinkerton, Allan. *The Mollie Maguires and The Detectives.* New York: G.W.

Carleton & Co., Allan Pinkerton's Detective Stories #6, 1877. Reprinted by New York: Dover Publications, 1973.

R Rattler, Corporal Morgan. *The Irish Claude Duval*. The Five Cent Wide Awake Library #487 (3 May 1882).

Sa 'Seyek.' *Ella Inness, A Romance of the Big Lockout; or, How the Knight Won the Prize. Labor Leader* 19 March 1887 — 30 April 1887.

Sb——— *John Behman's Experience; Or, A Chapter from the Life of a Union Carpenter. Labor Leader* 7 April 1888 — 26 May 1888.

T Turner, William Mason. *The Masked Miner; or, The Iron Merchant's Daughter. A Tale of Pittsburg. Saturday Journal* #15-26 (25 June 1870 — 10 September 1870). Reprinted in *Saturday Journal* #318-329 (15 April 1876 — 1 July 1876). Reprinted as *Doubly Disguised; or, The Young Miner's Merciless Foe. Banner Weekly* #398-409 (28 June 1890 — 13 September 1890).

U A U.S. Detective. *The Molly Maguire Detective; or, A Vidocq's Adventures Among the Miners*. The New York Detective Library #179 (8 May 1886).

WHa Wheeler, Edward L. *Deadwood Dick, The Prince of the Road; or, The Black Rider of the Black Hills*. Beadle's Half-Dime Library #1 (1877). Reprinted in *Eight Dime Novels*, edited by E.F. Bleiler. New York: Dover Publications, 1974.

WHb——— *Deadwood Dick On Deck; or, Calamity Jane, The Heroine of Whoop-Up. A Story of Dakota*. Beadle's Half-Dime Library #73 (17 December 1878). Reprinted in *Dime Novels*, edited by Philip Durham. New York: The Odyssey Press, 1966.

WM Whitman, Walter. *Franklin Evans; or, The Inebriate. A Tale of the Times. New World* Extra #34 (23 November 1842). Reprinted in *Uncollected Poetry and Prose of Walt Whitman*, edited by Emory Holloway. Volume Two. Garden City, N.Y.: Doubleday, Page and Company, 1921.

WTa Whittaker, Capt. Fred. *Nemo, King of the Tramps; or, The Romany Girl's Vengeance. A Story of the Great Railroad Riots. Saturday Journal* #564-576 (1 January 1881 — 26 March 1881). Reprinted in The New York Dime Library #1062 (July 1902).

WTb——— *John Armstrong, Mechanic; or, From the Bottom to the Top of the Ladder. A Story of How a Man Can Rise in America. Beadle's Weekly* #1-12 (18 November 1882 — 3 February 1883). Reprinted in Beadle's New York Dime Library #378 (20 January 1886).

WTc——— *Jaspar Ray, The Journeyman Carpenter; or, One Man as Good as Another in America. A Story of How a Carpenter Made His Way in the World. Beadle's Weekly* #19-31 (24 March 1883 — 16 June 1883). Reprinted as *Journeyman John, The Champion; or, The Winning Hand. A Story of How a Carpenter Made His Way in the World*. Beadle's New York Dime Library #445 (4 May 1887).

WTd——— *Larry Locke, The Man of Iron; or, A Fight for Fortune. A Story of Labor and Capital. Beadle's Weekly* #50-61 (27 October 1883 — 12 January 1884). Reprinted in The New York Dime Library #1079 (December 1908).

WTe——— *A Knight of Labor; or Job Manly's Rise in Life. A Story of a Young Man from the Country. Beadle's Weekly* #74-85 (12 April 1884 — 28 June 1884). Reprinted as *The Champion Coach-Maker; or, Job Manly, Apprentice and Proprietor. A Story of a Young Man from the Country. Banner Weekly* #572-583 (28 October 1893 — 13 January 1894).

Y The Author of 'Young Sleuth.' *Young Sleuth and the Millionaire Tramp; or, Diamonds under Rags*. Young Sleuth Library #113 (5 July 1895).

Bibliography

Adimari, Ralph. 1935. 'Saga of a Dime Novelist.' *American Book Collector* 6(January, February, March): 24-27, 72-75, 99-100.

——— 1956. 'Upton Sinclair, Last of the Dime Novelists.' *Dime Novel Round-Up* #285(June): 42-44; #286(July): 51-52. Followed by 'A Letter from Upton Sinclair.' #287(August): 62.

——— 1958. 'William J. Benners: The First Historian of the Dime Novel.' *Dime Novel Round-Up* #312(September 15): 121-128.

Alexander, James W. [Charles Quill, pseud.]. 1838. *The American Mechanic.* Philadelphia: Henry Perkins.

——— 1839. *The Working-Man.* Philadelphia: Henry Perkins.

Allen, James Smith. 1981. *Popular French Romanticism: Authors, Readers, and Books in the 19th Century.* Syracuse: Syracuse University Press.

——— 1983. 'History and the Novel: *Mentalité* in Modern Popular Fiction'. *History and Theory* 22(iii): 233-252.

Altick, Richard D. 1957. *The English Common Reader: A Social History of the Mass Reading Public, 1800-1900.* Chicago: University of Chicago Press.

Anderson, Benedict. 1983. *Imagined Communities: Reflections on the Origin and Spread of Nationalism.* London: New Left Books.

Appleby, Joyce. 1985. 'Republicanism and Ideology.' *American Quarterly* 37(iv): 461-473.

Aurand, Harold and William Gudelunas. 1982. 'The Mythical Qualities of Molly Maguire.' *Pennsylvania History* 49(April): 91-105.

Barnes, James J. 1974. *Authors, Publishers an Politicians: The Quest for an Anglo-American Copyright Agreement 1815-1854.* Columbus: Ohio State University Press.

Barthes, Roland. 1974. *S/Z.* New York: Hill and Wang.

Baym, Nina. 1978. *Woman's Fiction: A Guide to Novels By and About Women in America, 1820-1870.* Ithaca, N.Y.: Cornell University Press.

——— 1984. *Novels, Readers, and Reviewers: Responses to Fiction in Antebellum America.* Ithaca: Cornell University Press.

The Beadle Collection of Dime Novels. 1922. New York: New York Public Library.

'The Beadle Dime Novel.' 1900. *Publishers Weekly* 57 (June 16): 1187-1188.

Bellows, Robert Peabody. 1899. 'The Degeneration of the Dime Novel.' *The Writer* 12(July): 97-99.

Benjamin, Walter. 1936. 'The Storyteller: Reflections on the Works of Nikolai Leskov.' In *Illuminations.* New York: Schocken Books, 1969.

Bercovitch, Sacvan. 1978. *The American Jeremiad.* Madison: The University of Wisconsin Press.

Berman, Russell A. 1983. 'Writing for the Book Industry: The Writer under Organized Capitalism.' *New German Critique* #29(Spring/Summer): 39-56.

Bimba, Anthony. 1932. *The Molly Maguires*. New York: International Publishers.

Bishop, W.H. 1879. 'Story-Paper Literature.' *Atlantic Monthly* 44(September): 383-393.

Bisno, Abraham. 1967. *Abraham Bisno, Union Pioneer*. Madison, Wis.: University of Wisconsin Press.

Blake, Fay M. 1972. *The Strike in the American Novel*. Metuchen, N.J.: The Scarecrow Press.

Bloch, Ernst. 1986. *The Principle of Hope*. Cambridge: The MIT Press.

Blumin, Stuart M. 1984. 'Explaining the New Metropolis: Perception, Depiction and Analysis in Mid-Nineteenth-Century New York City.' *Journal of Urban History* 11(i): 9-38.

—— 1985. 'The Hypothesis of Middle-Class Formation in Nineteeth-Century America: A Critique and Some Proposals.' *American Historical Review* 90(ii): 299-338.

Bok, E.W. 1892. 'Literary Factories.' Reprinted from the *Boston Journal* in *Publishers Weekly* 42 (August 13): 231.

Bold, Christine. 1983. 'The Voice of the Fiction Factory in Dime and Pulp Westerns.' *Journal of American Studies* 17(i): 29-46.

Bouton, John Bell. 1855. *The Life and Choice Writings of George Lippard*. New York: H.H. Randall.

Boyer, Paul. 1968. *Purity in Print: The Vice-Society Movement and Book Censorship in America*. New York: Charles Scribner's Sons.

—— 1978. *Urban Masses and Moral Order in America: 1820-1920*. Cambridge, Mass.: Harvard University Press.

Boyle, Regis Louise. 1939. *Mrs. E.D.E.N. Southworth, Novelist*. Washington, DC: Catholic University of America Press.

Bremner, Robert. 1967. 'Introduction' to *Traps for the Young*, by Anthony Comstock. Cambridge, Mass.: Harvard University Press.

Broehl, Wayne G., Jr. 1964. *The Molly Maguires*. Vintage/Chelsea House.

Brooks, Jeffrey. 1985. *When Russia Learned to Read: Literacy and Popular Literature, 1861-1917*. Princeton, NJ: Princeton University Press.

Brooks, Peter. 1984. *Reading for the Plot: Design and Intention in Narrative*. New York: Alfred A. Knopf.

Brown, Bob. 1932. 'Swell Days for Literary Guys.' *American Mercury* 27(December): 480-485.

Bruce, Robert V. 1959. *1877: Year of Violence*. Chicago: Quadrangle Books.

Buchanan, Joseph R. 1903. *The Story of a Labor Agitator*. New York: The Outlook Company.

Buckley, Peter. 1984. *To the Opera House: Culture and Society in New York City, 1820-1860*. Unpublished Doctoral Dissertation: State University of New York at Stony Brook.

Burgess, Gelett. 1902. 'The Confessions of a Dime-Novelist.' *The Bookman* 15(August): 528-533.

[Burn, James Dawson]. 1865. *Three years Among the Working-Classes in the United States During the War*. London: Smith, Elder and Co.

Butterfield, Roger. 1955. 'George Lippard and His Secret Brotherhood.' *Pennsylvania Magazine of History and Biography* 79(iii): 285-309.

Carby, Hazel V. 1987. *Reconstructing Womanhood: The Emergence of the Afro-American Woman Novelist*. New York: Oxford University Press.

Carrier, Esther Jane. 1965. *Fiction in Public Libraries 1876-1900*. New York: Scarecrow Press.

Cawelti, John G. 1965. *Apostles of the Self-Made Man: Changing Concepts of Success in America*. Chicago: University of Chicago Press.

—— 1971. *The Six-Gun Mystique*. Bowling Green, OH: Bowling Green University Popular Press.

—— 1976. *Adventure, Mystery, and Romance: Formula Stories as Art and Popular Culture*. Chicago: University of Chicago Press.

Chatman, Seymour. 1978. *Story and Discourse: Narrative Structure in Fiction and Film*. Ithaca: Cornell University Press.

'The Cheap Libraries.' 1877. *Publishers Weekly* 12 (October 6): 396-397.

'Cheap Literature.' 1866. *Workingman's Advocate* 8 September: 2.

Cobb, Irvin. 1929. *Irvin Cobb At His Best*. Garden City, N.Y.: Doubleday, Doran & Company.

Cohen, Rose. 1918. *Out of the Shadow*. New York: George H. Doran Company.

Comstock, Anthony. 1882. *Traps for the Young*. Cambridge, Mass.: Harvard University Press, 1967.

'The Contributors' Club.' 1877. *Atlantic Monthly* 41(November): 619-620.

'The Contributors' Club.' 1878. *Atlantic Monthly* 42(September): 370-371.

Cook, William Wallace. [John Milton Edwards, pseud.]. 1912. *The Fiction Factory*. Ridgewood, NJ: The Editor Company.

Coryell, Russell M. 1929. 'The Birth of Nick Carter.' *The Bookman* 69(July): 495-502.

Couvares, Francis G. 1984. *The Remaking of Pittsburgh: Class and Culture in an Industrializing City, 1877-1919*. Albany: The State University of New York Press.

Cox, J. Randolph. 1981. 'The Detective-Hero in the American Dime Novel.' *Dime Novel Round-Up* #547(February): 2-13.

Curti, Merle. 1937. 'Dime Novels and the American Tradition.' *Yale Review* 26(Summer): 761-778.

Davidson. Cathy N. and Arnold E. Davidson. 1977. 'Carrie's Sisters: The Popular Prototypes for Dreiser's Heroine.' *Modern Fiction Studies* 23 (Autumn): 395-407.

Davidson, Cathy N. 1981. 'Laura Jean Libbey.' in *American Women Writers*, edited by Lina Mainiero. Volume Three. New York: Frederick Ungar.

Davies, Tony. 1983. 'Transports of Pleasure: Fiction and its Audiences in the Later Nineteenth Century.' In *Formations of Pleasure*. London: Routledge & Kegan Paul.

Davis, James J. 1922. *The Iron Puddler: My Life in the Rolling Mills and What Came of It*. Indianapolis: Bobbs-Merrill Company.

Davis, Michael. 1984. 'Forced to Tramp: The Perspective of the Labor Press, 1870-1900.' In *Walking to Work: Tramps in America, 1790-1935*, edited by Eric H. Monkkonen. Lincoln: University of Nebraska Press.

Denning, Michael. 1987. *Cover Stories: Narrative and Ideology in the British Spy Thriller*. London: Routledge & Kegan Paul.

De Grazia, Emilio. 1969. *The Life and Works of George Lippard*. Unpublished Doctoral Dissertation, Ohio State University.

Deutsch, James I. 1976. 'Jesse James in Dime Novels: Ambivalence Towards an Outlaw Hero.' *Dime Novel Round-Up* #517(February): 2-11.

Dobkin, J.B. 1986. 'Treatment of Blacks in Dime Novels.' *Dime Novel Round-Up* #580(August): 50-56.

Douglas, Ann. 1977. *The Feminization of American Culture*. New York: Avon Books, 1978.

Dredd, Firmin. 1900. 'The Extinction of the Dime Novel.' *The Bookman* 11(March): 46-48.

Duganne, Augustine Joseph Hickey [Motley Manners, pseud.]. 1851. *Parnassus in Pillory*. New York: Adriance, Sherman & Co.

Durham, Philip, ed. 1966. *Dime Novels*. New York: Odyssey Press.

Eagleton, Terry. 1982. *The Rape of Clarissa: Writing, Sexuality and Class Struggle in Samuel Richardson*. Minneapolis: University of Minnesota Press.

Eco, Umberto. 1979. 'Rhetoric and Ideology in Sue's *Les Mystères de Paris*.' In his *The Role of the Reader*. Bloomington: Indiana University Press.

Edholm, Felicity, Olivia Harris and Kate Young. 1977. 'Conceptualizing women.' *Critique of Anthropology* 3(ix-x).

Eisenstein, Sarah. 1983. *Give Us Bread But Give Us Roses: Working Women's Consciousness in the United States, 1890 to the First World War*. London: Routledge & Kegan Paul.

Engels, Friedrich. 1887. 'The Labor Movement in the United States.' In *Marx and Engels: Basic Writings on Politics and Philosophy*, edited by Lewis S. Feuer. Garden City, N.Y.: Anchor Books, 1959.

Enslin, Morton S. 1971. 'A List of Alger Titles.' *Dime Novel Round-Up* #467, 468: 74-84, 90-106.

Erlich, Heyward. 1972. 'The "Mysteries" of Philadelphia: Lippard's *Quaker City* and "Urban" Gothic.' *Emerson Society Quarterly* 18(1st Quarter): 50-65.

Everett, Edward. 1860. *The Mount Vernon Papers*. New York: D. Appleton & Company.

Everett, William. 1864. 'Critical Notices: Beadle's Dime Books.' *North American Review* 99(July): 303-309.

Ewen, Elizabeth. 1985. *Immigrant Women in the Land of Dollars: Life and Culture on the Lower East Side, 1890-1925*. New York: Monthly Review Press.

Feldberg, Michael. 1975. *The Philadelphia Riots of 1844: A Study in Ethnic Conflict*. Westport, Conn.: Greenwood Press.

——— 1980. *The Turbulent Era: Riot and Disorder in Jacksonian America*. Oxford: Oxford University Press.

Fiedler, Leslie A. 1966. *Love and Death in the American Novel*. New York: Stein and Day.

——— 1970. 'Introduction' to *The Monks of Monk Hall*, by George Lippard. New York: The Odyssey Press.

——— 1982. *What Was Literature? Class Culture and Mass Society*. New York: Simon and Schuster.

Fink, Leon. 1983. *Workingmen's Democracy: The Knights of Labor and American Politics*. Urbana, Ill.: University of Illinois Press.

Foner, Eric. 1980. *Politics and Ideology in the Age of the Civil War*. New York: Oxford University Press.

Foran, Martin A. 1872. 'Preface' to *The Other Side. Workingman's Advocate* 28 September 1872:1.

Fornet, Ambrosio. 1975. 'Reading: The Proletariat and National Culture.' In *Communication and Class Struggle*, Volume 2, edited by Armand Mattelart and Seth Siegelaub. New York: International General, 1983.

Foster, Frank K. 1901. *The Evolution of a Trade Unionist*. Boston: Frank K. Foster.

Foster, George G. 1850. *New York by Gas-Light: With Here and There a Streak of Sunshine*. New York: Dewitt & Davenport.

Foucault, Michel. 1978. *Discipline and Punish: The Birth of the Prison*. New York: Pantheon Books.

Fraser, John. 1982. *America and the Patterns of Chivalry*. Cambridge: Cambridge University Press.

Freibert, Lucy M. and Barbara A. White, eds. 1985. *Hidden Hands: An Anthology of*

American Women Writers, 1790-1870. New Brunswick, NJ: Rutgers University Press.

Fullerton, Ronald. 1977. 'Creating a Mass Book Market in Germany.' *Journal of Social History* 10(March): 265-283.

—— 1979. 'Toward a Commercial Popular Culture in Germany: The Development of Pamphlet Fiction 1871-1914.' *Journal of Social History* 12(Summer): 489-512.

Garrison, Dee. 1979. *Apostles of Culture: The Public Librarian and American Society, 1876-1920.* New York: The Free Press.

Geller, Evelyn. 1984. *Forbidden Books in American Public Libraries, 1876-1939.* Westport, CT: Greenwood Press.

Ginzburg, Carlo. 1980. *The Cheese and the Worms: The Cosmos of a Sixteenth-Century Miller.* Baltimore: The Johns Hopkins University Press.

Godfrey, Lydia S. 1983. 'The Influence of Dime Novels on Theodore Dreiser.' *Dime Novel Round-Up* #563(October): 66-71.

Gold, Louis. 1931. 'Laura Jean Libbey.' *American Mercury* 24(September): 47-52.

Gordon, David, Richard Edwards and Michael Reich. 1982. *Segmented Work, Divided Workers: The Historical Transformation of Labor in the United States.* Cambridge: Cambridge University Press.

Gramsci, Antonio. 1929-1935. *Selections from Cultural Writings.* Cambridge: Harvard University Press, 1985.

—— 1973. *Letters from Prison.* New York: Harper & Row.

Gray, William S. and Ruth Munroe. 1930. *The Reading Interests and Habits of Adults.* New York: The Macmillan Company.

Green, Martin. 1979. *Dreams of Adventure, Deeds of Empire.* New York: Basic Books.

Green, Samuel S. 1879. *Sensational Fiction in Public Libraries, and Personal Relations between Librarians and Readers.* Worcester, Mass.: Press of Chas. Hamilton.

Grimes, Mary C. ed. 1986. *The Knights in Fiction: Two Labor Novels of the 1880s.* Urbana: University of Illinois Press.

Grimsted, David. 1968. *Melodrama Unveiled: American Theater and Culture, 1800-1850.* Chicago: University of Chicago Press.

Gutman, Herbert. 1963. 'The Worker's Search for Power: Labor in the Gilded Age.' In *The Gilded Age: A Reappraisal,* edited by H. Wayne Morgan. Syracuse, N.Y.: Syracuse University Press.

—— 1976. *Work, Culture and Society in Industrializing America.* New York: Alfred A. Knopf.

Habegger, Alfred. 1981. 'A Well Hidden Hand.' *Novel* 14(Spring): 197-212.

—— 1982. *Gender, Fantasy, and Realism in American Literature.* New York: Columbia University Press.

Hall, Stuart. 1981. 'Notes on deconstructing "the popular".' In *People's History and Socialist Theory,* edited by Raphael Samuel. London: Routledge & Kegan Paul.

Halttunen, Karen. 1982. *Confidence Men and Painted Women: A Study of Middle-Class Culture in America, 1830-1870.* New Haven: Yale University Press.

Hanson, Russell L. 1985. *The Democratic Imagination in America.* Princeton, N.J.: Princeton University Press.

Harrison, Rev. Jonathan Baxter. 1880. *Certain Dangerous Tendencies in American Life, and Other Papers.* Boston: Houghton, Osgood and Company.

Hart, James D. 1950. *The Popular Book: A History of America's Literary Taste.* Oxford: Oxford University Press.

Hartsfield, Larry K. 1985. *The American Response to Professional Crime, 1870-1917.* Westport, CT: Greenwood Press.

Harvey, Charles M. 1907. 'The Dime Novel in American Life.' *Atlantic Monthly* 100(July): 37-45.

Harvey, Katherine. 1974. *The Best Dressed Miners*. Ithaca, N.Y.: Cornell University Press.

Heins, Marjorie. 1974. 'Horatio Alger: Symbol for Success.' *Dime Novel Round-Up* #505(October): 118-124; #506(November): 130-134.

Herminghouse, Patricia. 1985. 'Radicalism and the "Great Cause": The German-American Serial Novel in the Antebellum Era.' In *America and the Germans; Volume One: Immigration, Language, Ethnicity*, edited by Frank Trommler and Joseph McVeigh. Philadelphia: University of Pennsylvania Press.

Hicks, John D. 1931. *The Populist Revolt: A History of the Farmers' Alliance and the People's Party*. Minneapolis: University of Minnesota Press.

Hobsbawm, Eric. 1981. *Bandits*. New York: Pantheon Books.

Hohendahl, Peter U., ed. 1983. *Mass Culture in Imperial Germany 1871-1918*. A Special Issue of *New German Critique* #29.

Hoppenstand, Gary, ed. 1982. *The Dime Novel Detective*. Bowling Green, Ohio: Bowling Green University Popular Press.

Horkheimer, Max and Theodor Adorno. 1944. *Dialectic of Enlightenment*. New York: The Seabury Press, 1972.

Hudson, Frederic. 1873. *Journalism in the United States from 1690 to 1872*. New York: Harper and Brothers.

Humpherys, Anne. 1985. 'G.W.M. Reynolds: Popular Literature and Popular Politics.' In *Innovators and Preachers: The Role of the Editor in Victorian England*, edited by Joel H. Wiener. Westport, CT: Greenwood Press.

Ickstadt, Heinz. 1979. 'The Novel and the People: Aspects of Democratic Fiction in Late 19th Century American Literature.' In *Proceedings of a Symposium on American Literature*, edited by Marta Sienicka. Poznan: Institute of English, Adam Mickiewicz University.

James, Henry. 1888. 'The Art of Fiction.' In *Henry James: Selected Fiction*, edited by Leon Edel. New York, E.P. Dutton, 1964.

James, Louis. 1963. *Fiction for the Working Man 1830-1850*. Oxford: Oxford University Press.

Jameson, Fredric. 1972. *The Prison-House of Language: A Critical Account of Structuralism and Russian Formalism*. Princeton, NJ: Princeton University Press.

—— 1974. 'The Vanishing Mediator: Narrative Structure in Max Weber.' *Working Papers in Cultural Studies* #5(Spring): 111-149.

—— 1975. 'Magical Narratives: Romance as Genre.' *New Literary History* 7:135-163.

—— 1977a. 'Class and Allegory in Contemporary Mass Culture: *Dog Day Afternoon* as a Political Film.' *College English* 38: 843-859.

—— 1977b. 'Ideology, Narrative Analysis, and Popular Culture.' *Theory and Society* 4:543-559.

—— 1978. 'Imaginary and Symbolic in Lacan: Marxism, Psychoanalytic Criticism, and the Problem of the Subject.' *Yale French Studies* #55-56: 338-395.

—— 1979. 'Reification and Utopia in Mass Culture.' *Social Text* #1:130-148.

—— 1981. *The Political Unconscious: Narrative as a Socially Symbolic Act*. Ithaca, N.Y.: Cornell University Press.

—— 1982. 'Towards a New Awareness of Genre.' *Science Fiction Studies* #28: 322-324.

Jelley, S.M. 1887. *The Voice of Labor*. Chicago: A.B. Gehman & Co.

Jenks, George C. 1904. 'Dime Novel Makers.' *The Bookman* 20(October): 108-114.

Johannsen, Albert. 1950. *The House of Beadle and Adams and Its Dime and Nickel*

Novels: A Story of a Vanished Literature. Norman, Okl.: University of Oklahoma Press. Volume 1 and 2: 1950; Volume 3: 1962.

Johannsen, Albert. 1959. *The Nickel Library: Bibliographic Listing.* Fall River, Mass.: Edward T. LeBlanc.

Jones, Daryl. 1978. *The Dime Novel Western.* Bowling Green, Ohio: Bowling Green University Popular Press.

Kaplan, Justin. 1966. *Mr. Clemens and Mark Twain.* New York: Simon and Schuster.

Karetzky, Stephen. 1982. *Reading Research and Librarianship: A History and Analysis.* Westport, Conn.: Greenwood Press.

Kaser, David. 1984. *Books and Libraries in Camp and Battle: The Civil War Experience.* Westport, CT: Greenwood Press.

Katzman, David M. and William M. Tuttle, Jr., eds. 1982. *Plain Folk: The Life Stories of Undistinguished Americans.* Urbana, Ill.: University of Illinois Press.

Katznelson, Ira. 1981. *City Trenches: Urban Politics and the Patterning of Class in the United States.* New York: Pantheon Books.

Kelley, Mary. 1979. 'The Sentimentalists: Promise and Betrayal in the Home.' *Signs* 4(iii): 434-446.

——— 1984. *Private Woman, Public Stage: Literary Domesticity in Nineteenth-Century America.* Oxford: Oxford University Press.

Kessler-Harris, Alice. 1982. *Out to Work: A History of Wage-Earning Women in the United States.* Oxford: Oxford University Press.

Korey, Marie E. 1980. 'T.B. Peterson & Brothers.' In *Publishers for Mass Entertainment in Nineteenth Century America,* edited by Madeleine B. Stern. Boston: G.K. Hall & Co.

Lang, Lucy Robins. 1948. *Tomorrow is beautiful.* New York: The Macmillan Company.

Larcom, Lucy. 1889. *A New England Girlhood.* Gloucester, Mass.: Peter Smith, 1973.

Laurie, Bruce. 1980. *Working People of Philadelphia.* Philadelphia: Temple University Press.

Leavis, Q.D. 1932. *Fiction and the Reading Public.* London: Chatto and Windus.

Leenhardt, Jacques. 1980. 'Toward a Sociology of Reading.' In *The Reader in the Text,* edited by Susan R. Suleiman and Inge Crosman. Princeton, N.J.: Princeton University Press.

Lees, Lynn Hollen. 1979. 'Getting and Spending: The Family Budgets of English Industrial Workers in 1890.' In *Consciousness and Class Experience in Nineteenth-Century Europe,* edited by John M. Merriman. New York: Holmes & Meier Publishers.

Leithead, J. Edward. 1965-1971. 'The Anatomy of Dime Novels.' A series of 21 articles published in *Dime Novel Round-Up.* Eleven of the series were reprinted in *American Book Collector* 18-21(1968-1971).

Levasseur, E. 1900. *The American Workman.* Baltimore: The Johns Hopkins Press.

Levine, Susan. 1984. *Labor's True Woman: Carpet Weavers, Industrialization, and Labor Reform in the Gilded Age.* Philadelphia: Temple University Press.

Lewis, Ethel Clark. 1941. 'A Weaver of Romances.' *Dime Novel Round-Up* #110(October): 1-4.

Lingenfelter, Richard E. 1974. *The Hardrock Miners: A History of the Mining Labor Movement in the American West, 1863-1893.* Berkeley: University of California Press.

Lippard, George. 1848. 'Valedictory of the Industrial Congress.' *The Nineteenth Century* 2: 186-189.

Lynd, Robert S. and Helen Merrell Lynd. 1929. *Middletown: A Study in Modern American Culture*. New York: Harcourt Brace Jovanovich, 1956.

McConachie, Bruce A. 1985. '"The Theatre of the Mob": Apocalyptic Melodrama and Preindustrial Riots in Antebellum New York.' In *Theatre for Working-Class Audiences in the United States, 1830-1980*, edited by B.A. McConachie and D. Friedman. Westport, CT: Greenwood Press.

McNeill, George E., ed. 1886. *The Labor Movement: The Problem of To-Day*. Boston: A.M. Bridgman & Co.

McWatters, George S. 1871. *Knots Untied: or, Ways and By-Ways in the Hidden Life of American Detectives*. Hartford: J.B. Burr and Hyde.

Marx, Karl. 1852. *The Eighteenth Brumaire of Louis Napoleon*. In *Surveys from Exile*, edited by David Fernbach. New York: Random House, 1973.

—— 1867. *Capital: A Critique of Political Economy*. Harmondsworth: Penguin Books, 1976.

—— and Friedrich Engels. 1845. *The Holy Family, or Critique of Critical Criticism*. In *Karl Marx. Friedrich Engels. Collected Works*. Volume Four. New York: International Publishers, 1975.

Matthews, Brander [Arthur Penn, pseud.]. 1883. *The Home Library*. New York: D. Appleton and Company.

—— 1923. 'Certain Books in Black and Red.' *Literary Digest International Book Review* 1(June): 33-35.

Maurice, Arthur Bartlett. 1902. 'The Detective in Fiction.' *The Bookman* 15 (May): 231-236.

Messenger, Christian K. 1981. *Sport and the Spirit of Play in American Fiction*. New York: Columbia University Press.

Mitchell, Sally. 1981. *The Fallen Angel: Chastity, Class and Women's Reading, 1835-1880*. Bowling Green, Ohio: Bowling Green University Popular Press.

Modell, John. 1978. 'Patterns of Consumption, Acculturation, and Family Income Strategies in Late Nineteenth-Century America.' In *Family and Population in Nineteenth-Century America*, edited by Tamara K. Hareven and Maris A. Vinovskis. Princeton, N.J.: Princeton University Press.

Monaghan, Jay. 1952. *The Great Rascal: The Life and Adventures of Ned Buntline*. Boston: Little, Brown and Company.

Montgomery, David. 1967. *Beyond Equality: Labor and the Radical Republicans, 1862-1872*. New York: Vintage Books.

—— 1972. 'The Shuttle and the Cross: Weavers and Artisans in the Kensington Riots of 1844.' In *Workers in the Industrial Revolution*, edited by Peter N. Stearns and Daniel J. Walkowitz. New Brunswick, N.J.: Transaction Books, 1974.

—— 1976. 'Labor in the Industrial Era.' In *The American Worker*, edited by Richard B. Morris. Washington: US Department of Labor.

—— 1979. *Workers' Control in America: Studies in the history of work, technology, and labor struggles*. Cambridge: Cambridge University Press.

—— 1980. 'Labor and the Republic in Industrial America: 1860-1920.' *Le Mouvement Social* 111: 201-215.

Monkkonen, Eric H. 1984. *Walking to Work: Tramps in America, 1790-1935*. Lincoln: University of Nebraska Press.

Moretti, Franco. 1983. *Signs Taken For Wonders: Essays in the Sociology of Literary Forms*. London: Verso.

Mott, Frank Luther. 1947. *Golden Multitudes: The Story of Best Sellers in the United States*. New York: The Macmillan Company.

Murolo, Priscilla. 1981. 'The Working Girls' Clubs of New York City, 1884-1894: Cooperation, Self-Government, Self-Support.' Unpublished Essay.

Neider, Charles. 1982. *The Selected Letters of Mark Twain*. New York: Harper and Row.

Neuberg, Victor E. 1977. *Popular Literature: A History and Guide*. Harmondsworth: Penguin Books.

Nichols, Roger L. 1982. 'The Indian in the Dime Novel.' *Journal of American Culture* 5(ii): 49-55.

Noel, Mary. 1954. *Villains Galore: The Heyday of the Popular Story Weekly*. New York: The Macmillan Company.

Oberholtzer, Ellis Paxson. 1906. *The Literary History of Philadelphia*. Philadelphia: George W. Jacobs & Co.

Ogden, Rollo, ed. 1907. *Life and Letters of Edwin Lawrence Godkin*. Two Volumes. New York: The Macmillan Company.

Orsmbee, Hazel Grant. 1927. *The Young Employed Girl*. New York: The Womans Press.

Orwell, George. 1939. 'Boys' Weeklies.' In *A Collection of Essays*. Garden City, NY: Anchor Books, 1954.

Pachon, Stanley A. 1957. 'William Wallace Cook.' *Dime Novel Round-Up* #300: 67-75.

—— 1986. 'The Case of the Purloined Image.' *Dime Novel Round-Up* #577(February): 6-7.

Pam, Dorothy S. 1980. *Exploitation, Independence, and Solidarity: The Changing Role of American Working Women as Reflected in the Working-Girl Melodrama, 1870-1910*. Unpublished Doctoral Dissertation, New York University.

Papashvily, Helen Waite. 1956. *All the Happy Endings: A study of the domestic novel in America, the women who wrote it, the women who read it, in the nineteenth century*. New York: Harper & Brothers Publishers.

Patten, Gilbert. 1964. *Frank Merriwell's 'Father': An Autobiography*. Norman, Oklahoma: University of Oklahoma Press.

Pearson, Edmund. 1929. *Dime Novels; or, Following An Old Trail in Popular Literature*. Boston: Little, Brown, and Company.

Peiss, Kathy. 1986. *Cheap Amusements: Working Women and Leisure in Turn-of-the-Century New York*. Philadelphia: Temple University Press.

Penn, I. Garland. 1891. *The Afro-American Press, and its Editors*. Springfield, MA: Wiley & Co.

Peterson, Joyce Shaw. 1983. 'Working Girls and Millionaires: The Melodramatic Romances of Laura Jean Libbey.' *American Studies* 24(Spring): 19-35.

Peterson, Theodore. 1956. *Magazines in the Twentieth Century*. Urbana: University of Illinois Press.

Pinkerton, Allan. 1878. *Strikers, Communists, Tramps and Detectives*. New York: G.W.Carleton & Co.

Popular Memory Group. 1982. 'Popular Memory: Theory, Politics, Method.' In *Making Histories: Studies in History Writing and Politics*, edited by Richard Johnson, Gregor McLennan, Bill Schwarz, and David Sutton. Minneapolis: University of Minnesota Press.

Powderly, Terence V. 1940. *The Path I Trod*. New York: Columbia University Press.

Prawer, S.S. 1976. *Karl Marx and World Literature*. Oxford: Oxford University Press.

Przeworski, Adam. 1985. *Capitalism and Social Democracy*. Cambridge: Cambridge University Press.

Puffer, Nathaniel H. 1980. 'Frank Tousey.' In *Publishers for Mass Entertainment in Nineteenth Century America*, edited by Madeleine Stern. Boston: G.K. Hall & Co.

Radway, Janice A. 1984. *Reading the Romance: Women, Patriarchy, and Popular Literature*. Chapel Hill: University of North Carolina Press; 1987, London: Verso.

Rasche, William Frank. 1937. *The Reading Interests of Young Workers*. Chicago: University of Chicago Libraries.

Reilly, John M. 1976. 'Beneficent Roguery: The Detective in the Capitalist City.' *Praxis* #3:154-163.

Reynolds, David S. 1982. *George Lippard*. Boston: Twayne Publishers.

—— ed. 1986. *George Lippard, Prophet of Protest: Writings of an American Radical, 1822-1854*. New York: Peter Lang.

Reynolds, Quentin. 1955. *The Fiction Factory: or, From Pulp Row to Quality Street*. New York: Random House.

Richardson, Dorothy. 1905. *The Long Day: The Story of a New York Working Girl*. Reprinted in William O'Neill, ed. *Women at Work*. New York: Times Books, 1972.

Ridgely, J.V. 1974. 'George Lippard's *The Quaker City*: The World of the American Porno-Gothic.' *Studies in the Literary Imagination* 7(i):77-94.

Ringenbach, Paul T. 1973. *Tramps and Reformers 1873-1916: The Discovery of Unemployment in New York*. Westport, Conn.: Greenwood Press, Inc.

Robinson, Harriet. 1898. *Loom and Spindle, or Life Among the Early Mill Girls*. Kailu, Hawaii: Press Pacifica, 1976.

Robinson, Henry Morton. 1928. 'The Dime Novel is Dead, but the Same Old Hungers Are Still Fed.' *The Century Magazine* 116(May): 60-67.

Robinson, Henry Morton. 1929. 'Mr. Beadle's Books.' *Bookman* 69(March): 18-24.

Rodgers, Daniel T. 1978. *The Work Ethic in Industrial America 1850-1920*. Chicago: University of Chicago Press.

Rosenzweig, Roy. 1983. *Eight hours for what we will: Workers and leisure in an industrial city, 1870-1920*. Cambridge: Cambridge University Press.

Ross, Dorothy. 1979. 'The Liberal Tradition Revisited and the Republican Tradition Addressed.' In *New Directions in American Intellectual History*, edited by John Higham and Paul K. Conkin. Baltimore: The Johns Hopkins University Press.

Ross, Steven. 1985. *Workers on the Edge: Work, Leisure, and Politics in Industrializing Cincinnati, 1788-1890*. New York: Columbia University Press.

Rubin, Gayle. 1975. 'The Traffic in Women: Notes on the "Political Economy" of Sex.' In *Towards an Anthropology of Women*, edited by R.R. Reiter. New York: Monthly Review Press.

Ryan, Mary. 1979. *Womanhood in America: From Colonial Times to the Present*. New York: New Viewpoints, Second Revised Edition.

Saxton, Alexander. 1984. 'Problems of Class and Race in the Origins of the Mass Circulation Press.' *American Quarterly* 36(ii): 211-234.

Scharnhorst, Gary. 1980. *Horatio Alger, Jr*. Boston: Twayne Publishers.

—— with Jack Bales. 1985. *The Lost Life of Horatio Alger, Jr*. Bloomington: Indiana University Press.

Schick, Frank L. 1958. *The Paperbound Book in America*. New York: R.R. Bowker Company.

Schiller, Dan. 1981. *Objectivity and the News: The Public and the Rise of Commercial Journalism*. Philadelphia: University of Pennsylvania Press.

Schivelbusch, Wolfgang. 1979. *The Railway Journey: Trains and Travel in the 19th Century*. New York: Urizen Books.

Schudson, Michael. 1978. *Discovering the News: A Social History of American Newspapers*. New York: Basic Books.

Schulte-Sasse, Jochen. 1983. 'Toward a "Culture" for the Masses: The Socio-

Psychological Function of Popular Literature in Germany and the U.S., 1880-1920.' *New German Critique* #29(Spring/Summer): 85-105.

Scisco, Louis Dow. 1901. *Political Nativism in New York State*. Studies in History, Economics and Public Law: Volume XIII, Number 2. New York: Columbia University Press.

Seelye, John. 1963. 'The American Tramp: A Version of the Picaresque.' *American Quarterly* 15: 535-553.

Settle, William A., Jr. 1966. *Jesse James Was His Name*. Columbia, Mo.: University of Missouri Press.

Sewell, William H. Jr. 1980. *Work and Revolution in France: The Language of Labor from the Old Regime to 1848*. Cambridge: Cambridge University Press.

Shove, Raymond. 1937. *Cheap Book Production in the United States, 1870 to 1891*. Urbana, Ill.: University of Illinois Library.

Siegel, Adrienne. 1981. *The Image of the American City in Popular Literature 1820-1870*. Port Washington, N.Y.: Kennikat Press.

Simmons, Michael K. 1981. 'Nationalism and the Dime Novel.' *Studies in the Humanities* 9(i):39-44.

Slotkin, Richard. 1985. *The Fatal Environment: The Myth of the Frontier in the Age of Industrialization, 1800-1890*. New York: Atheneum.

Smith, Henry Nash. 1978. *Democracy and the Novel: Popular Resistance to Classic American Writers*. Oxford: Oxford University Press.

Smith, Henry Nash. 1950. *Virgin Land: The American West as Symbol and Myth*. Cambridge, Mass.: Harvard University Press.

Smith, Norman D. 1980. 'Mexican Stereotypes on Fictional Battlefields: or Dime Novel Romances of the Mexican War.' *Journal of Popular Culture* 13(iii): 526-540.

Smith, Ralph P. 1944. 'Barred by the Post Office.' *Dime Novel Round-Up* #145: 1-5.

Sollors, Werner. 1986. *Beyond Ethnicity: Consent and Descent in American Culture*. New York: Oxford University Press.

Soltow, Lee, and Edward Stevens. 1981. *The Rise of Literacy and the Common School in the United States: A Socioeconomic Analysis to 1870*. Chicago: University of Chicago Press.

Sorge, Friedrich A. 1891-1895. *The Labor Movement in the United States*. Westport, Conn.: Greenwood Press, 1977.

Stansell, Christine. 1972. 'Elizabeth Stuart Phelps: A Study in Female Rebellion.' *Massachusetts Review* 13(Winter/Spring): 239-256.

───── 1986. *City of Women: Sex and Class in New York, 1789-1860*. New York: Alfred A. Knopf.

Stearns, Peter N. 1975. *Lives of Labor: Work in a Maturing Industrial Society*. New York: Holmes and Meier Publishers.

Steckmesser, Kent Ladd. 1965. *The Western Hero in History and Legend*. Norman: University of Oklahoma Press.

Stedman Jones, Gareth. 1983. *Languages of Class: Studies in English Working Class History 1832-1982*. Cambridge: Cambridge University Press.

Stein, Leon and Philip Taft, eds. 1971. *Workers Speak: Self Portraits*. New York: Arno Press.

Steinberg, Hans Josef. 1976. 'Worker's Libraries in Germany Before 1914.' *History Workshop* 1: 166-180.

Steinberg, Heinz. 1972. 'Books and readers as a subject of research in Europe and America.' *International Social Science Journal* 24(iv): 744-755.

Stern, Madeleine B., ed. 1980. *Publishers for Mass Entertainment in Nineteenth Century America*. Boston: G.K. Hall & Co.

Stewart, R.F. 1980. *...And Always a Detective: Chapters on the History of Detective Fiction.* Newton Abbott: David & Charles.

Suleiman, Susan R. 1980. 'Introduction: Varieties of Audience Oriented Criticism.' In *The Reader in the Text,* edited by Susan R. Suleiman and Inge Crosman. Princeton, N.J.: Princeton University Press.

Susman, Warren I. 1984. *Culture as History: The Transformation of American Society in the Twentieth Century.* New York: Pantheon Books.

Taylor, George Rogers. 1977. 'Gaslight Foster: A New York "Journeyman Journalist" at Mid-Century.' *New York History* 58: 297-312.

Therborn, Göran. 1980. *The Ideology of Power and the Power of Ideology.* London: Verso.

Tompkins, Jane P. 1980. 'Sentimental Power: *Uncle Tom's Cabin* and the Politics of Literary History.' *Glyph* #5: 79-102.

—— 1985. *Sensational Designs: The Cultural Work of American Fiction, 1790-1860.* New York: Oxford University Press.

Trachtenberg, Alan. 1982. *The Incorporation of America: Culture and Society in the Gilded Age.* New York: Hill and Wang.

Trommler, Frank. 1983. 'Working-Class Culture and Modern Mass Culture Before World War I.' *New German Critique* #29(Spring/Summer): 57-70.

US Bureau of Education. 1876. *Public Libraries in the United States of America: Their History, Condition, and Management.* Part One. Washington: Government Printing Office.

US Senate, Committee on Education and Labor. 1885. *Report of the Committee of the Senate upon the Relations between Labor and Capital, and Testimony Taken by the Committee,* Four Volumes. Washington: Government Printing Office.

Utter, Robert Palfrey and Gwendolyn Bridges Needham. 1936. *Pamela's Daughters.* New York: The Macmillan Company.

Voloshinov, V.N. 1930. *Marxism and the Philosophy of Language.* New York: Seminar Press, 1973.

Walcutt, Sue G. 1971. 'Libbey, Laura Jean.' In *Notable American Women, 1607-1950: A Biographical Dictionary,* edited by Edward T. James. Volume Two. Cambridge, Mass.: Harvard University Press.

Walkowitz, Daniel J. 1978. *Worker City, Company Town: Iron and Cotton-Worker Protest in Troy and Cohoes, New York, 1855-84.* Urbana, Ill.: University of Illinois Press.

Wallace, Anthony. 1978. *Rockdale: The growth of an American village in the early Industrial Revolution.* New York: Alfred A. Knopf.

Waples, Douglas and Ralph Tyler. 1931. *What People Want to Read About: A Study of Group Interests and a Survey of Problems in Adult Reading.* Chicago: University of Chicago Press.

—— Bernard Berelson and Franklyn R. Bradshaw. 1940. *What Reading Does to People: A Summary of Evidence on the Social Effects of Reading and a Statement of Problems for Research.* Chicago: University of Chicago Press.

Warner, Sam Bass Jr. 1968. *The Private City: Philadelphia in Three Periods of Its Growth.* Philadelphia: University of Pennsylvania Press.

Webb, R.K. 1955. *The British Working Class Reader, 1790-1848.* London: George Allen & Unwin.

Whittaker, Frederick. 1884. 'Reply.' *New York Tribune* 16 March: 8.

Wilentz, Sean. 1984. *Chants Democratic: New York City and the Rise of the American Working Class, 1788-1850.* New York: Oxford University Press.

Williams, Raymond. 1977. *Marxism and Literature.* Oxford: Oxford University Press.

254

Wilson, Christopher P. 1983. 'The Rhetoric of Consumption: Mass-Market Magazines and the Demise of the Gentle Reader, 1880-1920.' In *The Culture of Consumption*, edited by Richard Wightman Fox and T.J. Jackson Lears. New York: Pantheon Books.

Wolff, Richard and Stephen Resnick. 1982. 'Classes in Marxian Theory.' *Review of Radical Political Economics* 3(iv): 1-18.

―――― 1986. 'Power, Property, and Class.' *Socialist Review* #86: 97-124.

Wright, Carroll D. 1884. *The Working Girls of Boston*. Boston: Wright & Potter Printing Co. 1889.

Wright, Erik Olin. 1985. *Classes*. London: Verso.

Wright, Lyle. 1969. *American Fiction, 1774-1850: A Contribution Toward a Bibliography*. San Marino, Calif.: The Huntington Library, Second Revised Edition.

―――― 1978a. *American Fiction, 1851-1875: A Contribution Toward a Bibliography*. San Marino, Calif.: The Huntington Library.

―――― 1978b. *American Fiction, 1876-1900: A Contribution Toward a Bibliography*. San Marino, Calif.: The Huntington Library.

Wright, Will. 1975. *Six Guns and Society: A Structural Study of the Western*. Berkeley: University of California Press.

Wyckoff, Walter A. 1898a. *The Workers: An Experiment in Reality. The East*. New York: Charles Scribner's Sons.

―――― 1898b. *The Workers: An Experiment in Reality. The West*. New York: Charles Scribner's Sons.

Wyman, Lillie B. Chace. 1888-1889. 'Studies of Factory Life.' *Atlantic Monthly* 62(July, September, November): 17-29, 315-321, 605-612; 63(January): 69-79.

Zahler, Helene Sara. 1941. *Eastern Workingmen and National Land Policy, 1829-1862*. New York: Columbia University Press.

Ziff, Larzer. 1981. *Literary Democracy: The Declaration of Cultural Independence in America*. New York: The Viking Press.

Index